Authority, Church,
and Society in George Herbert

Authority, Church, and Society in GEORGE HERBERT

Return to the Middle Way

Christopher Hodgkins

University of Missouri Press
Columbia and London

Copyright © 1993 by
The Curators of the University of Missouri
University of Missouri Press, Columbia, Missouri 65201
Printed and bound in the United States of America
All rights reserved
5 4 3 2 1   97 96 95 94 93

Chapter 7, "The Church Legible: Herbert and the Externals of Worship," was
previously published in *The Journal of Religion* (Spring 1991). Copyright © 1991
by The University of Chicago. All rights reserved. Chapter 8, "'Betwixt This World
and That of Grace': Herbert and the Church in Society," was previously published in
Studies in Philology 87 (Fall 1990). Both are reprinted by permission.

Library of Congress Cataloging-in-Publication Data

Hodgkins, Christopher, 1958–
    Authority, church, and society in George Herbert : return to the
middle way / Christopher Hodgkins.
        p. cm.
    Based on the author's thesis (Ph.D.—University of Chicago, 1988)
under the title: Returning to the middle way.
    Includes bibliographical references and index.
    ISBN 0–8262–0881–9 (alk. paper)
    1. Herbert, George, 1593-1633—Criticism and interpretation.
2. Literature and society—England—History—17th century.
3. Christian poetry, English—History and criticism.   4. Authority
in literature.   5. Church in literature.   I. Hodgkins, Christopher,
1958–   Returning to the middle way.   II. Title.
PR3508.H64   1993
821'.3—dc20   92–39416
                                                   CIP

⊛™ This paper meets the requirements of the
American National Standard for Permanence of Paper
for Printed Library Materials, Z39.48, 1984.

Designer: Rhonda Miller
Typesetter: Connell-Zeko Type & Graphics
Printer and Binder: Thomson-Shore, Inc.
Typefaces: Sabon and Caxton

The Dedication

Lord, my first fruits present themselves to thee;
Yet not mine neither: for from thee they came,
And must return. Accept of them and me,
And make us strive, who shall sing best thy name.
    Turn their eyes hither, who shall make a gain:
    Theirs, who shall hurt themselves or me, refrain.

Contents

Acknowledgments   ix

Abbreviations   xiii

Introduction   1

1. **The Exact Middle Way:** Herbert, the Elizabethan Settlement, and Calvinism   9

2. **The Bounds of Power:** Stuart Authority in Crisis   34

3. **Power Disabled:** Limited Authority in Herbert's "Lent"   64

4. **"Showing Holy":** Herbert and the Power of the Pulpit   87

5. **"Doctrine and Life":** Herbert's Protestant Priesthood   103

6. **Slowly to the Flame:** "The Priesthood" and Herbert's Hesitation   127

7. **The Church Legible:** Herbert and the Externals of Worship   149

8. **"Betwixt This World and That of Grace":** Herbert and the Church in Society   181

Epilogue   210

Bibliography   215

Index of Herbert Poems   225

General Index   227

Acknowledgments

I am that perhaps alarming type of dinner guest who, when asked what he would like before the meal, sometimes requests the family album. Then I make myself comfortable by the cheese tray, leafing through the progenitors, infancies, childhoods, adolescences, and recent developments in the lives of my hosts.

Similarly, I am a great reader of acknowledgment pages in others' books; here one finds intimations of the human context for an author's otherwise disembodied voice. Here one discovers, or can at least surmise, something about a book's ancestry, its genesis, its benefactors, and the domestic places in which it grew to its public self. If a book is a grateful and well-mannered book, it will acknowledge its origins—and its debts—eagerly and gladly. Of course, not all grateful books are smart books; but, I think, no smart book can be a truly good book unless it is grateful. So if you have read this far on this page, thank you. You are either, like me, peculiarly interested in reading such things, or you are looking for your name. Either way, I owe you a debt, probably an unpayable one. And unpayable debts are the only ones worth having.

This project began in 1985 as a dissertation at the University of Chicago, and it is to my mentors, teachers, and colleagues there that I owe much of its transformation into a publishable form. My advisors, Richard Strier and Janel Mueller, blessed my work with such fiercely nurturing attention that much of the originally fusty doctoralese was kneaded and knocked out of it by the time I finished my degree in 1988. They prodded, challenged, but most of all encouraged me at every stage, and they still do. I also am thankful for the very substantial attention, advice, and aid of David Bevington, Michael Murrin, Joshua Scodel, John Wallace, and the whole remarkable Renaissance Workshop, especially (then) fellow students Frances Dolan, Richard Duerden, and Jeffrey Nelson, all of whom read much of this work in draft. I also am grateful to Mark Kishlansky, then of

Chicago's history department, now of Harvard's, for reading a version of my second chapter and advising me on the substance of early Stuart church politics.

Other experts have given my manuscript the inestimable boon of a complete reading and thorough commentary, most notably Cristina Malcolmson of Bates College and Gene Edward Veith, Jr., of Concordia University; their improvements are inscribed throughout. John R. Roberts of the University of Missouri read a prospectus, and later all of chapter 4. Bruce Johnson of James Madison University responded helpfully to chapter 1. Furthermore, in the summer of 1990, I had the great pleasure of participating in the National Endowment for the Humanities "Protestant Imagination" seminar organized by John N. King at Ohio State University. There the book took something like its present form, with the careful help of Professor King and the whole delightful group—Catherine Cox, Bradford DeVos, Tamara Goeglein, Peter Herman, Mark Heumann, Stephen Honeygosky, Edna Anne Osmansky Loftus, Frances Malpezzi, Michael Mikolajczak, Helaine Ross, and Susanne Sklar. Chapters 1 and 7 in particular bear their mark.

My erstwhile (and much missed) colleagues at Calvin College brought their fine literary sense and theological sensibilities to numerous draft chapters. Charlotte Otten rescued chapter 7 from muddy terminology; Edward E. Ericson, Jr., drew my attention to some differences between Lutheran and Calvinist doctrine; Jeffrey Johnson and John Hare brought that attention back to the similarities; and John Netland, gentleman and scholar, praised my style and substance. He also shared with me the pleasure of a team-taught interim course on Herbert and Hopkins. The late Howard McConaughy encouraged me toward our common goal of discovering Herbert on his own terms.

I also wish to thank Emilie Mills, curator of Special Collections at the University of North Carolina at Greensboro, for permission to reprint an engraving from the extraordinary George Herbert Collection left to the University by Herbert's biographer, the late Amy M. Charles. In addition, I am grateful to James Evans and my colleagues in the UNCG English Department for their interest in and support of this project, most particularly in the form of a teaching load reduction to complete it. Thanks also to the fine students in my fall 1991 graduate seminar who read and responded to a version of chapter 4.

That's not all. After graduating from Chicago, while on a casual walk through the Regenstein Library stacks, I was astonished to discover that my bound dissertation actually had been *checked out* and, as it happened, *read in its entirety* by history of science graduate student James Altena, whose thorough knowledge of the Oxford Movement has saved me some embarrassments; and for years I have received valuable correspondence from history graduate student Gregory P. Randolph, whose county-to-county archival research on the Henrician Reformation he has generously shared with me. To Chicago's Sublime Society of Eutychus's Window—Fred Buettler, Lendol Calder, Julie Crutchfield, John Hand, Hope Howell Hodgkins, Mary Ann Kemp, Mike Kugler, Alan Savage, Wan-ling Wee, Young Whang, John Wicks, and others—I offer thanks for their insights into the relationship between Christian faith, doctrine, and history.

At the University of Missouri Press, Susan Denny and Beverly Jarrett saw this work through numerous evaluative readings with fairness and heartening care, while Jane Lago and Tim Fox have been thoroughly helpful in the preparation of the final text. I wish to thank the University of Chicago Press for permission to use material previously published by *Modern Philology* and the *Journal of Religion* (in the Introduction and chapter 7, respectively), and the University of North Carolina Press for permission to use material previously published by *Studies in Philology* (in chapter 8).

For financial assistance while in graduate school, I am grateful to my late grandmother, Mrs. Lyman J. Smith, and to the Mrs. Giles Whiting Foundation. For further support during the summer of 1990, I thank the National Endowment for the Humanities. For innumerable hours of good fellowship during the early years of the project, I thank my nearly innumerable apartment-mates at the godly commonwealth of "5470" (South Hyde Park Boulevard): Todd Arbogast, Gregg Bendrick, David Braddock, Mark Duban, John Hand, Douglas Honorof, Robert Hormann, James Jones, Edward Lewis, Tracy Miller, Brent Perry, Alan Savage, Arthur Weiner, Joel White, and John Wicks. Where else do doctors, physicists, biologists, accountants, sinologists and linguists, chemists, economists, lawyers, literary scholars, ad salesmen, political scientists, and mathematicians share rent, chores, discussion, laughter, prayer, and Crockpot chicken six nights a week? "Eche hath nede of other," right, guys?

My parents and siblings—Norman and Eleanor Hodgkins, and Craig, Catherine, and Charles—have always given me the inestimable gift of loving respect, which is, I suspect, why I have never seriously doubted the value of spending over seven years writing about a four-hundred-year-old poet. My daughter Mary has given me the invaluable gift of napping well in the afternoons. My daughter Alice, born just as this book goes to press, reminds me that "Daddy" is the most honorific of titles. Because I wrote most of this work in the white heat of bachelorhood, my wife Hope was mostly spared the agonies of the scholar's widow, and my reader is spared those confessions of book-induced irascibility and virtual abandonment that usually turn up at about this point in an acknowledgments section. (I must blame my failings on something else.) Yet Hope is a generous partner and colleague; she has read just about every page, many more than once, and her good sense is to be found everywhere. So this book is hers, as well.

One would hope that with all this help, I could get things right. I hope so, too; but I ask my reader's patient correction of the faults that remain.

Abbreviations

The following abbreviations are used throughout the text and notes to refer to frequently cited sources:

BH   Church of England. *Certaine Sermons or Homilies Appointed to be Read in Churches in the Time of Elizabeth I (1547–1571). A Facsimile Reproduction of the Edition of 1623 (The Book of Homilies).* 2 vols. in 1. Gainesville, Fla.: Scholars' Facsimiles and Reprints, 1968.

DNB   Sir Leslie Stephen and Sir Sidney Lee, eds. *Dictionary of National Biography.* 22 vols. Oxford: Oxford University Press, 1917.

ICR   John Calvin. *The Institutes of the Christian Religion.* 2 vols. Translated by Ford Lewis Battles. Edited by John T. McNeill. Philadelphia: Westminster Press, 1960.

LD   Lancelot Andrewes. *A Learned Discourse of Ceremonies Retained and used in Christian Churches.* London: Charles Adams, 1653

LEP   Richard Hooker. *Of the Laws of Ecclesiastical Polity.* 4 vols. Edited by W. Speed Hill. Cambridge: Harvard University Press, 1977.

OED   James A. H. Murray, ed. *The Oxford English Dictionary.* 10 vols. New York: 1888.

W   *The Works of George Herbert.* 2d ed. Edited by F. E. Hutchinson. Oxford: The Clarendon Press, 1964.

Authority, Church, and Society in George Herbert

Introduction

I joy, deare Mother, when I view
Thy perfect lineaments and hue
                    Both sweet and bright.
                    —"The British Church" (*W,* 109, ll. 1–3)

Brave rose, (alas!) where art thou? in the chair
Where thou didst lately so triumph and shine
A worm doth sit, whose many feet and hair
Are the more foul, the more thou wert divine.
                    —"Church-rents and schismes" (*W,* 140, ll. 1–4)

[W]ise men have thought it the best way of preserving a state
to reduce it to the principles by which it grew great.
                    —*The Countrey Parson* (*W,* 258)[1]

This book is about regenerative nostalgia—George Herbert's pow-
erful longing for a social order that was passing away, in Richard
Hooker's phrase, "as in a dream" (*LEP,* Preface.1.1).[2] This longing

---

1. Barnabas Oley's 1671 edition of *The Countrey Parson* seems to have added *The Priest to the Temple* to Herbert's original title; therefore, I have chosen to refer through-out to the work as Herbert did. See Joseph Summers, *George Herbert: His Religion and Art,* 13. As to Herbert's Latin poetry, all translations are my own. However, I have com-pared them throughout with those in *The Latin Poetry of George Herbert: A Bilingual Edition,* trans. Mark McCloskey and Paul R. Murphy.
2. Subsequent references to *LEP* are to book, chapter, and paragraph numbers. For Herbert's nostalgia, see Leah Sinanoglou Marcus, *Childhood and Cultural Despair: A Theme and Variations in Seventeenth-Century Literature,* 94ff. However, according to Marcus, Herbert's nostalgia is regressive rather than regenerative, a "retreat" from the disordered world without and his spiritual struggles within. For a fascinating account of how Herbert sought stability—not retreat—within the established church, see "George Herbert Pulling for Prime," in Anna K. Nardo, *The Ludic Self in Seventeenth-Century English Literature.*

carried Herbert an enormous social distance—from embittered, displaced courtier to diligent rural parson—and moved him to heart-searching eloquence in poetry and prose. It pointed him in his last few years to an audacious lifework, his long-sought "employment": to return his *Ecclesia Anglicana,* wounded by increasingly bloody-minded divisions, to the *via media* of the old Elizabethan Settlement. It is my purpose to rediscover and define Herbert's "middle way"—its theological and political configuration, its internal coherence and contradictions, and its motive power.

And indeed, Herbert has kept the power to move. It is remarkable that readers across the entire spectrum of English-speaking Christendom have admired and often claimed him, from the New England congregationalists who hailed him as a prophet to the Jesuit Gerard Manley Hopkins, who saw him as a spiritual and artistic forbear.[3] The key to Herbert's wide appeal, I argue, is not his "Catholicism" (as defined in terms of the Oxford Movement) but his catholicity. He was able to revive the symbols and cycles of ancient Christian tradition as emblems of an immediate spiritual experience that fulfills the grand imperative of Christ as understood by the Reformation: "ye must be born again." He believed that all human institutions, whether governmental, ecclesiastical, or social, are to be valued only insofar as they encourage a reformed faith and devotion in the individual believer's heart.

So, on the one hand, I argue that Herbert, even more than the Elizabethan Settlement, which formed his ecclesiastical ideal, was Calvinist in the essentials of theology. Thus when in the later 1620s the increasingly powerful "high-church" party led by William Laud sought to soften this strong Protestant distinctiveness and to reassert certain medieval traditions and practices, Herbert did not sympathize with their cause, although, ironically, some continue to identify him with it. Instead, he walked what I term the Elizabethans' "exact middle way": he preferred a constitutionally limited monarchy and episcopacy; he practiced and advocated a "godly" parish ministry like that of the moderate Puritans; he believed in passing important spiritual

3. See Cotton Mather, *Magnalia Christi Americana,* 89, 115, 371–72; W. H. Gardner, *Gerard Manley Hopkins, 1844–1889* 1:170–72, 2:73–74.

responsibility on to laymen; and he advocated simple, scriptural intelligibility in liturgy, in church architecture, and in poetry.

Yet on the other hand, Herbert was no Puritan; he was extraordinarily loyal to the established structure and ideals that he inherited from the Elizabethans, and he advocated them despite all of their critics, Roman and Puritan—and Laudian—alike. Like all aging revolutionary movements, the English Protestantism of Herbert's day was splintering, and he sought a return to the foundations that, in the 1560s, had been both emphatically Protestant in theology *and* episcopal in church government. Thus Herbert can often sound like a "Puritan" without being one or wanting to be one—"Old Conformists" of Herbert's type shared with Puritans the same base in Luthero-Calvinist biblicism, but they built (or wished to build) differently in matters of ecclesiastical polity.

Religion has tended to be for the twentieth century—at least for many twentieth-century intellectuals—what sex became to the nineteenth: a suspect, even guilty thing, best discussed (if at all) in other terms, and practiced (if at all) behind firmly closed doors. Thus my determination to treat Herbert and his poetry in their own religious terms—embedded as the man and his work were in a period of inflamed and explicit doctrinal passion—may discomfit some readers. And even readers not so innocent of Christian dogma may well object that a historical-theological approach threatens to be procrustean. Why not rather seek the deeply human Herbert, beneath or even apart from confining orthodoxies?

I answer that trying to understand Herbert apart from doctrinal constraints is as fruitless as trying to appreciate James Joyce apart from the confines of Dublin. It is of course possible to reduce Joyce to a pedantic gridwork of sites, statues, and allusions; but in Dublin—at least in his memory of Dublin—Joyce the artist lived and moved and had his being. There he found the concrete particularities for his artificing. Similarly, we should bear in mind Jeanne Clayton Hunter's caution that "Herbert's poetry is not a precise exposition of anyone's doctrine"; yet this is a generic distinction rather than a substantive one.[4] Lyric poems are not expositions, theological or otherwise, but

4. "'With Wings of Faith': Herbert's Communion Poems," 57.

this fact does not preclude what Herbert actually does: dramatize and realize in lyric form the confusions and resolutions that doctrine often works on the believer.

Herbert was one of those on whom ideas—in his case theological ideas—act like physical forces. John Bunyan was set upon and grasped and shaken out by biblical texts; John Henry Newman took his "first real hit" from Roman Catholicism through Augustine's anti-Monophysite arguments, and the blow gave him a stomachache. Likewise, Herbert, writes Richard Strier, was "'stirred to imaginative intensity' by, as Yeats put it, 'some form of propaganda.'" Thus, as Strier notes elsewhere, Helen Vendler's project of "humanizing" Herbert apart from "orthodoxy," while in some cases wonderfully illuminating, nevertheless greatly narrows her range of appreciation. For example, Vendler is led to pronounce "The Altar" incoherent, "Sion's" last stanza "curious and unconvincing," and all but the last stanza of "Lent" simply "dull."[5] On the contrary, my purpose, among others, is to provide context that will display "The Altar" as highly coherent, "Sion's" ending as deeply moving, and "Lent" as seriously flawed, but for politically fascinating reasons.

John N. Wall has different reasons for downplaying the importance of doctrine, particularly continental Protestant doctrine, in understanding Herbert's poetry. Wall argues that the distinctive character of the English Reformation lies in its having been "primarily a liturgical reformation, achieved through changing the religious behavior of England as a nation rather than by exchanging one theological formulary for another."[6] Wall's emphasis on how religion functions in society provides useful insights into Herbert's vision of an English church involved in, yet distinct from, the nation; and Wall is right to highlight important institutional differences between the English way and those of the continental Protestant churches. However, his externalist, behavioral approach slights a crucial question: was not the reformed English liturgy itself designed to teach? I argue that Herbert,

5. DNB, "Newman," 344a; Strier, Love Known: Theology and Experience in George Herbert's Poetry, xii; Strier, "'Humanizing' Herbert"; Vendler, The Poetry of George Herbert, 61–63, 191, 150–51.

6. Transformations of the Word: Spenser, Herbert, Vaughan, 3.

like Cranmer and the other Tudor Protestant reformers, saw the externals of worship—the sacraments, Prayer Book, music, vestments, calendar, and architecture of the church—as means toward pointedly evangelistic ends. What beliefs, then, did these outward things signify? How should they be made "legible" to the people? To what varieties of spiritual experience were these signs and beliefs supposed to lead? Again, we must know doctrine if we wish to know much of Herbert on his own terms.

Yet if we agree that reading Herbert requires a clearer theological context, which do we choose? His was a confused era, and theologies raged about him—Lutheran and Roman, hyper-Calvinist and Arminian, iconoclast and ritualist, episcopal absolutist and anticlerical. So, in a sense, we must agree with Rosemond Tuve, Louis L. Martz, Stanley Stewart, and others who argue that Herbert cannot be understood apart from medieval and counter-Reformation modes of devotion—to ignore them is to deplete the rich matrix of images and associations that are the stuff of his poetry.[7] But appropriation is not assent; these "Catholic" materials are usually present to be questioned, challenged, undermined, even overthrown. Of course Herbert, like the Elizabethan Settlement—and, surprisingly, like Calvin—was often liturgically inclusive and, again like Calvin, profoundly eucharistic. Yet everything that Herbert kept from the past is to some degree transformed—either reframed or remade.

I have already begun, like Herbert's parson preaching, to particularize—"This is for you, and This is for you." Besides speaking to "humanizing" work like Vendler's, "Protestantizing" work like Strier's, "externalizing" work like Wall's, and "Catholicizing" work like Tuve's, Martz's and Stewart's, this study also engages postmodern readings of Herbert as "self-consuming" and "self-fashioning." I display an obvious debt to Stanley Fish in my third chapter's extended reading of "Lent," as I discuss how Herbert's defense of state-mandated fasting collapses upon itself because he is uneasy about coercion in spiritual matters. Similarly, my fourth, sixth, and eighth chapters on Herbert's reconstituted identity as "country parson" have benefited from the

7. Gene Edward Veith, Jr., "The Religious Wars in George Herbert Criticism: Reinterpreting Seventeenth-Century Anglicanism," 21–22.

brilliant recent work of Michael C. Schoenfeldt and Cristina Mal-colmson.[8] Each treats Herbert's pastoral manual as a kind of cour-tesy book, demonstrating that both the manual and *The Temple* are permeated by the anxieties and the strategies of a courtier seeking "employment," yet in the court of the heavenly king.

However, some of these "self-consuming" and "self-fashioning" ap-proaches, especially Fish's, require correction by proper doctrinal context. Fish misunderstands the marrow of Herbert's Calvinist the-ology as the obliteration rather than the redemption of the distinct self—as if the corollary of the divine I AM were YOU AREN'T. Thus he nihilistically treats *The Temple* as an ontological battle between Herbert and God. So, for Fish's Herbert, the supreme act of piety is blank passivity and devotion's greatest expression is empty silence; just as any deed or word, even of worship, becomes necessarily an act of rebellion. Schoenfeldt, although less concerned with theology (and much more moderate in his claims), apparently makes a similar as-sumption, for he seems to regard Herbert's frequent prostrations be-fore the divine throne ultimately as self-empowerment tactics—as if Herbert believed that King Jesus, like King James, really could be flattered.

Instead, I argue that for Herbert, the redeemed individual becomes more distinct, not less, and that his spiritual "empowerment" is qual-itatively different from its courtly counterpart, being tempered by sin-cerely grateful humility. In the words of "The Holdfast," "all things" — the powers of willing obedience, trust, and confession—are "more ours by being [Christ's]," restored to the self by the Savior's redeem-ing conquest (*W,* 143, l. 12). Herbert loved and created for God be-cause, he believed, God had first loved and re-created him.

Since so much of this study depends on Herbert's place in the the-ological spectrum, I begin by defining both that place and that spec-trum in "The Exact Middle Way: Herbert, the Elizabethan Settlement,

---

8. Fish, *Self-Consuming Artifacts: The Experience of Seventeenth-Century Literature;* Schoenfeldt, *Prayer and Power: George Herbert and Renaissance Courtship,* "'Subject to Ev'ry Mounters Bended Knee': Herbert and Authority," and "Standing on Ceremony: The Comedy of Manners in Herbert's 'Love (III)'"; Malcolmson, "Society and Self-Defi-nition in the Works of George Herbert," and "George Herbert's *Country Parson* and the Character of Social Identity."

and Calvinism." Chapter 2, "The Bounds of Power: Stuart Authority in Crisis," sets the historical and political context for the increasingly tumultuous period of Herbert's maturity, the 1620s. Chapter 3, "Power Disabled: Limited Authority in Herbert's 'Lent,'" applies this theological-political context to an especially problematic poem, which displays Herbert at odds with himself over the issue of applying state coercion in spiritual matters. Chapter 4, "'Showing Holy': Herbert and the Power of the Pulpit," extends this discussion of authority into the parish by questioning the ethical pedigree of Herbert's rhetorical techniques for swaying and controlling his parishioners.

Chapter 5, "'Doctrine and Life': Herbert's Protestant Priesthood," continues inquiring into the parson's power and motives by surveying his remarkable array of responsibilities and comparing them with those specified in the pastoral manual written by Herbert's important Puritan imitator, Richard Baxter. Chapter 6, "Slowly to the Flame: 'The Priesthood' and Herbert's Hesitation," reads Herbert's lyric in the contexts both of his extraordinarily demanding pastoral vision and of his own notoriously protracted delay in becoming a pastor. Chapter 7, "The Church Legible: Herbert and the Externals of Worship," pursues two of Herbert's favorite themes—plainness and practicality—through his many poems dealing with church liturgy, architecture, vestments, and music; I ask what, in the end, these externals are worth to him. Chapter 8, "'Betwixt This World and That of Grace': Herbert and the Church in Society," addresses the issue that so dogged Tudor-Stuart England: the individual's sometimes conflicting obligations to church and nation. Finally, through comparison with a contemporary, Thomas Fuller, the Epilogue speculates on how Herbert might have reacted to the national upheaval that followed his death.

As even my chapter titles should suggest, this is fundamentally a reconstructive rather than a deconstructive or reductionist project. By classing Herbert as a very particular subspecies of *homo religiosus,* we will see him come to life in something more like foursquare reality: the arch young controversialist humbled and mellowed to a man of profound and firm principle; the troubled monarchist and churchman called to enforce an established faith at a time when king and bishop were uprooting the constitutional source of their legitimacy; the would-be privy councillor zealously combining pastoral care and statecraft in vanishingly obscure Bemerton; the repentant court flatterer mocking his former pretensions and methods with a fierce and even tearful piety; the poetic architect building his "Temple," his "Church," and his "Altar" only to make them disappear; and throughout, the dazzling rhetorician constantly damping his muse of fire to an intimate, domestic glow. It was Herbert's religion that created, sustained, and sometimes resolved these dynamic tensions, and understanding that religion better can only enrich our experience of his work. He was above all a Reformation poet, perhaps the greatest in any language—not only in his creed, but also in his habit of mind: he re-formed everything he touched.

1

The Exact Middle Way

Herbert, the Elizabethan Settlement, and Calvinism

> All . . . [the Country Parson] doth . . . as desiring to keep the middle way between superstition, and slovenlinesse, and as following the Apostles two great and admirable Rules . . . : The first whereof is, *Let all things be done decently, and in order:* The second, *Let all things be done to edification,* I Cor. 14. For these two rules . . . excellently score out the way, and fully, and exactly . . .
>
> —*The Countrey Parson* (W, 246)

> [It] is the greatest ability of a Parson to lead his people exactly in the ways of Truth.
>
> —*The Countrey Parson* (W, 230)

Any attempt to claim precision for the English *via media* is bound to arouse skepticism. It is common to hear the Settlement's *Articles of Religion* spoken of as deliberately vague, cannily inclusive, or, in Louis L. Martz's recent suggestive phrase, "generously ambiguous."[1] To many, an "exact middle way" will sound like merely another Elizabethan oxymoron—hot ice, indeed. Nevertheless, I claim a kind of exactness, both for the Settlement that formed Herbert's ecclesiastical and social ideal and, even more so, for Herbert himself—the exactness of the mid-sixteenth-century Protestant consensus of Luther, Martyr,

---

1. "The Generous Ambiguity of George Herbert's *Temple*." See also Wall, *Transformations of the Word,* 1–2.

Bucer, Bullinger, Cranmer, Ridley, Jewel, and, most comprehensively, of Calvin; in other words, the magisterial theology of *sola gratia, sola fide,* and, basic to both, *sola scriptura.*

My claim seems to enlist me as a "Roundhead" in the "wars of religion" that, as Gene Edward Veith, Jr., has noted, are being fought over again in Herbert criticism. Among the other "Roundheads," Veith numbers William H. Halewood, Barbara Kiefer Lewalski, Richard Strier, and himself—to whom I would add Ilona Bell, Daniel Doerksen, and Jeanne Clayton Hunter—who argue that Herbert can be best understood in terms of Protestant models. Among the "Cavaliers," he includes Rosemond Tuve, Martz, and Stanley Stewart—to whom again I would add C. A. Patrides and Diana Benet—"who insist that Herbert can scarcely be understood apart from the liturgy, the sacraments, and 'Catholic' means of devotion." The prize in this combat? Historically, the stakes are high—the meaning of "Anglicanism" and Herbert's place in it. Poetically, the stakes are perhaps even higher— the very nature of Herbert's aesthetic. Patrides writes, "[T]he Eucharist is the marrow of Herbert's sensibility."[2] If Patrides is right—as I believe he is, although not in the way commonly understood—then how can Herbert be explained, let alone assimilated, by a logocentric, even iconoclastic Protestantism? The seventeenth-century gap between "Puritans" and "Anglo-Catholics" seems to yawn anew.

But Veith believes, I think rightly, that resolution and true scholarly complementarity are possible if the parties will abandon these simplistic, often anachronistic, dichotomies. Instead he recommends a

---

2. Patrides, ed., *The English Poems of George Herbert,* 17. See also Veith, "Religious Wars," 18–19. For the "Roundheads," see Halewood, *The Poetry of Grace: Reformation Themes and Structures in English Seventeenth-Century Poetry;* Lewalski, *Protestant Poetics and the Seventeenth-Century Religious Lyric;* Strier, *Love Known;* Veith, *Reformation Spirituality: The Religion of George Herbert;* Bell, "'Setting Foot into Divinity': George Herbert and the English Reformation"; Doerksen, "Recharting the *Via Media* of Spenser and Herbert"; and Hunter, "Herbert's 'The Water-Course': Notorious and Neglected," and "'With Wings of Faith': Herbert's Communion Poems." For the "Cavaliers," see Tuve, *A Reading of George Herbert;* Martz, *The Poetry of Meditation;* Stewart, *George Herbert;* Patrides, *English Poems;* Benet, *Secretary of Praise: The Poetic Vocation of George Herbert;* and (with some qualifications) Terry G. Sherwood, *Herbert's Prayerful Art.* Wall's *Transformations of the Word* differentiates itself from both camps, analyzing Herbert largely in terms of corporate religious behavior rather than in terms of doctrine and inner experience.

less binary, more modular approach: to ask separate questions about a person's understanding of predestination, the sacraments and liturgy, and church government.[3] Thus, for example, it was quite possible in the period to be an arch-Calvinist arch-Episcopalian, like King James; an Arminian high-churchman, like Lancelot Andrewes; or an Arminian low-churchman, like John Milton—to name only a few of the more famous permutations. Likewise, I place Herbert more definitely on the politico-religious spectrum of the later 1620s and earlier 1630s, and I reread his poetry and prose in this context.

To Veith's vital questions about salvation, sacraments, liturgy, and church polity, I add others about preaching style, pastoral theology, and, especially, royal and episcopal absolutism. My fundamental claim is that as the gap widened between Puritan "Non-Conformists" and William Laud's "New Conformists," Herbert walked the increasingly lonely way of the Elizabethan "Old Conformists." To be painfully precise: in the conflict between Arminian absolutist high-church Episcopalians (New Conformists) and Calvinist antiabsolutist low-church Presbyterians (Non-Conformists), Herbert kept to the "middle way" of his boyhood church, as a Calvinist nonabsolutist lower-church Episcopalian (Old Conformist). He emphasized God's loving, unconditional, irresistible grace—the Strength that "makes his guest" (*W,* 156, l. 8); he preferred a powerful but constitutionally limited monarchy and episcopacy; he preached and ministered in the authoritative plain and practical style of the moderate Puritans, passing important spiritual responsibility onto laymen; and he advocated simple, scriptural intelligibility in liturgy, church architecture, and poetry.

Anyone who has endured the previous paragraph knows that precision has its dangers. One worries about murdering to dissect. Once we have Herbert fixed in a formulated phrase, pinned and wriggling on a wall, what does it profit? My answer, as already suggested in my Introduction, is that this is fundamentally a reconstructive rather than a reductionist project. As when applying any conceptual system to literature, reductionism and tendentiousness are dangers; certainly it is possible to inflict on literary readers not only *odium theologicum* but also *odium psychologicum, odium oeconomicum,* and even *odium*

---

3. "Religious Wars," 21–22.

neo-historicum. Still, such conceptual and contextual readings can be enriching rather than impoverishing if we remember that poetry no more reduces to mere ideology or doctrine than a harvest reduces to the seed. Yet the seed produces the harvest. This chapter carefully identifies the theology from which *The Temple* grew. Succeeding chapters will consider the distinctly English soil and the changeable political weather.

A worse danger is recalled by an epithet current in Herbert's day— Protestant malcontents were called not only "Puritans" but also "precisians." To invert Martz's phrase, this study risks being ungenerously precise. It argues, for instance, that Herbert went beyond the 1563 *Articles of Religion* by assenting explicitly to that most notoriously exclusive doctrine, double predestination. If "the sweet singer of *The Temple*" was really a Calvinist at heart, will not the poetic landscape go grayer from the pale Genevan's breath? In Martz's terms, will not the "Lord of Power" defeat the "Lord of Love"?[4] Thus it appears that redefining the Elizabethan and Herbertian middle way requires rightly defining "Calvinism" as well, and Calvin's relation to this study.

Calvin, "Learned Ignorance," and "Calvinism"

It is nearly axiomatic that the zealous disciple is the dead master's bane. The transferred mantle seldom brings an equal, let alone a double, measure of Elijah's spirit. Brian Gerrish has noted that Calvin, not the Lutheran Philip Melanchthon, was Luther's true disciple in the sense of preserving the master's emphasis on the incomprehensible and radically gratuitous nature of salvation.[5] Calvin was similarly unfortunate in his designated successor, Theodore de Bèze (Beza), and in many of Beza's English followers, who created a neo-scholastic, hyper-dogmatized "Calvinism." Ironically, as Calvin's name became more and more identified with English Protestantism, Beza departed

---

4. "Generous Ambiguity," 35–36.
5. "John Calvin on Luther." Calvin always saw among the major reformers and himself, in his words, a "remarkable consensus . . . on all that is essential to godliness," despite his famous disagreement with Luther and Lutherans over the nature of the eucharist. As we will see, in this important eucharistic controversy, the Elizabethan Settlement and Herbert are reformed/Calvinist rather than Lutheran. See also Robert Ellrodt, *L'Inspiration personelle et L'Esprit du temps chez les poetes metaphysiques anglais.*

increasingly from Calvin's original emphases and even his substance. It is my thesis that Herbert, in following the Elizabethan middle way, is closer to the heart of Calvin's "Calvinism" than were many of the reformer's most ardent English and Continental devotees.

My warrant for such a revisionist claim is found in the Protestant watchword, *sola scriptura,* and its rejection of rationalistic speculation. In Calvin's *Institutes of the Christian Religion* we see this scripturalist emphasis not only in frequent assertions of biblical preeminence but also in the very order of his discussion. He roughly approximates the structure of Paul's argument in Romans, postponing the potentially thorny topic of free will until the second of the four books (chapters 2–6), well after Book One (chapters 1–6) has laid the foundations of God's incomprehensibility. Like Luther and others before him, Calvin insists that man is utterly unable to know saving truth apart from scriptural revelation, and that scripture clearly teaches what Luther called "the bondage of the will": the total inability of the fallen person to choose good works pleasing to God apart from God's grace. The even thornier issue of predestination Calvin places yet later, near the end of Book Three, "How We Receive the Grace of Christ" (chapters 21–24).[6] (Similarly, in Romans, a letter now conventionally divided into sixteen chapters, Paul deals with the natural man's enslavement to sin in chapter 3 and with predestination in chapters 8:28–11:36.) Again, Calvin takes pains to reproduce Paul's and Augustine's stress on God's will as entirely just yet utterly unfathomable. "The Word of the Lord is . . . the *sole* light to illumine our vision . . . let us not be ashamed to be ignorant of something in this matter, wherein is a certain *learned ignorance*. Rather, let us willingly refrain from inquiring into a kind of knowledge, the ardent desire for which is both foolish and dangerous, nay, *even deadly*" (*ICR* 3.21.2, emphases mine). Consistent with such strong caution, Calvin brackets the free-will/election sections with warnings about the twin perils of these topics: that ignoring them may wrongly give man the credit for his own salvation, but that handling them speculatively may throw people into despair and unclean living (*ICR* 2.2.1).

---

6. Martin Luther, *The Bondage of the Will.* In all subsequent references to *ICR,* book, chapter, and paragraph numbers are provided.

In fact, Calvin concludes his famously pointed defense of double predestination by rebuking the "curiosity" of "those foolish teachers and foreboding prophets" who presume to know the reprobate from the elect. Instead, he says, scripturalist "learned ignorance" should make believers, in Augustine's words, "'so minded as to wish that *all men* be saved.' So shall it be that we try to make *everyone* we meet a sharer in our peace" (*ICR* 3.24.14, emphases mine). Calvin presents election and damnation as God's secret business from first to last; the believer's business is to love all people as God's image-bearers (*ICR* 3.7.6–7) and invite all to be his spiritual children. Thus Calvin attacks the parsimonious exclusivity so often attributed to him and to his doctrine.

Calvin's caution on these issues reveals his differences from the "systematizing and logicalizing theology" of Beza, who had little patience with oxymorons like "learned ignorance." In the decades following Calvin's death in 1564, Beza raised a question that Calvin clearly thought speculative, namely, the order of God's decrees in predestination.[7] The effect of this seemingly subtle shift on Protestant theological discussion was enormous. Predestination, which before had been a doctrine clearly subsidiary to *sola gratia,* was now thrust into the foreground of debate, and indeed it became the linchpin of what I will call a developing "neo-Calvinist" theology. This difference in emphasis amounted to a difference in substance, because, by the later 1580s, all other doctrinal questions were being referred and subordinated to this overriding interest in God's absolute decrees.

Nowhere was this shift felt more acutely than in England, where William Perkins and William Whitaker translated Beza's new emphases into highly influential vernacular sermons and treatises. Perkins's *Whether a man* (1589) takes as its theme the multifarious ways in which the reprobate—those "elected unto death" by God—can display the outward and inward signs of holiness and still, inevitably, be damned in the end. In *A Golden Chaine* (1591), Perkins expands these arguments and concretizes them in a precise and orderly chart, borrowed from Beza, of God's decrees, chronologically arranged. In only thirty

---

7. R. T. Kendall, "The Puritan Modification of Calvin's Theology," 201, 206.

years, double predestination has gone from Calvin's *decretum quidem horribile fateor*—"a decree of which it is terrifying to speak"—to a kind of spiritual periodic table.[8]

In England, the issue first came to a head in 1595, when Archbishop Whitgift, on Whitaker's advice, promulgated the highly controversial Lambeth Articles, intended to quash nascent "Pelagianism" at Cambridge.[9] These nine articles stress the strictly limited number of the saved and foreground God's absolute decree of "reprobation unto death." Formally, they say nothing that Calvin had not taught, but the very prominence of their promulgation and the speculative neo-Calvinism that produced and interpreted them would probably have brought strong warnings, if not rebukes, from Calvin had he been living.

Not surprisingly, the Lambeth Articles accelerated the polarization that they sought to resolve. In 1600, the Dutch divine Jacob Arminius reacted to Perkins and Whitaker by returning to Erasmus's Pelagian "free-will" arguments that had provoked Luther's seminal *Bondage of the Will* seventy-five years earlier. Like Erasmus, Arminius taught that depravity is partial, not total, so that the will is free to choose independently against sin; that election is conditional upon foreseen faith and works; that Christ's atonement is universal and hypothetical; that God's saving grace can be resisted; and that the true believer can lose salvation. "Arminianism" threw the Netherlands and all of Protestant Europe into an uproar, and in England some churchmen—among them Lancelot Andrewes and William Laud—came out publicly in support of the anti-Calvinists. In 1618–1619, at the international Synod of Dordrecht (Dordt) in Holland, the various reformed churches, including King James's Church of England, strongly rebuffed the Arminians with what have come to be called the "five points of Calvinism": total depravity, unconditional election, limited atonement, irresistible grace, and the perseverance of the elect.[10] However, these official pronouncements did little to resolve the controversy in England, where by 1625

8. Kendall, "Puritan Modification," 204; see also John A. Garraty and Peter Gay, eds., *Columbia History of the World,* 529.

9. Peter Lake, *Moderate Puritans in the Elizabethan Church,* 201ff.

10. Veith, *Reformation Spirituality,* 26–27.

James's Arminian son was king, and the newly favored Laudian party was beginning to harry Calvinists with a will.

The portentous departures of speculative neo-Calvinism from Calvin's doctrinal caution not only incited the even more speculative Arminians to action; they also highlight for us Calvin's affinities with the paradoxically "exact middle way" of the old Elizabethan Settlement, which couches its strongly Protestant affirmations in the same scripturalist language of "learned ignorance." Once we observe these affinities we can better understand how Herbert, looking back after the "foul worm" of Arminian-Calvinist controversy had done much of its damage, could long for what was, at least in relative terms, a golden age of Protestant harmony.

Predestination: The *Articles* and Herbert

The 1563 *Articles,* like the Edwardine *Articles* that they largely duplicate, and like the magisterial reformers who contributed their theological substance, unequivocally affirm the primacy of scripture (Article 6). The Bible is in turn said to teach the "bondage of the will" —"that we have *no* power to do good works . . . without the grace of God by Christ preventing [preceding] us" (Article 10, emphasis mine) —and justification by faith alone—that "[w]e are accounted righteous before God, *only* for the Merit of our Lord and Saviour Jesus Christ by Faith, and *not* for our own works or deservings" (Article 11, emphasis mine). The *Articles* also teach "predestination to life" in a particularist rather than a universalist sense as "the everlasting purpose of God, whereby . . . he hath constantly decreed . . . to deliver from curse and damnation those whom he hath chosen in Christ *out of mankind*" (Article 17, emphasis mine). Consideration of "predestination to life," the article warmly continues, "is full of sweet, pleasant, and unspeakable comfort to godly persons, and such as feel in themselves the working of the Spirit of God," since it deepens their assurance of salvation and "kindles" their love for God.

However, as Martz has noted, Article 17 stops short of stating the obvious corollary of "predestination to life"; that, as Herbert affirms in "The Water-course" (*W,* 170), God

<pre>
                            {Salvation.
        gives to man as he sees fit {
                            {Damnation.
                              (l. 10)
</pre>

It is this omission that, more than anything else, confirms for Martz the "generous ambiguity" of the Elizabethan Settlement, especially compared to the later Lambeth Articles with their focus on "reprobation unto death." It is the tenets of Lambeth, Martz argues, that "would underlie a truly Calvinist Church of England."[11] Their absence in the 1563 *Articles* indicates that the English church was not "truly Calvinist."

If Martz meant only that the Thirty-Nine Articles speak for the mid-sixteenth-century reformed consensus, which was not unique to Calvin, and that they do so well before the heated neo-Calvinist predestinarian debates of the 1590s and beyond, he would be right. Calvin's direct influence on the *Articles,* while important, was probably strongest in eucharistic doctrine, since the soteriological core of *sola gratia, sola fide* was already present in Cranmer's earlier Edwardine *Articles,* under the strong epistolary influence of Bullinger, and personal influence of immigrants Martyr and Bucer.[12]

However, what Martz means by "not truly Calvinist" is that the 1563 *Articles* are "frequently, indeed pervasively, so vague, so guarded, so ambiguous that people of anti-Calvinist persuasion could and did, in good conscience, swear allegiance to them, while making their own interpretations."[13] Appropriately, Martz's prime example of an anti-Calvinist interpreter is John Henry Newman, the formative genius of the nineteenth-century Anglo-Catholicism that, among its other accomplishments, revived interest in George Herbert as its spiritual forebear. Martz begins his essay by quoting from Newman's famous Tract No. 90 of 1841, which argues that "the Articles are not framed on the principle of excluding those who prefer the theology of the early ages to that of the Reformation. . . . [T]heir framers constructed them in such a way as best to comprehend those who did not go so far

---

11. "Generous Ambiguity," 33.
12. Kendall, "Puritan Modification," 200, 199.
13. "Generous Ambiguity," 32.

in Protestantism as themselves."[14] Indeed, Newman here claims that some of the most important articles—like Article 11 on justification—are capable of a fully Roman Catholic interpretation.

However, Martz does not discuss the equally famous aftermath of No. 90, narrated so compellingly by Newman in *Apologia Pro Vita Sua*. "From the end of 1841"—scarcely ten months after No. 90—"I was on my deathbed as regards my membership in the Anglican church."[15] He was coming reluctantly to admit that the *via media* was far more exclusively and intransigently Protestant than he had thought. By October 14, 1843, he would write,

> I fear I must confess, that in proportion, as I think the English Church is showing herself *intrinsically* and *radically* alien from Catholic principles, so do I feel the difficulties of defending her claim to be a branch of the Catholic Church. It seems a dream to call a communion Catholic, when one can neither appeal to any clear statement of Catholic doctrine in its formularies, *nor interpret ambiguous formularies* by the received and living Catholic sense, whether past or present.[16]

Newman resolved his dilemma with dramatic integrity—he retracted all that he had said against Rome, resigned his living at St. Mary the Virgin, and, within two years, was received as a Roman Catholic.

That a man of Newman's brilliant interpretive resources and obvious persistence, with every personal and professional reason to do otherwise, should be compelled to acknowledge English doctrine's radical alienation from Catholicism is certainly no evidence for Martz's claims about Anglican ambiguity. Indeed, the range of this ambiguity seems remarkably narrow. If the Thirty-Nine Articles are vague, their vagueness is of a strangely exact kind.

To return, then, to double predestination, so conspicuously absent from Article 17: it is one thing for the *Articles* to gesture vaguely, as Newman originally had claimed, at a number of possible doctrinal paths at once; it is quite another thing for the *Articles* to set the reader

14. *DNB*, "Newman," 344b.
15. *Tracts for the Times, Remarks on Certain Passages in the Thirty-Nine Articles*, No. 90, 81–82; as in Martz, "Generous Ambiguity," 32.
16. *Apologia Pro Vita Sua, Being a History of His Religious Opinions*, 200, emphases mine.

on a markedly Protestant path—sufficiency of scripture (Article 6), bondage of the will (Articles 9–10), rejection of merit/justification by faith (Articles 11–15), predestination to life (Article 17)—without forcing him to the full predestinarian conclusion. No doubt the reprobation decree troubled many minds, including Calvin's. Archbishop Matthew Parker, who drafted the *Articles,* is said to have harbored reservations on this point, although the text of Article 17 is identical with the Edwardine Article authored by Cranmer.[17] Nevertheless, we should bear in mind the obvious generic difference between the *Institutes* and the *Articles:* Calvin's treatise was intended primarily for the learned, for divines, and for pastors, while the *Articles* are an official document, soon published in English (1571) and read to all subjects, with subscription required of all officeholders. So it is probable that the *Articles'* reticence on reprobation results not only from statesmanlike equivocation but also from pastoral caution. As we have seen, one could be convinced of double predestination and yet fear, like Calvin—and probably like Cranmer—that a cursory public proclamation of the doctrine could have dangerous effects on the hearers.

Hence we find strong words at the end of Article 17 warning against the curiosity of "carnal persons," for whom "to have before their eyes the sentence of God's Predestination, is a most dangerous downfall . . . either into desperation, or into wretchlessness of most unclean living." Like Calvin, the *Articles* will not have election misapplied or "turned into a curse" (*ICR* 3.23.14). Then the last paragraph of Article 17 concludes the matter by warning against speculation: "We must receive God's promises in such wise, as they be generally set forth in holy Scripture." This final caveat does not, as Martz suggests, undercut the Article's previous assertions by "leav[ing] the whole matter open to personal interpretation according to scripture";[18] instead, it seems to parallel Calvin's response to objections that teaching predestination will diminish faith in the straightforwardness of the gospel promises. "When we receive the promises in faith," he writes, "we

17. V. J. K. Brook, *A Life of Archbishop Parker,* 131. See also Charles Hardwick, *A History of the Articles of Religion,* 310–14 for the Latin and English texts of the *Articles* of 1553, the Latin *Articles* of 1563, and the English translation of 1571.
    18. "Generous Ambiguity," 38.

know that then and only then do they become effective in us . . . his mercy is extended to all, provided that they seek after it and implore it. But only those whom he has illumined do this. . . . The latter possess the sure and unbroken truth of the promises" (*ICR* 3.24.17). For Calvin, whosoever *will* may come. Believers can and should take Christ's words at face value, assuming that if they have the will to seek forgiveness, the promises are for them.

So the difference between Calvin's thinking the damnation decree "terrifying to speak of" and the *Articles*' finding it *too* terrifying to speak of seems surprisingly small; indeed small enough, as I have suggested, to be a difference in genre and social context. I have belabored what is probably the least loved doctrine in Christendom because adherence to or rejection of it is still treated as the litmus test for the honor, or the onus, of the label "truly Calvinist." Yet we have seen that caution or reticence about the doctrine did not denote rejection of it, let alone of the reformation's distinctive theological core. So I will assume throughout this study that the Elizabethan Settlement was, in its doctrine of salvation, profoundly Protestant and—how shall I say it—very nearly Calvinist. Very, very nearly.

However, when we turn to Herbert himself, the evidence points to his having been in fact "truly Calvinist." No doubt his Trinity College divinity reading included the *Institutes*;[19] and in his early anti-Puritan work, *Musae Responsoriae,* he begins his attack on the Scots Calvinist Andrew Melville by agreeing with Melville's theology and choice of "sacred authors," including not only the ancient Fathers, but also Martyr, Bucer, Beza, Whitaker, and, of course, Calvin. All of them, as Herbert says of Melville and himself, "revere the Divine Will."[20] It is on this common ground of predestinarian theology that Herbert engages the Puritans in controversy over church government and ritual. Furthermore, in commenting on Juan de Valdes's statement that God has "two wills . . . one Mediate . . . and the other Immediate," Herbert notes approvingly that "[h]e meanes a mans fre-will is only in outward, not in spiritual things." Yet he concludes by echoing Cal-

19. Kendall, "Puritan Modification," 202.
20. Epigram 33, ll. 3, 6 and Epigram 4, l. 6; *W,* 398 and 386, respectively. In the original of Epigram 4, "Numen & ipse colo."

vin's own pastoral caution: "This doctrine however true in substance, yet needeth discreet, and wary explaining" (*W,* 313–14).

As "discreet and wary" as Herbert was, nevertheless "The Water-course" explicitly affirms double predestination. Jeanne Clayton Hunter has shown how the poem adopts the same water imagery used by Preston, Sibbes, and especially Calvin, who writes, "We shall never be clearly persuaded, as we ought to be, that *our salvation flows from the wellspring of God's free mercy* until we come to know of his eternal election, which illuminates God's grace by this contrast: that he does not indiscriminately adopt all into hope of salvation but *gives to some what he denies to others*" (*ICR* 3.21.1, emphases mine). Martz's attempt to distinguish a "Calvinist tone" in this poem from "Calvinist doctrine" seems forced and artificial. He suggests that, for Herbert, God's giving salvation or damnation "as he sees *fit*" implies that election may after all be fitted to—conditional upon—man's foreseen faith and foreknown remorse.[21] But Martz's introduction of such conditions contradicts not only the English Church's free-will and justification articles (10–11) but also Herbert's own denial of grief's merit in poems from "The Reprisall" to "The Holdfast" to "Love" (III).

We also should remember that "The Water-course" does not appear in the Williams manuscript (*W,* liv–lv), and therefore that Herbert seems to have added the poem, along with many others, relatively late. By 1632–1633, when Herbert was putting *The Temple* into its final form for possible publication, he must have known of the strongly anti-Calvinist policies being enforced at court and at the universities. Less than two years earlier, Laud had called John Davenant, Herbert's own bishop at Salisbury, to kneel before the council and be harshly rebuked for discussing predestination and election in a court sermon. In such a tense political context, with Arminian-controlled censors at Cambridge, the eye-catchingly emblematic "Water-course" seems, if anything, obtrusively Calvinist.[22]

---

21. Hunter, "Herbert's 'The Water-course,'" 310–12; Martz, "Generous Ambiguity," 38–39.

22. *DNB,* "Davenant," 551a,b. In fact, the vice-chancellor of Cambridge did refuse for some time to license *The Temple* because he suspected that "The Church-militant" expressed sympathy for the Massachusetts Bay Puritans because of its lines (*W,* 235–36, 196) about true religion's immanent flight "to the *American* strand." See *W,* lxxii, 547.

The same tense context of doctrinal enforcement seems relevant to "Perseverance" and the question of its exclusion from *The Temple*. Only the Williams manuscript contains this fine poem (*W*, 204–5), which Martz rightly calls "a cry of deep anguish"—the anguish of a soul, I would argue, that successively doubts God's good will to save, and Christ's power to save:

> My God, the poore expressions of my Love
> Which warme these lines & serve them vp to thee
> Are so, as for the present I did moue,
>   Or rather as thou mouedst mee.
>
> But what shall issue, whither these my words
> Shal help another, but my iudgment bee,
> As a burst fouling-peece doth saue the birds
>   But kill the man, is seald with thee.
>
> (ll. 1–8)

These stanzas sound like uneasy broodings induced by the neo-Calvinism of Beza and Perkins. The speaker begins by claiming some spiritual initiative—"as for the present I did moue"—but then quickly, and rather woodenly, corrects himself—"Or rather as thou mouedst mee." Orthodoxy superficially restored, the second stanza dramatizes, in the image of the exploding gun, the terrible possibility speculated upon by Perkins: that a man may be spiritually warmed and moved to help others and yet, finally, "reprobated unto death" at God's pleasure. The speaker fears that God's inscrutable hand may yet make him the object of what amounts to an exceedingly grim practical joke —as if all of his life were a set-up for a damning slapstick conclusion. The note of helplessness grows oppressive with the awareness in line 8 that the outcome is fatally "seald with thee." Neo-Calvinist speculation is well on its way to producing despair.

Then, in the next stanza, the speaker entertains a theologically opposite, but equally chilling alternative:

> ffor who can tell, though thou hast dyde to winn
> And wedd my soule in glorious paradise,
> Whither my many crymes and vse of sinn
>   May yet forbid the banns and bliss?
>
> (ll. 9–12)

We might call this the "Arminian" stanza, because it rebounds from the damning fatalism of the second stanza to a damning freedom—freedom to fall. Contrary to the reformed belief in the "perseverance of the saints," Arminius taught that, despite Christ's hypothetical atonement for all mankind, and despite his wooing by the Spirit, true believers can finally separate themselves from God through their sins.[23] Arminius, like Pelagius and Erasmus before him, considered this possibility a goad to moral living; but for this poem's speaker, it seems merely another route to despair. Humans need saving, but human freedom means divine impotence.

Caught between these alternatives—both resulting, Calvin would say, from extra-scriptural speculation—the speaker casts himself on the God of scripture, of "whosoever will may come," in the superbly emotive final stanza:

> Onely my soule hangs on thy promisses
> With face and hands clinging vnto thy brest,
> Clinging and crying, crying without cease,
>   Thou art my rock, thou art my rest.
>   (ll. 13–16)

These lines brilliantly fuse the images of the terrified soul dangling from a rocky precipice and the terrified infant sobbing on his parent's chest. The internal echoes of "clinging" and "crying" resound off the "rock," but the rock is—suddenly and wonderfully—a maternal breast, and finally a "rest." Implicit in the one image is the hungry abyss below; but implicit in the other, and subsuming both, are the motherly Father's strong "everlasting arms" (Deut. 33:27). In the solipsism of fear, the child who grasps the "promisses" may feel that he is doing all the grasping; but what nurturing father or mother will not clasp a crying child? The Judge is also the Savior, and a kind of nurse, perhaps like Christ weeping over Jerusalem (Luke 13:34). Thus Calvin wrote that the frightened believer should look neither to God's secret decrees nor to his own works or sins when questioning his salvation, but only to his heavenly Father's gospel promises (*ICR* 3.24.7).

---

23. Veith, *Reformation Spirituality,* 26–28.

So the pathos of this poem's parent-child image, and the characteristically Herbertian reliance at the end on terse scriptural bedrock, place "Perseverance" on an unmistakable trajectory toward "Calvinist" assurance.[24] The saints persevere because God preserves them, even when the saints are too frightened to notice. Nevertheless, Herbert omitted the poem from *The Temple*. Why?

First, *implicit* indictment of speculative errors and *implicit* assurance are not quite the things themselves. Furthermore, the Arminianism of the third stanza may have worried Herbert, especially since, in the Williams manuscript, he had placed the poem prominently in "The Church," only sixth from the end (*W*, lv). Perhaps, as Martz suggests, its outcry seemed to conflict with the assured mood that dominates the last fifteen poems in the Bodleian manuscript. One could wish, with Martz, that Herbert had found a place for "Perseverance" earlier in the collection. However, the most reasonable explanation for its final absence would not seem to be that it "raised a controversial issue"—so did "The Water-course"—but that it sounded Arminian.[25] No doubt, accustomed as we are now to free speech and free press, Herbert's decision to cut one poem here and add another there hardly seems to us a ringing manifesto. But we should remember that two controversial *lines* nearly kept *The Temple* from seeing print at all. The mature Herbert of *The Temple* was no longer the brash polemicist of the *Musae Responsoriae;* yet he had become a man of strong and settled reformation principles. He knew that Laud was redrawing the boundaries of belief. Before delivering his manuscript to Ferrar, Herbert almost certainly counted the cost, and left the poems as stones of remembrance, recalling the contours of the older order. It is possible to take a stand without shouting.

The Eucharist: The *Articles* and Herbert

Besides these hotly contested points of predestinarian doctrine, the other theological formulation most commonly assumed to distinguish

24. See Psalm 19:14, "The Lord is my rock and my fortress and my deliverer, / My God, my rock in whom I take refuge" and Psalm 37:7, "Rest in the Lord and wait patiently for him" (Revised Standard Version).
25. Martz, "Generous Ambiguity," 38.

the English *via media* and Herbert from "strict Calvinism" is that of the Eucharist. Both Martz and Stanley Stewart point to Herbert's avoidance of dogmatism in this matter as evidence that he is truly "Anglican" rather than strictly Protestant or Calvinist.[26] However, there is a difference between dogmatism and affirmation, so that this contrast between ambiguity and punctiliousness is again misleading.

No doubt, the fruitless eucharistic debates between Zwinglians and Lutherans, which disastrously affected the cause of Protestant unity, seem a textbook case of ungenerous precision. Both Zwingli and Luther rejected medieval "transubstantiation"—the Scholastic doctrine that priestly consecration transforms the physical substance of bread and wine into the physical substance of Jesus' body and blood—only to fall out intractably over an alternative interpretation. Zwingli's "memorialism" understood Christ's words "This is my body. . . . This is my blood" (Mark 14:22, 24) as purely metaphorical and the Lord's Supper as only a symbolic memorial; Luther insisted on the "Real Presence" of Christ *physically, along with* the substance of the elements. Luther's position, commonly called "consubstantiation"—though not by Luther and Lutherans—grows from the belief that Christ, as God, is "everywhere present throughout his creation as a sustaining and animating force," including "in, with, and under" the Communion elements.[27]

So it is crucial to note that, as Jeanne Clayton Hunter writes, Calvin's eucharistic theology appeared in its own day "as the *via media* between Zwingli and Luther."[28] In fact, Calvin sought to mediate between the two parties, warning against complex and speculative solutions to the true nature of Christ's presence. Instead, as when discussing predestination, he recommends a learned—and reverent—ignorance: "Now, if anyone should ask me how [the believer's feeding on Christ] takes place, I shall not be ashamed to confess that it is a secret too lofty for either my mind to comprehend or my words to declare. . . .

26. Martz, "Generous Ambiguity," 40; Stewart, *George Herbert,* 48.

27. See Roland H. Bainton, *Here I Stand: A Life of Martin Luther,* 140. In the actual Lutheran language, Christ is present "[i]n, with, and under the in-substance-unchanged bread and wine" (*in, mit, und unter dem der Substanz nach unveränderlen Brode und Weine*). See *OED,* "consubstantiation."

28. "'With Wings of Faith,'" 59.

I rather experience than understand it" (ICR 4.17.32, emphasis mine).
Again, Calvin opposes doctrinaire "curiosity" and calls instead for
awe in the face of a tremendous mystery.

Nevertheless, as Hunter makes clear, Calvin's middle way does pos-
sess its own internal logic. While rejecting as speculative Luther's be-
lief in the ubiquity of Jesus' resurrection body—that, in other words,
the risen Christ is physically present everywhere, especially in the
Communion elements—Calvin also rejected the "bare memorialism"
of Zwingli's empty sign—sometimes parodically called the "Real Ab-
sence."[29] Instead, Calvin affirmed a doctrine of spiritual "Real Pres-
ence," arguing that the soul's mysterious feeding takes place after the
Holy Spirit raises the believing communicant up to union with Christ
in heaven. As Hunter notes, the ascension metaphor is essential for Cal-
vin, who writes that the believing communicant, "having surmounted
the world *on wings of faith, soars up to heaven*" (ICR 4.17.24, em-
phasis mine). To Calvin, this kind of metaphysical soul-feeding is far
more "real" than any physical feeding—his insistence on its "spir-
ituality" is in no way to be confused with Zwingli's "memorialism,"
let alone with modern materialist uses of "spiritual" to mean "unreal"
or "insubstantial." True feeding depends for Calvin not on Christ's
physical substance in the elements, but on the communicant's receiv-
ing the elements with a "lively faith" in Christ's atoning passion and
resurrection. Hence Calvin's "Real Presence" view is often called
"receptionist."

Hunter's illuminating discussion of Calvin's *via media* is exceed-
ingly relevant to the English church's 1563 sacramental articles (25–
31)—indeed, much more relevant than Hunter herself claims. Although
she rightly sees Herbert's Communion poems as "closely allied" to
Calvin's eucharistic theology, she still, like Martz and Stewart, sees
the *Articles* themselves as ambiguously Anglican.[30] Certainly, as in
Article 17 on predestination, a range of ambiguity exists; but again,
this range is surprisingly narrow, indeed narrower than on predes-
tination, so that in the end there is practically no distinction between
the English position and Calvin's own. In fact, on only one eucha-

29. Ibid., 60.
30. Ibid., 57–58.

ristic matter do the *Articles* seem less than clearly Calvinist: from Article 28, the convocation deleted a section, based on the similar Edwardine Article, that strongly denied the Lutheran "ubiquity of Christ" doctrine—that Christ is everywhere present—the doctrine crucial to so-called "consubstantiation."[31]

However, the ambiguity that convocation gives with one hand it takes away with the other. Even without the "ubiquity" clause, Article 28 rules out Luther's position, and it duplicates Calvin's: "The Body of Christ is given, taken, and eaten in the Supper, *only* after a heavenly and spiritual manner. And the *means whereby the Body of Christ is so received* and eaten in the Supper, is Faith" (emphases mine). Then Article 29 stresses that "the wicked, and *such as be void of a lively faith,* although they do carnally and visibly press with their teeth . . . the Sacrament . . . , yet *in no wise are they partakers of Christ:* but rather, to their condemnation do eat and drink" (emphases mine). Stewart writes, like many others, that English eucharistic doctrine "bore the impress of [Elizabeth's] determination to establish a middle ground between the extremes of Luther and Zwingli, on the one hand, and Rome on the other."[32] However, this middle ground is misplaced. Actually, the "extremes" between which Articles 25–31 navigate are Zwingli's and Luther's. Rome is off the map—dismissed with the kind of stinging language that Newman was to find so intractable.[33] Furthermore, the middle ground between these Protestant extremes had long been occupied by Calvin. In 1563 it came again to be shared officially, as in Edward's time, by the Church of England.

What then of Herbert's Communion poems? Although it is unnecessary to recapitulate Hunter's finely nuanced argument in full, Martz's "ambiguity"-based readings require some response, especially in light of the eucharistic articles' relative exactness. We should bear in mind, as we have already noted, that Herbert's lyrics are not doctrinal ex-

---

31. Brook, *Archbishop Parker,* 133.
32. *George Herbert,* 48.
33. For example, to quote only from the sacramental articles themselves: "The Sacraments were not ordained of Christ to be gazed upon, or to be carried about" (Article 25). "Transubstantiation . . . is repugnant to the plain words of Scripture, overthroweth the nature of a Sacrament, and hath given occasion to many superstitions" (Article 28). "[T]he sacrifice of Masses . . . are blasphemous fables, and dangerous deceits" (Article 31).

positions, let alone polemics. We should remember too that, as Hunter reminds us, Herbert seems to have experienced some uncertainty about the mode of receiving Christ in Communion—an uncertainty that occurs in one of the seven poems that she discusses.[34] Hunter notes that in "The Invitation" (*W*, 179–80) the speaker offers the Communion cup to the repentant as that which "*before* ye drink is bloud" (l. 12). This line, she admits, "could be read as evidence of Roman transubstantiation or Lutheran consubstantiation. But the larger body of evidence shows that Herbert clearly embraces ascension to the body of Christ and within that context I have read this line"— which she interprets as a poetic compression of the "receptionist" theory: "the signified received."[35] In any case, Herbert's debt to Calvin is clear, both in general tone and in actual imagery, so we should not hesitate to see the poet, like his church, agreeing in this matter with Geneva.

Both Martz and Stewart build much of their argument on Herbert's dislike of theological disputes. Martz notes rightly that these lines from "Divinitie" (*W*, 134–35) "serve well as an attack on excessive doctrinal controversy":

> But he doth bid us take his bloud for wine.
> Bid what he please; yet I am sure,

34. "The Banquet," "Love Unknown," "The Invitation," "The H. Communion," "The H. Communion" (Williams manuscript), "The Agonie," "Love" (III). Like Martz, Hunter also discusses the one communion poem excluded from *The Temple*—the Williams manuscript's "H. Communion" (*W*, 200–201). Martz and Hunter agree—rightly—that despite its tone of uncertainty, the piece clearly rejects transubstantiation (ll. 19–30). Hunter concludes that Herbert cut the poem as too polemical and discursive ("'With Wings of Faith,'" 69); Martz explains its exclusion as a "surprisingly clumsy and uneasy" piece ("Generous Ambiguity," 42). Martz seems closer to the truth—the poem is indeed rough going, and *The Temple* does take on controversial topics, e.g. in "The Water-course," "Lent" (see my chapter 3), and "The Church-militant." Yet the last two stanzas of the Williams "H. Communion" do anticipate Herbert's Calvinist resolution of eucharistic dilemmas in the clearly superior "H. Communion" found in "The Church" (*W*, 52–53). The Williams version admits that "[i]nto my soul this [the "fleshly" communion elements] cannot pass; / fflesh (though exalted) keeps his grass / And cannot turn to soule" (ll. 37–39). Thus the concluding cry—"My God, give me all Thee" (l. 48)— while vague, does gesture toward the "receptionist" position. Reverent ignorance desires spiritual "Real Presence."

35. "'With Wings of Faith,'" 65 n. 19.

> To take and taste what he doth there designe,
>   Is all that saves, and not obscure.
>   (ll. 21–24)

Yet the wittily reverent agnosticism of this stanza is in no way inconsistent with Calvin's "reverent ignorance" about Christ's Real Presence—"I rather experience than understand it." It may seem strange to hear this kind of humble devotionalism from a man like Calvin, who published hundreds of tightly argued pages on the subject. But he believes that if ignorance is truly "learned," it will know the limits of knowing. At Communion time, Calvin, as Hunter observes of Herbert, "drops argument for experience."[36] Since the saving work is all God's, the communicant need not comprehend God's means, but only obey his commands and receive his grace.

Besides overlooking this antispeculative affinity between reformer and poet, Martz and Stewart also neglect the important Calvinist motif of eucharistic "ascension," which, as Hunter demonstrates, appears repeatedly in these poems, most particularly in "The Banquet" (W, 181–82), where

> Having rais'd me to look up,
>   In a cup
> Sweetly he doth meet my taste.
> But I still being low and short,
>   Farre from court,
> *Wine becomes a wing at last.*
>
> *For with it alone I flie*
>   *To the skie . . .*
>   (ll. 37–44, emphasis mine)[37]

36. Ibid., 69.
37. See also the second half of the two-part "H. Communion," which, following the ingestion of the elements in part one, begins by remembering the ascent and rapture that ensued:

> Give me my captive soul, or take
>   My bodie also thither.
> Another lift like that will make
>   Them both to be together.
>   (ll. 25–28)

Images of flight and lightness permeate the poem; the eucharist restores man to prelapsarian ease, when "[h]e might to heav'n from Paradise go, / As from one room, t'another"

Herbert seems actually to have read and borrowed Calvin's governing metaphor here—the communicant is mounting up "on wings of faith." Furthermore, as Hunter shows, "ascension anticipates Real Presence."[38] Once on the wing, the communicant, in Calvin's words, "soars up to heaven,"

> Where I wipe mine eyes, and see
> What I seek, for what I sue;
> > *Him I view,*
> Who hath done so much for me.
> > (ll. 45–48, emphasis mine)

It is this progression—ascension to Real Presence—that makes possible the true communion of "The Banquet."

Significantly, Martz appears to read "The H. Communion" (*W*, 52–53) in a "receptionist" sense, writing that "only the *spiritual* presence of Christ can penetrate to the soul."[39] However, he does not seem to realize how this admission works against his attempt to distance Herbert from Calvin. It is precisely Calvin's claim that, in Herbert's words,

> Onely thy grace, which *with* these elements comes
> Knoweth the ready way,
> > And hath the privie key,
> Op'ning the souls most subtile rooms . . .
> > (ll. 19–22, emphasis mine)

Christ's spiritual substance comes *with*, not *in* the elements. He is received only by "a lively faith." Similarly, in "The Priesthood" (*W*, 160–61), God "become[s] our fare" when he "vouchsafeth" (l. 15)—when he condescends graciously to allow the believer into his presence. Then and only then do the "holy men of God"—Herbert's Protestant

---

(ll. 35–36). See also the fifth stanza of "The Invitation," the poem that immediately precedes "The Banquet," where eucharistic ascension is parodied by the worldling's "dove" of erotic "love," which sexually "exalts you to the skie" (*W*, 179–80).

38. "'With Wings of Faith,'" 64.
39. "Generous Ambiguity," 45.

"priests"—"convey him [Christ], who conveys their hands" (l. 16).[40] There is Real Presence here; however, there is no so-called "consubstantiation," let alone transubstantiation—despite the echoes of Thomas à Kempis (*W,* 534).

How then are we to regard Patrides's oft-quoted claim that "the Eucharist is the marrow of Herbert's sensibility"? As absolutely correct, though not in the way that he intended and is usually understood. For underlying this claim is the assumption that Herbert and the English *via media* are far more "sacramental" than Calvin and other "strict Protestants," far more devoted to the mysteries of Christ's Real Presence and Passion than their logocentric brethren. Nowhere do "Anglo-Catholic" readings more profoundly misunderstand the Elizabethan Settlement, Herbert, or Calvin. We have already observed Calvin's scripturalist insistence on the *magnum mysterium* of the Real Presence. I will mention only one more (amazingly) overlooked fact: that if frequency of observance is any measure of how important one considered Communion, no one in Reformation-era Christendom, Protestant or Roman Catholic, was more devoted than Calvin. In a period when it was customary for English churchmen to celebrate Communion three times a *year* (*W,* 259), and for Roman Catholics to receive it *once* a year (*ICR,* 4.14.44 nn. 41–42), Calvin writes that "the Lord's Table should [be] spread at least once a *week*" (*ICR* 4.17.46, emphases mine). "It was ordained to be frequently used among all Christians," he writes, "in order that they might frequently return in memory to Christ's Passion, and by such remembrance to sustain and strengthen their faith" (*ICR* 4.17.44).

Thus when Herbert, in *The Countrey Parson,* recommends that the Parson celebrate Communion "if not duly once a *month,* yet at least five or six times in the year" (*W,* 259, emphasis mine), he indeed seems to be walking a "middle way" between the reformer and Rome—but with Calvin at the "sacramentalist" extreme! Clearly, the Eucharist was at least as near the marrow of Calvin's sensibility as Herbert's; they share a devotional sensibility of communion, rapture, and thanksgiving for sheer grace. In fact, Herbert's "Calvinist" devotion to the

---

40. See my discussion of the "Protestant Priesthood" in chapter 5, and my full treatment of this autobiographical lyric in chapter 6.

Eucharist appears to have inspired his desire to exceed the "Anglican" minimum. Nowhere do we grasp so fully the ironic truth of William J. Bouwsma's claim that "Calvinism was the creation of a devout sixteenth-century French Catholic."[41]

Calvin's *Via Media*

If the arch-Protestant himself can sound so disconcertingly Catholic, we have come full circle to the question of how the supposedly "Anglo-Catholic" Herbert could be a Calvinist. For Calvin, again unlike many of his later disciples, was as much an inclusivist as an exclusivist, as much a relativist as an absolutist. His certainty on a core of absolutes—*sola scriptura, sola gratia, sola fide*—made him loath to absolutize in other areas. Nowhere did he dogmatize against Episcopalianism, nowhere did he attack all church ceremonies, or recommend the eradication of all local traditions, let alone undervalue the Eucharist.[42] Each of these issues, he wrote, "ought to be variously accommodated to the customs of each nation and age . . . we ought not to charge into innovation rashly, suddenly, for insufficient cause. But love will best judge what may hurt or edify; and if we let love be our guide, all will be safe" (*ICR* 4.10.30). Again, in Herbert's words, "the Apostles two admirable Rules: *all things done decently, all things done to edification.*" This is the *via media* that Herbert shared with Calvin: moderate precision in the service of love.

Few in any age let love be their guide, especially in ages of controversy. Certainly Michael Servetus and the Anabaptists had cause to doubt Calvin's charity. Herbert's own age was especially contentious, and it grew far more so after his death. He knew painfully well how easily the language of truth and precision became the language of hate and loathing, and how theological exactness came to gleam on the edge of a sword. Yet he believed God's truth to be the foundation of human love, and feared loving exactness no more than a builder

---

41. *John Calvin: A Sixteenth-Century Portrait,* 11. On Calvin and the frequency of the Eucharist, see also Kilian McDonnell, O.S.B., *John Calvin, the Church, and the Eucharist,* 190.
    42. Veith, *Reformation Spirituality,* 32.

fears a sound foundation. So, with a "learned ignorance" and a "discreet boldness" (*W,* 226) he set out to Bemerton on a path of charitable precision, with an errand into a milder sort of wilderness.[43] As the old Elizabethan social edifice creaked and crumbled around him in the larger world, he would seek to rebuild it to exact scale in a rural hamlet—lay again its foundations and raise its walls anew, commit its plan to poetry and prose, and God willing, publish the blueprint for all the builders and rebuilders of the kingdom, that righteous brotherhood of godly parsons.

As we will see, Herbert's surprisingly quixotic errand was, at least in its contemporary political effects, a poignant failure; the Elizabethan Settlement collapsed within the decade, and Herbert's ideal did vanish like a dream. Nevertheless, the poetic fruits of his vision continue to fascinate us. Thus this chapter has been a work of archaeology, diagraming the theological foundations on which Herbert sought to build. The succeeding chapters reassemble the superstructure—its doctrines of kingly power, pastoral duty, external worship, and social mission. Though Calvin would have been horrified to hear anyone called "Calvinist" (he had himself buried in an unmarked grave), I have so called Herbert, and have described his church's doctrinal base as "very, very nearly Calvinist"—so nearly, in fact, that frequently the distinction will be meaningless, and, for economy's sake, I often will forgo it. Neither Herbert nor Calvin would wish me to be overprecise.

43. See Perry Miller, *Errand into the Wilderness.*

2

The Bounds of Power

Stuart Authority in Crisis

> That thou may'st rightly obey power, her bounds know;
> Those past, her nature and name's chang'd; to be
> Then humble to her is idolatrie.
> —Donne, *Satyre III, Religion* (ll. 100–102)[1]

George Herbert produced much of his greatest poetry during the 1620s, a decade marked by increasingly deep and bitter divisions in church and state. During this decade, the constitution inherited from the Elizabethans foundered on the nature and extent of authority, particularly authority over spiritual matters. Though King James claimed absolute powers for himself, he left these claims largely unenforced. However, when James died in 1625, the new regime—King Charles, the Duke of Buckingham, William Laud, and the so-called "Arminian" party—decided to stand for their own. Laud and his party aggressively asserted, against most Calvinists—whether Presbyterian or Episcopalian—that kings and bishops ruled by divine right, without accountability to human law. Furthermore, the emerging regime sought to de-emphasize England's Protestant distinctiveness (also inherited from the Elizabethans) and to restore some medieval church liturgy, ceremony, and ornamentation that, they believed, had been wrongly eradicated during the Reformation.[2] So the coming conflict began to

---

1. *The Satires, Epigrams, and Verse Letters,* 14.
2. In my first chapter, I have already implied that despite persistent divisions between Conformists and Puritans, a far deeper cleavage existed in the 1620s between the Calvinists and the anti-Calvinists, or Arminians. Patrick Collinson writes, quoting Nicholas

take shape; Laud had an ambitious program of restoration afoot, and the rationale, temperament, and means for enforcement.

Yet despite their other widening differences, the absolutists and non-absolutists of the 1620s still spoke a common monarchist language, both groups framing arguments that appealed to the "Defender of the Faith and Supreme Governour of the Church" in terms of his self-interest. Thus in a sermon on the opening of Parliament in February 1626, Laud warned that the critics of "divine right" episcopacy, for all their assurances of loyalty to the king, "will not spare (if ever they get power) to have a pluck at the throne of David."[3]

Yet on the non-absolutist side of the controversy, monarchist rhetoric persisted. The Commons' subcommittee for religion insisted in the *Heads of Articles* of February 1629 that Laud's "Arminian sect," by then in possession of the most powerful bishoprics in England, posed a "great danger . . . to the Church and State, by divers courses and practices tending to the change and innovation of religion . . . within his Majesty's own dominions."[4] Even in 1640, when Charles himself publicly expressed the fear that the detractors of episcopacy "aim at our royal person," the "Root and Branch" petitioners spoke as royalists, calling for the abolition of episcopacy on the grounds that the bishops' claim to derive their authority "immediately from the Lord Jesus Christ . . . is against the Laws of the kingdom, and derogatory to his Majesty and his state royal."[5]

We certainly should note the important differences between the *Heads*

Tyacke, that until the mid-1620s, Calvinist theology formed "'a common and ameliorating bond' uniting conformists and moderate Puritans" and providing "the theological cement of the Jacobean Church." In contrast, the Arminians, led by Laud,

> inverted what the religious majority believed to be the true order of things. . . . [T]hat majority, "a society steeped in Calvinist theology," believed Calvinism and the religious practice associated with Calvinist belief to be the true orthodoxy. . . . Such an understanding of "orthodox protestant religion," with a suspicious fear of "innovation," was shared by a majority of the bishops, [who formed] "the mainstream of Calvinist episcopalianism."

See Collinson, *The Religion of Protestants: The Church in English Society, 1559–1625,* 81–82; and Tyacke, "Puritanism, Arminianism and Counter-Revolution," 120–24.

3. *The Works of the Most Reverend Father in God, William Laud* 1:83.

4. William Cobbett, ed., *The Parliamentary History of England* 2:483–84.

5. Church of England, *Synodalia. A collection of articles of religion, canons and proceedings of convocations in the province of Canterbury . . . 1547–1717* 1:380; J. Rushworth, ed., *Historical Collections of Private Passages of State* 5:93.

of Articles, an episcopal Calvinist complaint against the policies of Arminian bishops addressed by Parliament to the king, and the "Root and Branch Petition," an anti-episcopal tract addressed in the name of fifteen thousand private subjects to the Parliament.[6] But having noted these differences, we must admit that even in 1640, and certainly during the 1620s, any member of either ecclesiastical party who advocated a program for the church intended it to be adopted and enforced "by authority"; and that he believed this authority to reside finally, if not exclusively, in the person of the king.

But could authority go too far? Could the king, or the king-in-Parliament, make and enforce laws for the church that would somehow overturn the foundation on which his Supremacy stood, so that, in Donne's words, authority's "nature and name's chang'd," and previous claims to obedience qualified? When the early seventeenth-century Englishman sought to know the bounds of power, he usually sought to understand its purpose over and in the church. How, he would ask, does scripture relate to secular authority? Is the Bible a source, a limit, or both? What is the role of tradition in the commands of men? Do considerations of spiritual edification and personal conscience qualify the state's imperative to maintain order and uniformity? Finally, if it is against conscience to submit when authority has passed its bounds, what then is the subject—not only the earl or knight or bishop, but the common Christian—to do in response?

My purpose is to answer these and related questions, as far as possible, from Herbert's viewpoint: that is, from what Nicholas Tyacke and Patrick Collinson have called "the mainstream of Calvinist episcopalianism."[7] For Herbert, devoted both to the first principles of Protestantism and to the established forms of the British mother church, the growing crisis over authority during the 1620s must have caused painful inner conflicts, quite apart from his other well-known "afflictions" of poor health and frustrated ambition. The times confronted Herbert with what were, for him, two unpalatable options: on the one hand, could he bear to watch the "fine aspect and fit aray" of

6. J. P. Kenyon, ed., *The Stuart Constitution, 1603–1688: Documents and Commentary,* 152.
7. See note 2, above.

Elizabethan church order defaced by Puritan attack? Yet, on the other hand, the Arminian bishops were moving boldly to reassert the sacerdotal and secular powers that they believed had been yielded wrongly to the laity. Could Herbert stand by while, in his view, they shut up the windows of plain gospel preaching and neglected the altar of the heart in their zeal to edify stone and glass?

In facing these issues, Herbert appears to have stood as a true son of the church settled under Elizabeth. It should surprise no one to observe that he loved "order" and "decency," and that he conscientiously deferred to authority in "things indifferent." But to define *order, decency,* and *indifference,* we must examine the sixteenth-century origins of the royal Supremacy over the church. We will see that the Tudor apologists for Conformity do prescribe limits to kingly power over the church, and therefore allow (and sometimes demand) passive resistance when rulers violate these limits; the Christian must "obey God rather than men."

Herbert, unlike Laud and his bishops, held to this Elizabethan doctrine of a limited authority. The looming conflicts over church and state did make him carefully, even painfully, reticent about controversial matters; yet his silence was not total, as this chapter and the next will show.

Herbert and the Old Conformity

The church settlement that Herbert saw degenerate to the point of collapse had its origins in conceptual and political upheavals between 1530 and 1560. As A. G. Dickens notes, the initial conflict between church and state did not center solely around the problem of Henry VIII's divorce from Queen Katherine.[8] However, the divorce was more than a mere "occasion." By alienating Henry finally from the pope, it provided the necessary catalyst by which humanist aspirations, biblical proof-texts, and constitutionalist claims could combine to produce that distinctively English form of Erastianism that made the monarch "Supreme Governor" of the church within the bounds of the common

8. *The English Reformation*, 83.

law.[9] Yet in its early stages, this process increased rather than decreased royal power. Years before England's break with Rome, Erasmus and his humanist disciples were trying to groom a new generation of literate, virtuous princes, including Henry, dedicated (the humanists believed) to maintaining just and tranquil realms that would foster the new learning and revitalize the church.[10] Sir Thomas Elyot, Henry's exact contemporary and a follower of Erasmus and More, expresses this strain of optimistic royalism in his *Book Named the Governor,* which praises absolute monarchy as reflecting God's unitary nature on earth.[11]

While the humanists strengthened the royal arm to usher in their golden age, the early Protestants, particularly Luther, were providing an even more influential boost to absolute monarchy by discovering an imperative to obey the higher powers in the newly proclaimed supreme authority of scripture. Dickens writes, "[T]he initial perusal of the Scriptures tended to enhance rather than undermine monarchical power. In the Old Testament one read much concerning godly kings, while the New Testament at least gave Caesar his due. In both Testaments one . . . could sense singularly little of the medieval or Renaissance papacy."[12] In the early years of the Reformation, Luther saw the spiritual and temporal powers of the papacy as the chief evils to be attacked, and since the secular authorities protected and aided the fledgling movement, Luther's writings spoke of the state as the executor of God's wrath against evildoers and declared that active resistance to the prince is always wrong. Although Luther periodically

9. So called after the Swiss Zwinglian theologian Thomas Erastus (1524–1583), whose doctrine made the Christian magistrate supreme over church affairs. See Ruth Wesel-Roth, *Thomas Erastus.*

10. See e.g. Erasmus's words to Wolsey in a letter written during the second decade of the sixteenth century: "I see, I see, an Age truly Golden arising, if that mind of yours should prevail with some number of others. He [Henry VIII], under whose auspices they are made, will reward your most holy efforts. And eloquence, alike in Latin and in Greek, will celebrate with eternal monuments your heart, born to help the human race." The subject is Wolsey's efforts in behalf of the new learning (R. W. Chambers, *Thomas More,* 168).

11. Elyot writes that "undoubtedly the best and most sure governance is by one king or prince. . . . For who can deny but that all thing in heaven and earth is governed by one God, by one perpetual order, by one providence? One sun ruleth over the day, and one moon over the night. [Among the bees] one principal bee, who excelleth all other in greatness" (*The Book Named the Governor,* 7).

12. *English Reformation,* 137.

berated the princes for abusing power, the overall effect of his political doctrine of submission, which he drew from Pauline and Petrine texts, accelerated the increase and consolidation of civil power and gave the idea of "divine-right monarchy" great prestige in the developing Protestant mind.[13]

This effect was particularly strong in England, where, haltingly under Henry VIII, then forcefully under Edward VI, the Protestant movement united under the banner of the royal Supremacy to reform the church by decree and by policy. The break with the pope, the publication of a vernacular Bible, the new stress on preaching, and the reform of the liturgy were all accomplished by a coalition of Protestant clergy under the aegis of the monarch and his Parliament. Even before Parliament in 1533 acknowledged Henry to be "Supreme Head of the English Church," the early English Protestant William Tyndale had written in *The Obedience of a Christen Man* (1528) that "ye kinge is in this worlde without law & maye at his lust doo right or wronge and shall geve acomptes but to God only."[14] "Yee kinges," wrote the anonymous author in the 1547 homily "Of Obedience," "haue all their power and strength not from Rome, but immediately of God most Highest . . . [they] doe exercise Gods roome in iudgement" (*BH* 1:70–71).

This new exaltation of the royal power is well illustrated by Thomas Becon's argument in *A Potation for Lent* (1541–1542). He writes that all subjects should obey King Henry's 1539 order requiring auricular confession, on the grounds that submission to the king is in itself a visible good work that will give glory to God and thereby lead others to salvation: "Above all things . . . be obedient to the king's grace's majesty, yea, and that not only for fear, but much more for conscience' sake . . . and in all your words and deeds, *let your light so shine before men, that they may see your good works, and glorify your father which is in heaven.*"[15] Becon, an otherwise sturdy Protestant, attempts to make Henry's imposition of a basically Roman practice acceptable to reformed consciences. To realize how far Becon had to bend, we

---

13. Winthrop S. Hudson, *John Ponet (1516?–1556): Advocate of Limited Monarchy*, 118.
14. *The Obedience of a Christen Man*, leaf xxxii, verso.
15. *The Early Works of Thomas Becon*, 121.

need only turn to the other five of Henry's Six Articles, which maintain the essence of medieval religion—transubstantiation, Communion in one kind, celibate priests, religious vows, and private masses—and which threaten dire penalties: burning for denying transubstantiation, forfeiture of all property and imprisonment for opposing the rest.

While Becon's "justification" of Lenten confession is ultimately subversive of the practice, he rationalizes not only from fear and prudence, but also from principle.[16] For at this first stage of the Reformation he probably believed, like most English Protestants, that scripture lays an overriding burden on Christian consciences to obey the king when at all possible, especially when the king appears to have made great progress by breaking with the pope and publishing an English Bible.

Thus in the early days of the independent national church, Henry rode the crest of the absolutist wave, claiming and receiving the title of "supreme head and king . . . [of] the body politic, compact of all sort and degrees of people divided by names of spiritualty and temporalty." He derived his claim to headship of church and state solely from God; Parliament did not invest him with the Supremacy, he said, but merely confirmed it as the restoration of his true position according to common law. Furthermore, he personally exercised in fact all of the ecclesiastical powers once yielded to the pope; he controlled the church's laws, its courts, its appointments, its revenues, and also its doctrine and ceremonies. Henry was, as G. R. Elton notes, a lay bishop, with complete personal supremacy.[17]

However, this initial fusion of humanist and biblicist absolutism was soon countered by the third major conceptual component of the Elizabethan Settlement of 1559: a growing stress on the legitimating power of the "ancient constitution." So while Elizabeth claimed a Supremacy like her father's, she really occupied a weaker position, both theoretically and actually. The intervening reigns of Edward and Mary

16. Despite Becon's submissiveness, the authorities recognized his ability to fill Catholic forms with Protestant meanings, so that only a few months after he published the *Potation*, they forced him to recant and to burn all of his books at Paul's Cross. At this time Becon became a fugitive, and he wrote more boldly in the same "heretical" vein (*DNB*, "Becon," 93).

17. *The Tudor Constitution: Documents and Commentary*, 344, 332–33.

had not only brought an infusion of Calvin's more constitutionalist doctrines through the Marian exiles, but also had eroded the basically personal nature of the Supremacy, giving Parliament the upper hand in matters of doctrine and ceremony.[18] Thus, under the Elizabethan Settlement, the final authority now rested with the "queen-in-Parliament" rather than with the queen alone. In addition, Elizabeth relinquished the title of "Supreme Head" and called herself instead "Supreme Governour" of the church. With the claim to headship went the quasi-episcopal status of the crown, so that, in Elton's words, the queen now "governed the spiritualty from the outside."[19]

But Elizabeth was followed by James, and it is important to note the major legal differences between Tudor and Stuart views of the royal prerogative. For unlike the Stuarts and their partisans, who claimed that the prerogative came *jure divino,* the more constitutionalist Tudor spokesmen admitted, indeed insisted, that the royal power derived from the common law and was limited by the common law. No doubt this insistence served at first as an antidote to possible Parliamentary claims. Only a year after Henry's death in 1547, William Stanford writes, "[T]his Parliament maketh no part of the king's prerogative, but long before it had his being by the order of the common law."[20] But by the 1590s, this resort to the common law becomes, in Richard Hooker's hands, a robust celebration of limited monarchy:

Happier that people whose law is their king in the greatest things, than that whose king is himself their law. . . . [By law] I mean not only the law of nature and of God, but very national or municipal law consonant thereunto. . . . In which respect, I cannot choose but commend highly their wisdom, by whom the foundations of this commonwealth have been laid; wherein though no manner person or cause be unsubject to the king's power, yet so is the power of the king over all and in all limited, that unto all his proceedings the law itself is a rule. The axioms of our regal government are these: "Lex facit regem" ["Law

18. Calvin discusses how constitutionally established magistrates are "to restrain the willfulness of kings" in an enormously influential passage of the *Institutes,* 4.20.31. See also John T. McNeill's note on how this passage influenced Calvinist resistance theorists from England's John Ponet, to the Huguenots, to the Scot Samuel Rutherford (*ICR,* 1518–19 n. 54).
19. *Tudor Constitution,* 335–36.
20. *An Exposition of the King's Prerogative,* fol. 5.

makes the king"]: *the king's grant of any favor made contrary to law is void.* "Rex nihil potest nisi quod jure potest" ["The king can do nothing but that which he is enabled to do by law"]. (*LEP* 8.2.12–13)

Here we can begin to appreciate the quite substantial difference between Elizabethan claims and those of the Stuarts. Where James and Charles claim to hold their power directly from God, to be responsible only to God, and to be over and even over against the earthly law, Hooker's monarch is subject to the common law of the land, insofar as it conforms to reason and scripture.[21] Indeed, the king is so much a creature of the law—*Lex facit regem*—that his actions outside the law lose their force. The law, that it might be executed, enables the king; the king, by transgressing the bounds of the law, disables himself—at least in that particular instance.

John Donne probably wrote his *Satyre III* in the 1590s, within only a few years of Hooker's *Laws,* and Hooker serves as an excellent gloss on the young poet's assertion that once power has passed her bounds, "her nature and name's chang'd." Hooker, quoting Archytas, writes that where the king does not rule according to the law, "it cometh by transgression thereof to pass that the king grows a tyrant; he that ruleth under him abhorreth to be guided and commanded by him; the people, subject under both [king and law], have freedom under neither; and the whole community is wretched" (*LEP* 8.2.12). Thus transgressing, "power" has a new name: tyranny.

Hooker's constitutionalism most affects authority in the church through his holding the Supreme Governor subject to specific human laws, which are themselves subject to reason and scripture. Thus the king becomes a tyrant in the ecclesiastical realm when he makes laws and policies that thwart the fundamental purpose of his Supremacy— the establishment of "good order" and the edification of the people. In the *Laws,* Hooker presses home the need for this universal secular regnum: "that kings should be in such sort supreme commanders over all men we hold it requisite as well for the ordering of spiritual as of civil affairs; inasmuch as without universal authority in this kind they should not be able when need serves to do as virtuous kings have done"

21. Elton, *Tudor Constitution*, 18.

(LEP 8.8.2). For Elizabeth and her Parliaments "to do as virtuous kings have done" meant, after thirty years of ecclesiastical upheaval under Henry, Edward, and Mary, to achieve a politically workable settlement of religion, both in doctrine and in outward observance, that would show forth the spiritual and temporal unity of the commonwealth in a uniform practice. Thus uniformity was to be enforced not only in the case of the central Protestant doctrines stated in the Thirty-Nine Articles and generally acknowledged to be explicit in scripture, but also in the case of certain church offices, ceremonies, and traditions admitted by all concerned to be neither commanded by scripture nor contrary to it, "things indifferent."

Herbert believed strongly in this authority of the king-in-Parliament to decide such ambiguous, "indifferent" matters. Privately, he lived in remarkable obedience to the established order of the British church, and as a pastor he worked diligently to edify his spiritual charges within the guidelines of that order. Herbert's most revealing statements about the nature of and reason for Conformity appear incidentally in *The Countrey Parson* as he discusses one or another matter of pastoral practice. In "The Parson's Accessory Knowledges" (*W,* 229–30), he calls in authority to tip the scales in favor of preaching "by way of expounding the Church Catechisme," because, while it is *"indifferent in it self to choose any Method* [of preaching], *that is best to be chosen,* of which there is likeliest to be most use. Now Catechizing being a work of singular, and admirable benefit to the Church of God, and *a thing required under Canonicall obedience,* the expounding of our Catechisme must needs be the most usefull form" (emphases mine). Significantly, it is typical of Herbert, as it is of Hooker, to recommend Conformity not as an end in itself, but as a means to order and edification, without which God cannot be glorified.

Herbert sounds even more like Hooker when discussing catechizing in chapter 21 of the pastoral manual. He notes that the parson "preferreth the ordinary Church Catechism," he says, "partly for obedience to authority, partly for uniformity sake, that the same common truth be everywhere professed, especially since many remove from Parish to Parish, who like Christian souldiers are to give the word, and satisfie the Congregation by their Catholick answers" (*W,* 255). Like Hooker, he justifies the Supremacy primarily by arguing that it is needed to express the commonwealth's spiritual and temporal unity through a uniform doctrine and practice; in other words, authority is valuable because it is useful.

Such utilitarianism is also seen in Herbert's claim that authority aids the believer by establishing set times and forms that he can then fill with devotion. In considering "The Parson's State of Life," he writes that an unmarried pastor, and probably any pastor, "thinkes it not enough to observe the fasting dayes of the Church, and the dayly prayers enjoyned him by auctority, *which he observeth out of humble conformity, and obedience;* but adds to them, out of choyce and devotion, some other dayes for fasting, and hours for prayers" (*W,* 237, emphasis mine). As we shall see in the lyric "Lent," Herbert believes fasting to be a spiritual and physical good in and of itself, so he sees the state-mandated fasting days as opportunities to do *with* the church what he is already more than willing to do on his own.

Thus Herbert most values a brimming piety that fills and overflows the authorized forms of worship. He praises such devotion even amid the barbs of the *Musae Responsoriae.* In defending the Prayer Book rubric for the "churching," or purification, of women after childbirth (*W,* Epigram 12, 390), Herbert states, "For godly souls, any occasion they have to pour out prayers from a humble heart is a rich gain" (pijs animis quaeuis occasio lucro est, Qua possint humili fundere corde preces, ll. 11–12). He claims that authority performs a spiritual service by creating and protecting a space for devotion, space which is to be filled by the grace of God acting in the worshiper. Thus, he would say, the form should not be blamed if the fervor is absent, because true devotion is the work of God alone.

Interestingly, Herbert praises spiritual rules most extravagantly in a passage that does not refer to established authority at all. Instead, he does so while explaining his own purpose in composing *The Countrey Parson.* The manual is no book of enforceable minimal standards, like the *Canons Ecclesiastical,* but written so "that I may have a Mark to aime at: which also I will set as high as I can, since hee shoots higher that threatens the Moon, then hee that aims at a Tree. Not that I think, if a man do not all which is here expressed, hee presently sinns, and displeases God, but that *it is a good strife to go as farre as wee can in pleasing of him, who hath done so much for us*" (*W,* 224, emphasis mine). It is this guiding principle, that the believer should do as much as possible to *please* God, and that we should do so out of sheer gratitude, which to a great degree gave Herbert such appeal with the Puritans. They and their successors saw the Conformists as establishing not only a policy of minimums but also a prevailing attitude of minimalism, a scrupulous carefulness to give God "no offense," but, perhaps, to feel or do little of positive value.

Thus, for John Whitgift, Elizabeth's chief spokesman for Conformity, to say that church doctrine and practice should be "agreeable, or not contrary to God's holy word" is only to say the same thing in two different ways.[22] But, as John S. Coolidge shows, the Puritan kept asserting, to the confusion, exasperation, and eventual provocation of the authorities, that a nonnegative did not amount to a positive.[23] For although the Puritan was usually willing to admit the logical equivalence of the two phrases, he would not agree to their theological equivalence. Thomas Cartwright, Whitgift's main Puritan opponent in the Admonition Controversy of the early 1570s, writes:

> For albeit it cannot be but that . . . which is not against the word of God is agreeable unto it; yet he that saith that certain things must be done *not against the word,* that he will not also accord that they should be done *according to the word,* giveth thereby to understand that there is some star or light of reason or learning or other help whereby some act may be well done, and acceptably unto God, *in which the word of God was shut out* and not called to counsel. (emphases mine)[24]

In responding to Cartwright's distinction, Hooker claims a logical triumph, commenting that it "is in effect to say, 'We know not what to say well in defence of this position; and therefore lest we should say it is false, there is no remedy but to say that in some sense or other it may be true, if we could tell how'" (*LEP* 3.8.1). But in claiming this triumph, Hooker, like most defenders of the establishment (including Herbert himself in the *Musae Responsoriae*) fails to respect or even

22. John Bridges, *A Defence of the government established in the Church of England for ecclesiastical matters,* 56.

23. *The Pauline Renaissance in England: Puritanism and the Bible,* 10–11.

24. *The Second Replie of Thomas Cartwright: Agaynst Maister Doctor Whitgiftes Second Answer, Touching the Church Discipline,* 55–56.

acknowledge the Puritan's obsession with *pleasing* God. This obsession led Puritans to insist, in Coolidge's words, that

> obedience to God's word must be something more than a rational adjustment of man's behavior to God's truth, although undoubtedly it is that. [The Puritan] insists on trying to hear God's voice of command in all his thoughts and cannot feel that he is obeying God if it is 'shut out.' Directions simply found out by reason, reliable or not, can no more be equivalent to scriptural direction for him than a good map of the country could have done duty for the pillar of cloud that went before the people of God in Exodus.[25]

Indeed, Cartwright seems to have the "pillar of cloud" in mind. "It is necessary," he writes, "to have the word of God *go before us* in all our actions . . . for that we cannot otherwise be assured that they please God" (emphasis mine).[26] At root, the Puritan believed that one cannot hope to please God merely by not offending him. Indeed, he believed that an emphasis on not offending is a kind of offense to God, who might conclude that "this people honor me with their lips, but their hearts are far from me" (Isa. 29:13). The Puritan thought that, at the worst, a Conformist might be damned by his own faint praise.

So it is that although Conformist and Puritan approach "things indifferent" with the same scriptural rules, they diverge; yet Herbert, the model of Conformity, won the hearts of Conformity's critics. He voices, at least in his English writings, the Puritan's common concern that the life of the spirit be excessive—excessive, at least, of the "decent," "inoffensive" forms made by men. Indeed, there is a certain extravagance to the controlling image of Herbert's prefatory paragraph that would excite the Puritan frame of mind and, perhaps, mystify the "judicious Hooker." For if a reasonable man were told to aim high, he might aim even at a treetop; but Herbert would have his conforming country parson "threaten the Moon." For Herbert, this suggestion of holy lunacy, of striving for the outer limits in God's service, is what Christ himself has made "the argument of a Pastour's love" (*W*, 224).

25. *Pauline Renaissance*, 11.
26. *Second Replie*, 61.

Yet it is probably this same tendency to exceed the established minimum and shoot for the high mark that made Herbert so attractive to Walton as a subject for Conformist hagiography. Walton no doubt felt the deep admiration that he expresses for "the holy Mr. Herbert," and indeed he compares his work in composing Herbert's *Life* to a famously extravagant spiritual act, Mary Magdalen's anointing of Christ's feet with precious ointment.[27] But since it is also clearly Walton's polemical purpose to apply Herbert's acknowledged spiritual luster to the tarnished edifices of the Restoration establishment, there is irony in the fact that he chose as a model of Conformist sanctity a parson whose work far outstripped the minimalism typical of establishment pluralists and their ill-trained, often negligent curates.[28] Walton decidedly mutes the exertions of Herbert's spiritual and pastoral regimen in order to enhance his portrait of a meek, contemplative ritualist, yet he exalts the holy character that this strenuousness produced. For here, at last, was a loyal Conformist cleric who gave the lie to Puritan complaints.

Conformity and Enforcement

But for all of Herbert's efforts at showing how the flowers of devotion can and should spring up within the church's decent bounds, the fact remains that ultimately, Conformity meant not merely suggestion or persuasion, but enforcement. Under the royal Supremacy, ecclesiastical canons were laws of the realm, with the power of the sword behind them. As a pastor, Herbert was not only a minister of Christ, but also of the king, and was under orders to ensure that his parishioners obeyed the king's ecclesiastical decrees.

The difference between Herbert and Laud on enforcement was not merely one of temperament, but one of principle. Laud and his allies introduced another rule into the already unstable complex of church authority, a rule that, as they saw it, conflicted with neither the rule of

27. *The Lives of John Donne, Sir Henry Wotton, Richard Hooker, George Herbert, and Robert Sanderson*, 258–59.
28. Clayton D. Lein, "Art and Structure in Walton's Life of Mr. George Herbert," 162–65.

scripture nor with the king's Supremacy. This rule was the principle of divine-right episcopacy, and it became the Arminians' chief defense, their main weapon, and, in the end, their greatest liability. The root of the controversy over divine right lay in the question of who, finally, would exercise the spiritual headship of the church, thus acting as the authoritative interpreters of the infallible scripture, and as formulators of official doctrine and practice.

By taking the title of Supreme Governor, Elizabeth had relinquished the quasi-episcopal claims of her father's headship, leaving the locus of doctrinal supremacy constitutionally vague. Certainly doctrine and ceremony were to be determined "by authority"; but by which authority, practically speaking? Although Archbishop Whitgift claimed in the early 1570s that doctrine was an affair for bishops only, he was thwarted at the time by Parliament, which claimed this power, and on which such decisions actually tended to devolve. Furthermore, under the influence of Calvinism, even Conformists generally admitted, as we have noted, that government by bishops is an indifferent thing, not essential to a true church. In fact, some churchmen, like Edmund Grindal, Elizabeth's crypto-Puritan Archbishop of Canterbury, merely tolerated episcopacy as necessary for the times, and they hoped for its eventual disappearance as the Reformation made greater headway.[29] Others, like Ireland's Archbishop Ussher, who was Laud's contemporary in the church, advocated a plan for a modified episcopacy approaching Presbyterianism.[30]

However, as J. P. Kenyon writes, "the advent of Laud and Charles I . . . killed the vague assumption, encouraged by Elizabeth and not vigorously discouraged by James I, that the episcopal establishment, abolished in all the other reformed churches, would soon wither away in England, too."[31] So what Elizabeth left undefined for political reasons, and James mainly from neglect, Laud specified with dogmatic certainty: that all ecclesiastical power not exercised directly by the king himself belongs to the bishops by a direct grant from Jesus Christ;

29. See for example Grindal's grudging comments on the retention of certain old forms in Hastings Robinson, ed., *The Zurich Letters,* 169ff.
30. Summers, *George Herbert: His Religion and Art,* 50.
31. *Stuart Constitution,* 147.

that, in other words, episcopacy is no mere "indifferent thing," but rather the very essence of the church, the bishops alone determining doctrine and ceremonies under the king.

So, in his *Apologia* for the condemnation of Bastwick, Burton, and Prynne in Star Chamber in June 1637, Laud, at the height of his power, declares that "from the Apostles' times, in all ages, in all places, the Church of Christ was governed by bishops, and lay elders never heard of till Calvin's newfangled device in Geneva." Furthermore, he argues, this divine order of bishops does not run opposite to the royal power, but rather complements it. "[O]ur being bishops *jure divino*," he claims, "takes nothing from the King's right or power over us. For though our office be from God and Christ immediately, yet we may not exercise that power, either of order or jurisdiction, but by and under the power of the King given us to do so." The difference on this point between the Old and the New Conformity is stark. Hooker, with his belief in constitutionally limited monarchy, notes approvingly that English kings, "when they take possession of the room they are called unto, have it painted out before their eyes, even by the very solemnities and rights of their inauguration, *to what affairs by the said law their supreme authority and power reacheth*" (*LEP* 8.2.12, emphasis mine). Laud, in contrast, paints out for the people how far their king's authority, and his own with it, overreaches and transcends the law. All who oppose divine-right episcopacy "are against the King and the Law, and can have no other purpose than to stir up sedition among the people." James I had said "no bishop, no king."[32] Laud transforms the bishop into a kind of king.

Such a doctrine as Laud's was certain to arouse resistance, and to prescribe its suppression. English Erastianism had in fact never allowed much room for conscientious objection to church policy. From the writers of the *Book of Homilies* to Herbert himself, apologists for Conformity had always portrayed the presently established doctrine and order as well within scriptural guidelines, so that, in their view, objections could arise only in confused or really seditious minds. Of course, even establishment spokesmen admitted that rulers had opposed true religion in ancient, pagan times; nevertheless, these spokesmen

---

32. Laud, *Works of Laud* 6:43, 46; Collinson, *Religion of Protestants*, 11.

unfailingly portrayed their own regimes as dedicated to preserving and advancing the reformed faith and their subjects' spiritual welfare. In this vein, the author of the homily "Of Obedience" declares that Christ, in submitting to Pilate, "taught vs plainely, that even the wicked rulers haue their power and authorities from God, and therefore it is not lawfull for their Subiects to withstand them, . . . much lesse then it is lawfull for subiects, to withstand their godly and Christian princes, which doe not abuse their authoritie, but use the same to Gods glory, and to the profite and commoditie of Gods people" (*BH* 1:72).

In the same vein, Cranmer, attributing to Henry a thoroughgoing Protestantism that he never exhibited, classes the deceased monarch with the godliest kings of Judah:

> Honour bee to God, who did put light in the heart of his faithfull and true minister, of most famous memorie King Henry the eight, and gaue him the knowledge of his word, and an earnest affection to seek his glory, and to put away all such superstitious, and Pharisaicall sectes by Antichrist inuented, and set up againe the true word of God, and glory of his most blessed Name, as he gaue the like spirit vnto the most noble and famous Princes, Josophat, Josias, and Ezekias. (*BH* 1:38)

The clear intent of these and many similar passages is to forestall any possible objections from conscientious subjects by assuring them that the present occupant of the throne shares their zeal.

Scripturalism and Conscience

However, despite Henry's claims of absolute authority over church and state, two key elements of later Henrician policy drastically undermined this authority for Henry's successors: the distribution and study of the English Bible, and the subordination of the clergy to the laity in deciding ecclesiastical policy. As to the first policy, by 1545 the vernacular Bible was coming into the hands of Everyman, and authority told him that it was not only his privilege but also his duty to read it. So Cranmer lays the cornerstone of the *Book of Homilies,* and indeed of the new order, with "A Fruitfull Exhortation to the reading and knowledge of holy Scripture." Here he asserts that "as many as bee desirous to enter into the right and perfect way vnto

God, must applie their mindes to know holy scripture, without the which, they can neither sufficiently know God and his will, neither their office and duty" (*BH* 1:1). To Cranmer, the word of God is not only the great book of salvation, but also the mandate for a just and ordered society, a pattern that enables each man to discover for himself his proper "office" in the church and the body politic and to do his duty there.

Indeed, Cranmer voices enormous confidence in not only the spiritual and social efficacy of scripture, but also in its clarity for all. To those who would decline to read the Bible, protesting their ignorance, he answers, "[H]e that is so weake that he is not able to brooke strong meat, yet he may sucke the sweet and tender milke, and deferre the rest, untill they wax stronger, and come to more knowledge." "God leaveth no man vntaught, that hath good will to know his word," promises the marginal gloss; to those who study with a "burning desire," the Lord will "send him some godly doctour, to teach him" (*BH* 1:5). Thus for Cranmer, the goal of Bible study is to build each individual toward spiritual maturity, which means drinking deliberately from the "Well of Life" and deliberately rejecting "the stinking puddles of mens traditions" (*BH* 1:6)—in other words, deciding spiritual matters for oneself.

Indeed, Cranmer declares, God is so eager for the edification of each Christian that even "if we lacke a learned man to instruct and teach vs, yet God himself from aboue, will giue light vnto our mindes, and teach us those things which are necessary for vs, & wherein we be ignorant" (*BH* 1:5). This guarantee of personal divine instruction is qualified by a warning against arrogant rashness in jumping to conclusions and by an exhortation to "aske of other that know" about questionable interpretations. Yet Cranmer stresses that "the humble man may search *any* trueth boldly in the scripture, without *any* danger of errour" (*BH* 1:5, emphases mine). This is strong language. Once a man heeds Cranmer's call and studies to understand biblical salvation for himself, he enjoys a less dependent relationship to his "godly doctour" than to his parish priest under the old religion. For the means of grace—the scripture and the Spirit of God—are in his possession as well as the cleric's. The learner needs to return for further instruction, but this basic biblical knowledge is his.

Of course, the widespread publication of *verbum dei* had a second, inevitable result, which Cranmer and his fellow Erastian Protestants did not clearly anticipate: the more scripturally literate the layman became, the more independent he felt of authority for understanding the rules by which the church was to be governed. Dickens writes that after the first official printing of the vernacular Bible in 1538,

> further attempts to restrict access proved half-hearted and ineffective. . . .
> [T]he English Bible was destined to cripple caesaro-papalism. . . . [M]en
> rapidly sensed that after so many centuries of hierarchical and autocratic
> Christianity they were only demanding a liberty which early Christians had
> assumed as a matter of course. A Christian country could not educate its laity
> and then prohibit their access to the written sources of Christian belief. Tudor
> laymen had to be treated like adults because they believed themselves to be
> such. Though the art of State-propaganda was now advancing, Tudor govern-
> ments could neither suppress the appetite for the Bible, once they had whetted
> it, nor could they successfully prescribe the conclusions to be drawn from
> biblical study.[33]

So for Hooker, or even James, to assert that kings ruled the church under God's law was a claim practically quite different from what was technically the same claim made by Henry sixty years earlier. For despite short-lived attempts to limit Bible reading to the middle and upper classes, and later persecutions of Non-Conformists by Whitgift, by the century's end nearly every plowboy and weaver owned a bound copy of God's law and took in eternal truth with his meat.[34] More-over, after years of being told by his superiors that the Bible was the standard and guide for everything done in his church, he was now more able and inclined to hold the standard up to the reality for a private measure.

As a pastor, Herbert was himself one of the "godly doctours" sent by authority to preach the gospel and to ensure its "proper" inter-pretation—"proper," that is, in maintaining the established doctrines of salvation by grace and of submission to authority. We have noted that at least from a Puritan viewpoint, his position as a minister of

33. *English Reformation,* 137.
34. David Little, *Religion, Order, and Law: A Study in Pre-Revolutionary England,* 136.

both Christ and of establishment authority made him suspect as a servant of two masters. But throughout his writings Herbert seems convinced that no final conflict is involved—if his earthly master is in submission to the heavenly.

Like Cranmer, Herbert emphasizes the efficacy and clarity of God's word as the ultimate source and limit for church authority. In "The Parson Arguing," he asks rhetorically whether the church "be a rule to it selfe," or "whether it hath a rule," and whether that rule "be obscure" (W, 263). He answers throughout *The Countrey Parson* and elsewhere that the church's one rule, like the individual Christian's, is scripture; the Bible is assumed clearly to answer all questions of faith and provide explicit general rules that govern in obscurer matters of external practice (W, 246–47). Like Cranmer, he believes that he and others can arrive at a clear knowledge of the Bible's message, because all scripture has been "penn'd by the one and self-same Spirit" (W, 229), so that "what the scripture teacheth, the spirit teacheth, the holy spirit indeed sometime doubly teaching both in penning and applying" (W, *Notes on Valdesso,* 317). Herbert regards commentaries as good and necessary checks on private interpretation, but "he doth not so study others, as to neglect the grace of God in himself, and what the Holy Spirit teacheth him" (W, 229). The ultimate focus of Christian knowledge is in the individual believer.

So Herbert, by maintaining the emphasis of the early English reformers on the efficacy and clarity of scripture, and particularly on the interpretive guidance of the Holy Spirit, creates room in which personal consciences can move, and grounds on which people of common principles can meet to discuss differences. Herbert clearly believes that the laity owe respect and obedience to the ecclesiastical decisions of their superiors; however, he seems to believe that this obedience is owed not because the decision makers are superior, but because the decisions themselves conform to scripture.

Lay Authority in the Church

This assertion of scriptural authority and clarity contributed to a second major trend in Henrician and Edwardine policy—substantially greater lay authority over church affairs. Dickens notes that when, on

December 26, 1547, "the failing ruler nominated a Council of Regency for his son . . . [v]irtually all its sixteen members belonged to the 'new' families, and its strong personalities leaned toward Protestantism."[35] Such "new men," nobles, gentry, and clerics, eagerly crusaded against the institutional developments of the late medieval and Renaissance papacy, to which they owed nothing and from which enormous economic spoils were to be gathered. Conveniently delivered under Henry from "popish" beliefs in the sacrosanctity of church lands, they raided the monasteries. After Henry's death freed them from the king's remaining Catholic scruples, these "new men," led by Cranmer and Somerset, attacked the heart of the old religion by abolishing the priestly consecration of the Eucharist and by allowing priests to marry, thus reducing the social distance between clergy and laity.[36] Such a change, taken together with the acceptance of Parliament into the Supremacy under Elizabeth, signaled the triumph of the laity over the clergy.

This substantially increased lay role extended into the parish. The *Constitutions and Canons Ecclesiastical of 1604* make it clear that the laymen elected locally to serve as churchwardens are the true advance guard of church discipline. It is they, not the bishops, deacons, or the local minister, who are mainly responsible to discover, admonish, and, if necessary, present for judgment those parishioners who violate the canons. These canons encode both explicit scriptural commands and instructions about "things indifferent," now made more than indifferent by authority. Thus the wardens and their assistant "Sidemen" must ensure that no one attacks the church's Prayer Book and *Articles of Religion,* its apostolic legitimacy, or its government by "Archbishops, Bishops, etc." Nor are the wardens to allow any separatist "Schismatickes" to absent themselves "from the Communion of Saints in the Church of England accounting the Christians who are conformable to be prophane and vnmeete for them to join with in Christian profession."[37]

Although the *Canons'* clear emphasis in order, length, and language

35. *English Reformation,* 195.
36. Elton, *Tudor Constitution,* 387–88.
37. Ibid.; Church of England, *Canons,* Canons 2, 4, 5, 3, 7, 8, respectively.

is on the "wicked errors" of Non-Conformists, they nevertheless al-
low for more breadth than one might first suppose. The Non-Con-
formists and "Schismatickes" so harshly denounced are those who
insist that the English church's doctrine, its sacraments, its forms of
worship, and its government are manifestly "Anti-Christian or repug-
nant to the word of God," and who therefore flatly deny that church
to be "true and Apostolicall."[38] While it is true that not only Roman
Catholics but also Brownists and other Protestant separatists made
many of these claims from the 1580s on, the latter were not typical of
Puritanism, under either Elizabeth or James.[39] Even the zealous Cart-
wright would not claim that the church's forms and practices were
"repugnant to scripture," much less that the English church under the
monarch was not a true church. Cartwright spoke as a member of the
church—albeit a marginal and disgruntled one—and, like most other
Puritans before the 1640s, he hoped to reform the church from within,
by constitutionally established means.[40]

So when Herbert exhorts his churchwardens to make the *Canons*
their rule and to set about the work of local reform, he very probably
does not intend them to harry Puritans out of the parish, simply be-
cause few Puritans actually fit the canonical definition of a "Non-
Conformist." Until the full force of Laudian "thorough" came to be
felt, with its new doctrine of divine-right episcopacy, most advocates
of further reform in the church could and did still accept with clear
consciences the Jacobean *Canons* as at least a temporary modus vivendi.

In addition, nearly all Puritans would have shared Herbert's objec-
tion to the abuses that he particularly mentions—"negligence in re-
sorting to church" and "disorderly carriage in time of divine service"
(*W,* 269). The canon that forbids the latter abuse would raise some
Puritan criticism because, as part of "orderly carriage," it calls for
kneeling during prayers as well as "due and lowly reuerence [when]
the Lord IESVS shalbe mentioned." However, the canon also calls for
general quiet cooperation and attention, to which no disciplined Pres-
byterian could take exception.[41] It appears from chapter 29 of *The*

38. Church of England, *Canons,* Canons 109, 9.
39. M. M. Knappen, *Tudor Puritanism,* 303ff.
40. Summers, *George Herbert: His Religion and Art,* 50–54.
41. Church of England, *Canons,* Canon 18.

Countrey Parson that Herbert wished to emphasize those aspects of canonical obedience that involve personal edification and absolutely necessary church order. His instructions differ notably from Laud's of 1633, which focus on kneeling and bowing as the primary matters for enforcement.[42]

In any case, the points that most concern Herbert in this chapter on churchwardens are the corresponding *secular* authority and *spiritual* dignity of the churchwarden's lay calling. "[The] Parson suffers not the place to be vilified or debased," he writes, "it being the greatest honor *of this world,* to do God and his chosen service. . . . Neither hath the place its dignity from the Ecclesiasticall Laws only, since *even by the Common Statute-Law* they are taken for a kind of Corporation, as being persons enabled by that Name to take moveable goods, or chattels, and to sue . . ." (*W,* 269–70, emphases mine). Conversely, Herbert says, the churchwarden, although not ordained, has a spiritual mission nonetheless, because he has a ministry of correction and exhortation in the church. He is "enabled" in this mission by both church and statute law, all under supreme authority of the king-in-Parliament.[43]

Herbert's emphasis on secular statute as a warrant for spiritual mission appears to have two related purposes: first, to increase the appeal of the office to the "best rank" of men in the parish by "shewing that they do not loose, or go lesse, but gaine by it," and second, to give the warden greater authority to withstand the resistance not only of the common people, but also of his social "betters." Herbert writes that the parson wishes his church wardens "by no means to spare any, though never so great; but if after gentle, and neighborly admonitions they still persist in ill, to present them [in the ecclesiastical court]; yea though

42. T. Rymer and R. Sanderson, eds., *Foedera, conventiones, literae et cuiuscunque generis acta publica* 2:109–13.

43. For example, Michael Dalton's *The Countrey Ivstice, Containing the practice of the Ivstices of the Peace out of their Sessions* (1618), the standard seventeenth-century handbook of the law recommended by Herbert himself (in *The Countrey Parson,* chapter 23, "The Parson's Completenesse"), mentions the churchwardens at least three times on equal terms with local constables, with whom they share the authority for fining irresponsible alehousekeepers, delinquent fishmongers, and for generally keeping the peace. The empowering statutes were enacted by Parliament during the first four years of James's reign (*The Countrey Ivstice,* 25–26, 48).

they [the wardens] be tenants, or otherwise ingaged to the delinquent: for their obligation to God, and their own soul, is above any temporall tye. Do well, and right, and let the world sinke" (*W,* 270). Here Herbert makes one of his strongest leveling statements. Only a few sentences earlier he had seemed to exclude men of "lower rank" from the churchwarden's office, and even to encourage an appeal to worldly ambition for church service. But here he insists that men of at least relatively lower rank can and must exercise direct authority in office over their social and economic "betters," both because the laws command and empower him, and, finally, because God has told him to do so.

Herbert's assertion of equality before the law derives from one of the Jacobean canons that laments that churchwardens often "forbeare to discharge their duties through feare of their Superiours."[44] So it is not only Herbert, but also the Jacobean establishment itself, that places a potent measure of ecclesiastical authority in the hands of laymen, whose election depends on the congregation as well as the minister, whose authority transcends social and economic rank, and who are legally semi-independent of the episcopal hierarchy for their power.

One can see how, given the situation that developed after Laud acceded to Canterbury, these especially "enabled" laymen might give their secularly grounded authority primacy over their obedience to the bishops in certain matters. Indeed, H. R. Trevor-Roper notes that the Laudian policies of the 1630s encountered some of their greatest local opposition from the churchwardens themselves.[45] For although the wardens were sworn to enforce the *Canons of 1604,* it was not clear that they were sworn to enforce Laud's particular interpretations and additions. Among other things, Laud commanded the placing and railing of the Communion table "altarwise" under the east window of every chancel, as well as the silencing of the Puritan "lecturers" so popular in many counties. Both of Laud's policies notably exceeded the letter of the Jacobean Canons. So, hypothetically, those churchwardens who regarded the moving and railing of the Communion table as a "popish innovation," or who approved of lectureships,

44. Church of England, *Canons,* Canon 113.
45. *Archbishop Laud, 1573–1645,* 155.

could claim that they were not under the direct authority of the epis-
copal hierarchy, but rather under the Supremacy of the king-in-Parlia-
ment, to whom both laity and clergy were subject. Therefore, they
might say that since the Parliament, which did not meet during that
decade, had not approved Laud's additions to the *Canons,* the king-
in-Parliament could not be said to have approved them, and their oath
did not require them to enforce the new measures.

It is not clear that any of the many churchwardens who resisted
Laudian "thorough" ever enunciated such a perilous claim, since it
flatly contradicts Stuart absolutist notions that the king is above the
law—and Charles had personally authorized Laud's measures.[46] How-
ever, we can see better how the elements that made up the Elizabethan
concept of "authority" could be set against each other.

Again, Herbert's own position on canonical obedience is clear: all
the *Canons of 1604* must be enforced, despite highborn or wealthy
opposition. Churchwardens are to do their duty both for the sake of
necessary church order and for the sake of their consciences. How-
ever, it is also clear that here, as elsewhere, Herbert greatly prefers a
reasoned appeal to the offender's conscience and devotion rather than
threats of force. So, in discussing the proper posture for taking Com-
munion in chapter 22 of *The Countrey Parson,* Herbert glosses the
canon that requires kneeling by giving a reason behind the order, thereby
revealing a predisposition to persuade rather than coerce: "The Feast
indeed requires sitting, because it is a Feast; but man's unprepared-
nesse asks kneeling. Hee that comes to the Sacrament, hath the confi-
dence of a Guest, and he that kneels, confesseth himself an unworthy
one, and therefore differs from other Feasters: but hee that sits, or
lies, puts up to an Apostle: Contentiousnesse in a feast of Charity is
more scandall than any posture" (*W,* 259). Sitting, he concedes, can
indicate godly confidence in one's state of grace, but more probably
indicates a scandalous overconfidence, "putting up to an Apostle";
kneeling speaks of humility. Since man's natural state is one of un-
readiness, this posture is therefore spiritually "safer" in public wor-
ship. Therefore authority, to prevent confusion and dissention, has
declared that all shall kneel. Anyone who contends with this decision

46. Kenyon, *Stuart Constitution,* 159–64.

becomes the worst kind of stumbling block: he thwarts the main purpose of the Eucharist by turning a "feast of Charity" into a wrangle.

Interestingly, for Herbert, "contentiousnesse" is not only a scandal in the parishioner, but in the parson as well. In "The Parson Arguing," he devotes a whole chapter to the means for returning Roman Catholics and schismatics "to the common Faith." These means are first, prayer; second, "a very loving, and sweet usage of them"; and third, a well-reasoned, humble, and "ingenuous" removing of "the main foundation, and pillar of their cause" (W, 262–63). To these means he adds "two great helps and powerfull perswaders on his side; the one, a strict religious life; the other [a manner] unmoved in arguing, and voyd of all contentiousnesse." Significantly, he does not mention external compulsion.

The difference between Herbert and the Laudians on the use of force is singularly important in placing him on the ecclesiastical spectrum of his day. Apparently, Herbert would rather not discuss enforcement in reference to "things indifferent," and when he does in speaking of church wardens, he would have them exercise their power only after "neighborly admonitions," and mainly against those who either avoid or disrupt services. He prefers reason in matters of conscience because he wants to make real converts, not mere outward Conformists. The Arminians, on the other hand, and especially their leader, were of the opposite inclination. Trevor-Roper writes that it was fully in keeping with Laud's character to despise "bandying words" with Puritans and separatists. "He hated discussion, and only entered upon controversy unwillingly. The way to secure orthodoxy was not, he believed, to prove the doctrine true but to enforce it, and to silence all disputation which tended to reopen a closed question." While Laud was the most notable devotee of coercion, all of his assistants—Montague, Cosin, Heylin, Wren, Brent—shared his spirit to a significant degree, summarily executing God's will and their own decrees as one and the same thing. As Montague wrote to Cosin in 1624, "it will never be well until we have our Inquisition."[47]

47. Trevor-Roper, *Laud,* 85, 103.

Herbert and Private Conscience

So Herbert's approach to Conformity is basically that of the Elizabethan Settlement, though he is less inclined than they to call for coercion. But if "authority"—the king-in-Parliament over convocation—is ultimately the judge of whether a certain practice or teaching is scriptural, who or what, on earth, is to check or limit authority? What if authority errs and ceases to fulfill its proper ends? What, after all, about private conscience? We have seen that sixteenth-century Conformists like Cranmer were willing to admit, at least hypothetically, that princes could and often did pervert their powers by persecuting the faith.

Thus, after pages of denouncing all who pose armed opposition to princes, the author of the homily "Of Obedience" turns abruptly to a strong qualification that rings strangely like a command: "Yet let vs beleeue vndoubtedly, (good Christian people) that we may not obey Kings, Magistrates, or any other, (though they be our own fathers) if they would command vs to doe any thing contrary to Gods commandments. In such a case wee ought to say with the Apostle, Wee must rather obey God then men" (*BH* 1:74). Herbert may well have heard these words yearly as a churchgoer, and as a pastor he probably proclaimed them more than once to his own Bemerton parishioners. They make three important points about the practical limits of royal power.

First, they acknowledge and even require that the individual's conscience have a role in understanding scriptural commandments, and thus in deciding whether the king has violated these commandments. For if authority transgresses the doctrines that it formerly defended and preached, everyone must fend for himself. Second, the absolute terms of this injunction—"undoubtedly," "ought," and "must"—positively obligate the subject to passive resistance. Third, and perhaps most importantly, the writer admits that sometimes the Christian's obligation to obey God amounts to "not obeying" men, even those men who speak in the name of God as "authority." So when the king's commands overturn the divine commands that enable kings to rule, he disables himself of any influence over the consciences of his subjects and is left with only the power of the sword to force his will on their bodies and property. Under such circumstances, the Christian is under divine orders to suffer and die rather than cooperate.

In contrast, the royal absolutists were determined to close even this small loophole. In a 1610 speech to Parliament, King James himself places overriding stress on his prerogative, to the complete exclusion of any earthly legal or constitutional check. His subjects, far from possessing a responsibility for passive resistance or a legitimate exercise of personal conscience, are rather "like men at chess—a pawn to take a bishop or knight," who owe him unconditionally "the affection of the soul and the service of the body." And the Laudian Robert Sibthorpe, in a 1627 sermon, proclaims that if a king commands against the law of God the people are quietly "to yield a passive *obedience* where they cannot yield an active one" (emphasis mine).[48] Thus, under the New Conformity, the subject's conscience is subsumed entirely into the royal will. The interpretation of God's law becomes effectively the prerogative of the king and his bishops, with only their consciences to limit them.

This claim to divine right buttressed Laud's twin goals: to eliminate what he saw as lay meddling in sacred affairs, and to reassert direct clerical control over the dispensation of God's grace. The Laudian bishops showed themselves hostile to any lay initiative by ordering churchwardens to enforce Laud's canonical changes as if the wardens were mere episcopal servants, with no discretion or legal independence of their own. In addition, Laud, while still Bishop of London, declared in Star Chamber his general dislike of vestries, those committees of parish laymen responsible for maintaining and outfitting church buildings. He had encountered repeated opposition from vestrymen over the relocation of Communion tables and over other "innovations." Laud particularly objected to the intervention of Parliament, which, he claimed, existed for the sole purpose of submissively raising funds to finance the king's policies.[49]

To understand better Laud's animosity to these lesser lay governors, we should note that many churchwardens and vestrymen, and nearly all members of Parliament, came from higher social and eco-

48. King James I, *Works,* 529–30; Sibthorpe, *Of Apostolique Obedience,* 15.
49. Trevor-Roper, *Laud,* 110–11; Laud, *Works of Laud* 1:112.

nomic classes than Laud and his fellow Arminians. Nicholas Tyacke writes that the Laudians "were in any case completely dependent on royal protection, [and] [e]vidence exists to suggest that one of the factors involved here was a desire to compensate for a sense of social inferiority. Certainly the Calvinist bishops had better blood relations with the gentry and aldermanic classes than did their Arminian successors, and there was some substance to Lord Brooke's derogatory remarks in 1641 about low-born prelates."[50] The descendants of Tudor "new men" were by now well established and had shut other would-be newcomers out of the secular corridors to power. So the Arminians, like "the butcher's son" Wolsey in Henry's early days, found tremendous opportunities for advancement through the church. And, quite apart from theological considerations, it was clearly in their material interests to protect and expand their monopoly by eliminating competition from the gentry and nobility, whether locally or in Parliament.

However, we cannot finally explain Laud or the Laudian opposition to lay "interference" merely in terms of personal ambition and material gain. Laud, at least, lived like a Spartan and died for his beliefs.[51] Ultimately, Laud and his bishops moved to restore clerical supremacy (under the king) and opposed all lay intervention because they were devoted to a revived medieval sacerdotalism, which accompanied their rejecting Calvin's doctrine of grace. They reinvested the name of "priest" with much of its old power, at the expense of the word preached and read. We have seen how Cranmer commends the individual study of scripture as the entrance "to the right and perfect way vnto God" (*BH* 1:1). Moreover, as Tyacke writes,

> [f]rom the Calvinist standpoint preaching, whether by a beneficed incumbent or a lecturer, was the chief means of salvation. Only an episcopate dominated by Arminians could contemplate with equanimity, and indeed with pleasure, a diminution in the number of sermons preached. . . . At the same time [Laud's] reassertion of sacramental grace lent itself to the view that clerics were almost a caste apart.[52]

50. "Puritanism, Arminianism, and Counter-Revolution," 139–40.
51. Trevor-Roper, *Laud,* 53.
52. "Puritanism, Arminianism and Counter-Revolution," 138–39, 140.

Once established at Canterbury in 1633, Laud did more than con-
template the curtailing of preaching—he decreed it. Empowered by
Charles, he immediately dissolved the Feoffees for Impropriations, a
corporation of clergy, lawyers, and merchants that financed licensed
lecturers, and in the *Instructions of 1633* he ordered that "in all par-
ishes the afternoon sermons be turned into catechizing by questions
and answers."[53] Furthermore, this catechizing was to be strictly lim-
ited, it having become an offense to expound the Catechism or the
Thirty-Nine Articles in any predestinarian sense. These and other
changes led Herbert's Bishop, John Davenant of Salisbury (a Cal-
vinist whom Laud had humiliated over predestination in Council) to
ask why "that should now be esteemed Puritan doctrine, which those
held who have done our church the greatest service in beating down
Puritanism [?]"[54] In less than a decade, the once overwhelming Cal-
vinist consensus of England's episcopal hierarchy had declined to the
point that for a bishop to speak publicly of sovereign grace or divine
election made him a "Puritan" or even a "Non-Conformist" in the
eyes of authority. The surviving Calvinist bishops, and lesser clergy
like Herbert, found themselves in another world.

53. Rymer and Sanderson, eds., *Foedera* 19:470.
54. Tyacke, "Puritanism, Arminianism, and Counter-Revolution," 139.

3

Power Disabled

Limited Authority in Herbert's "Lent"

> GODS Church ought not, neither may it be so tyed to . . . any
> . . . order now made, or hereafter to be made and deuised by
> the authoritie of man, but that it may lawfully for iust causes,
> alter, change, or mitigate those Ecclesiastical decrees and orders,
> yea, recede wholy from them: and breake them, when they tend
> either to superstition, or to impietie.
>
> —*BH* (2:90)

> Every subject's duty is the king's; but every subject's soul is his
> own.
>
> —*Henry V* (4.1.185–86)

The growing national schism of the 1620s seems to have cast Herbert into a "discreet and wary" silence. Yet he did not, or could not, refrain entirely from comment on the issues. We have seen that he deliberately shows his hand on the forbidden topic of predestination in "The Water-course"; similarly (though less deliberately) he speaks his mind about the limits of state authority while discussing fasting in *The Countrey Parson* and, especially, in "Lent." In this lyric, Herbert prudently hesitates to raise a controversial matter except for some "edifying" purpose. Yet his words necessarily possess a political edge; for at the very moments when he comes closest to defending something that sounds like Laudian policy, he turns to reveal his deep temperamental and doctrinal divergence from the Laudians. He concludes by qualifying his apparently "high-church" assertions to the vanishing point.

"Lent" (*W*, 86–87) has attracted little critical comment, apparently because it is thought to display Herbert at his most straightforwardly "Anglo-Catholic," and it has been praised, maligned, or ignored as such. Helen Vendler, the only modern reader of Herbert who gives any significant attention to the lyric, regards it as a notable failure, "an unexceptionably dull homily" marred by clichés and forced exhortations, yet with an ending "so plain, dry, and fine that it deserves to belong to a better poem."[1] Of course, given her unfortunately procrustean thesis that a Herbert poem "is only 'helped to wings' when it is entirely personal"—his mind being "resolutely unphilosophic and wholly restricted to the private case"—she could hardly conclude otherwise. "Lent" is, indeed, about an "impersonal" matter of doctrine and is addressed to the decidedly public case of a growing controversy.

However, when read with a proper appreciation for its theological and social context, "Lent" is hardly dull, or even impersonal. For while it must be numbered among Herbert's artistic failures, its very failure makes it a literary artifact intriguingly marked, formed, and even deformed by the conflicting pressures of a time and an order in which religion and politics were virtually identical. Herbert's defense of Lent is logically and rhetorically fragmented because he is psychologically and pastorally at odds, not only with state authoritarianism, but also with himself. Wishing to persuade the doubtful to love fasting for its own sake, he is thwarted in his appeal by the threats of authority, which would make Herbert's hearers submit, if at all, out of fear.

Thus "Lent" preserves the evasions and qualifications of Herbert's mind when confronted by the contradictions inherent in the old Elizabethan Conformity and magnified by Laud's new regime. He attempts unsuccessfully to reconcile his and others' consciences with an order that sought to instill inward devotion by ultimately coercive means. The poem's coherence is that of the Old Conformity itself, as are its

---

1. *Poetry of George Herbert,* 150–51. See C. A. Patrides, ed., *George Herbert: The Critical Heritage,* 206, 260, 262, 313; and William Ingraham Kip, *The History, Object, and Proper Observance of the Holy Season of Lent,* 2, for "Anglo-Catholic" treatments of the poem.

tensions, flaws, and self-contradictions. Significantly, when the twists and turns of "Lent" have ceased, Herbert has chosen a position that might have set him against Laudian policy, had he lived, but yet not made him a Puritan.

Much of the poem's difficulty lies in the fact that it treats a number of separate, though related, questions in a fragmentary way. Herbert attempts to provide answers consistent with multiple guiding principles that were increasingly in conflict. The poem successively discusses the feast of Lent, the goodness and proper method of fasting, and the role of tradition in guiding the believer's devotional life. However, once Herbert has engaged these issues, he cannot ignore the overwhelming question: namely, the purpose and limits of authority in prescribing Christian behavior for "things indifferent."

For as everyone agreed, Lent was an indifferent matter. It was one of those festivals mentioned by Hooker as neither commanded by nor "repugnant" to scripture, and which the queen-in-Parliament had thought sufficiently edifying to modify and retain in the calendar of the reformed church (*LEP* 3.5.1). Its defenders noted that while Lent per se could not be proven out of scripture, yet in scripture the "gouernours of the Jewes" repeatedly ordained fasts at their discretion, "rather of devotion, then by any expresse commandement giuen from God" (*BH* 2:83). The Prayer Book collect for Ash Wednesday voices a thoroughly Protestant call for mercy, without any implications of justification through self-denial,[2] and the homily on fasting takes special pains to condemn any belief in works-righteousness as "a divelish perswasion, . . . so far of[f] from pleasing of God, that it refuseth his mercy, and is altogether derogatory to the merites of Christs death, and his pretious bloodshedding" (*BH* 2:85).

So Lent was "indifferent"; but this does not mean that the Puritans were indifferent toward it. They claimed that, however well-laundered the collects and homilies may be, the feast itself was indelibly tainted through its long and guilty associations. Anthony Gilby's attack of 1581 against the cap and surplice might just as well have been aimed at Lenten rites, as far as many Puritans were concerned: "Now, these

2. Church of England, *The Book of Common Prayer, 1559: The Elizabethan Prayer Book,* 108.

[things] which in popery have belonged to Idols, are filthy Idolothytes, that served unto Devils. Therefore they are against Christian liberty. Again, to bind men to [use] Idolothytes, were against Christian liberty."[3] Many of those who flatly rejected the Conformist decrees pointed for support to the scriptural command against "giving offense" (Rom. 14:13–15). They protested that, were they to observe the forty days of Lent as commanded by authority, they would make their "weaker brothers"—those still inclined to Roman piety—stumble, and thus they, the stronger, would abuse their own freedom in Christ. Further-more, Puritans would have opposed strongly the reveling tradition-ally practiced immediately before Lent, between Quinquagesima Sunday and Shrove Tuesday. Certainly, they would admit, there was no collect for Mardi Gras in the Prayer Book; but some would argue that for the church to make repentance a seasonal matter, as if all days were not for returning to God, amounted to much the same thing.

The Conformist Sermon

So, in defending the observation of Lent, Herbert probably has in mind two main audiences, in addition to those more sympathetic souls whose devotion is already both heartfelt and conformable. First, of course, are the Puritans, especially those approaching or actually com-mitted to illegal separation from the established church. However, of almost equal concern to Herbert are those brethren whose reaction to Lent is not one of zealous opposition but of carnal neglect; who would rather continue to gorge throughout on their Shrove Tuesday cakes and ale and, perhaps, toast the Lord for their Christian liberty. It is to both spirits that Herbert addresses his exhortation. "Welcome deare feast of Lent": he begins,

> who loves not thee
> He loves not Temperance, or Authoritie,
> But is compos'd of passion.
>
> (ll. 1–3)

3. *A Pleasaunt Dialogue, Between a Souldior of Barwicke, and an English Chaplaine,* Sig. K7 and verso.

Immediately Herbert characterizes the apparently divergent opposition as sharing a common source: both are "compos'd of passion." He implies that two kinds of passion cause a coldness to this otherwise welcome, "deare" guest—the libertine's passion against temperate self-rule, and the schismatic's passion against rule by the divinely ordained authorities. Since self-control and submission are spiritual fruits essential to the Christian life, it is not enough merely to tolerate or respect these virtues. Rather the believer must "love" them, and show it by eagerly welcoming the feast, when he can specially exercise "Temperance" and submit to "Authoritie."

That Herbert "loved authority," defined in Elizabethan terms, we have already seen. There is also abundant evidence of his love for temperance. His most notable contribution to the literature of diet and appetite is *A Treatise of Temperance and Sobrietie,* his translation of the Venetian Luigi Cornaro's mid-sixteenth-century *Trattato de la vita sobria* (*W,* 291–303). However, Herbert seems to have valued Cornaro's method chiefly for physical rather than directly spiritual reasons.[4] Walton claims that, through "a spare diet" advised by Cornaro, Herbert sought to remedy his many digestive ailments and "became his own Physitian, and cur'd himself of his Ague."[5] In fact, much of Herbert's discussion of fasting in *The Countrey Parson* deals with the effects that particular foods had on the "great obstructed vessel" that was Herbert's tubercular body (*W,* 241–42). Thus in later stanzas of "Lent," Herbert's medical concerns tend to overshadow his treatment of the spiritual benefits associated with physical abstinence.

Like Herbert, Thomas Becon, a Henrician Protestant defender of Lent, also links the libertine and the separatist to a common motive of "passion." In *A Potation for Lent,* Becon speaks against the "gross gospellers" who, "condemning all kinds of godly fasting, give themselves to gluttony and drunkenness, persuading themselves to be the best Christian men when they are furthest from Christianity."[6] Although it is not possible to tell precisely about whom he is speaking,

---

4. Cornaro was, of course, a Roman Catholic, his work translated from Italian into Latin by the Jesuit Lessius. Herbert omits Cornaro's jabs at the "unhappy" vice of Lutheranism from his translation (*W,* 565).

5. *Lives,* 284.

6. *Early Works,* 104.

he could mean any number of antinomian groups who had attacked fasting on spiritual grounds, but from a decidedly sensual motivation.

But while Becon's "gross gospeller" seems compatible with the intemperate and insubordinate passions of which Herbert speaks, it is unlikely that Herbert believed the Puritans to be secret sensualists. Rather, Elizabethan Puritans had been notable—and notorious—fasters, frequently joining day-long fasts "to prayer and the preaching of the word in public assemblies." Early in Elizabeth's reign, much of the pressure for officially sanctioned regional fasts seems to have come from Puritans.[7] Indeed, in September of 1642, on the eve of its great war against prerogative rule, the Puritan Parliament, while closing the theaters and ejecting Capuchin friars from the land, proclaimed "set-times" of national fasting.[8] What made public Puritan fasts different from those of the established church was that the Puritans fasted not according to the cycles of a liturgical calendar, but only ad hoc, for a particular purpose.

Herbert understands this Puritan notion of ad hoc fasting and recognizes it as a major point of contention, so in turning first to the Puritans in his audience, he comes immediately to the point: "The Scriptures bid us *fast;* the Church says, *now*" (l. 4). That "the Scriptures bid us fast" no Puritan would deny, for Christ himself gives explicit directions for fasting in the Sermon on the Mount (Matt. 6:16–18). It is only the time and duration of fasting that are "indifferent." So the Puritan and Conformist fundamentally disagree over the church's right to determine external forms of worship when a clear scriptural warrant is lacking. For the lover of "Authoritie," or at least of Conformity, the Church's saying "now" would happily settle the matter. But not for the Puritan.

It is worth noting that if William Laud had written "Lent," it would consist of only these first four lines, and end, "the Church says, *now.*" Herbert's mere inclination to engage his nonconforming brethren in a reasoned dialogue in itself distinguishes him importantly from the Arminians. Also, Herbert softens his tone by beginning his case with a sentimental, if somewhat topically barbed, appeal:

7. Patrick Collinson, *The Elizabethan Puritan Movement,* 214–15.
8. *Journals of the House of Commons,* vol. 3, September 2 and 7, 1642.

> Give to thy Mother, what thou would allow
> To ev'ry Corporation.
>
> (ll. 5-6)

As in "The British Church" and "Church-rents and schismes" (though nowhere else), the church is Mother to the believer, bringing him forth by the word of truth, nourishing him on the pure spiritual milk, providing him with shelter and comfort in the world. "Certainly," Herbert might say, "you owe her some debt of gratitude. Whatever you may think her faults to be, it was from her that you first learned the faith of Christ. Obeying in this indifferent matter is the least one can do."

Topically, he calls Puritan sincerity into question by pointing out that their scruples against submitting to authority seem suddenly to vanish in the case of "corporations" with a merely legal or economic purpose. *The Oxford English Dictionary* defines the "corporation" of Herbert's day as "a body corporate legally authorized to act as a single individual; an artificial person created by royal charter, prescription, or act of the legislature, and *having authority to preserve certain rights in perpetual succession*" (emphasis mine; definition 3). Herbert might argue, "You grant the municipal corporation of your city government the right to act on your behalf and regulate your behavior. The Church is also a legal Corporation, and much more. Why not allow her the same perpetual rights?" An answer to this implied question is suggested by another sense of "corporation" as "an incorporated body of traders," a legal entity that provides a specifically economic strength and protection to its members.

Christopher Hill notes that in Jacobean and Caroline England, "corporations" of this kind protected not only financial but also religious interests. Mercantile and town corporations were usually composed of Puritan merchants who often endowed lectureships as a way of legally circumventing the establishment's doctrinal monopoly. "The lecturer might preach quite a different theology in the afternoon from that which the incumbent preached in the morning. Lectureships gave those who financed them a great measure of control, since the stipend could be withdrawn, increased, or diminished at the will of the contributors."[9] These were corporate bodies to which the Puritan could

9. Hill, *The Century of Revolution, 1603–1714*, 89–90.

submit with a clear conscience, for they represented what he felt to be his true interests. Submission became a very different kind of act when it meant obeying policies that one had had a voice in forming. Not surprisingly, the episcopal hierarchy was alarmed by this democratic leaven in the land. "Looking back after 1660," says Hill, "Archbishop Sheldon thought that 'nothing had spoiled the late king's affairs so much as the credit that the factious lecturers had in all corporations.'"

It is unlikely that Herbert viewed corporately endowed lectureships with as much animosity as did Sheldon, but we can be sure that he looked skeptically on the conscientious objections of Puritans and separatists, given his argument in the following stanza:

> The humble soul compos'd of love and fear
> Begins at home, and layes the burden there,
>   When doctrines disagree.
> He sayes, in things which use hath justly got,
> I am a scandall to the Church, and not
>   The Church is so to me.
>   (ll. 7–12)

Here, in contrast to those unruly souls "compos'd of passion," we see Herbert's Conformist, "compos'd of love and fear." Even when this man feels certain reservations about church practice in a matter of doctrinal dispute like Lent, he looks first to the beam in his own eye, laying the "burden" of doubt "at home," on himself. He is moved by the "love" of God and of the good—any good—that he finds or that he can do within the forms of the church; and he "fears," not punishment, but offending the Lord by setting up his own inclinations as truth.

Furthermore, this "humble soul" respects tradition, believing that the weight of corporate Christian experience over the years should give him pause. If long "use" has "justly got" the practice of public fasting during the forty days before Easter, and if fasting is itself commanded in the Bible, then a humble, reasonable man will question his own scruples rather than accuse most of his fellow Englishmen, at least since the Reformation, of using "filthy Idolothytes." For Herbert, this is not to become a "traditionalist," a lover of the old ways per se, for his emphasis here is not on the antiquity of the "use" but on its "justice," its conformity to the scriptural rules of order and edification. As he writes in "The Parson's Condescending," "The Countrey Parson is a Lover of old Customes, if they be good and harmlesse; . . . If there be any ill in the custome, that may be severed from the good, he pares the apple, and gives [his people] the clean to feed on" (W, 283–84). The Conformist is not willing that any good opportunity should go to waste, and since authority has already pared the Lenten apple, he refuses to begrudge the custom its age.

To do otherwise—to defy authority for a personal scruple with no clear scriptural warrant—is to become a stone of stumbling oneself. "In disobeying," Herbert writes elsewhere, "there is scandall also" (W, 263). So "Contentiousnesse in a feast of Charity is more scandall" than any particular rite or order causing offense to the overdelicate conscience (W, 259). Similarly, Elizabeth's first Archbishop of Canterbury, Matthew Parker, writes, "[I]f law foreseeing harms [to Christian conscience] and providing quietness, have taken lawful order therein [by determining the public use of indifferent things], offence is taken, and not given, when the subject doth his duty in obedience, so severely enjoined him by God's word."[10]

Yet in exhorting the scandalized Puritans to welcome Lent, Herbert is not insisting that they become establishment zealots unable to acknowledge flaws in the mother church. Herbert admits that sometimes "doctrines disagree," and in fact, even in the midst of the hyperbolic *Musae Responsoriae* he concedes that "imperfections and stains" (Labeculas maculasque) still cling to the church. "Why?" he asks. "Is it that strange? We are travelers," he explains (Quid? Hoccine est mirum? Viatores sumus; W, 393, Epigram 22, ll. 1–2). Since all are travelers, he might say, all need to travel with the church. By leaving the fold, the "precisian" risks not only his own loss, but also the loss of leading others to stumble into the sin of rebellion.

Having thus tried to finesse the thorny "Puritan" problem of scandal with an appeal to humility, Herbert continues on his course of moving the godly to the love of Lent. Having attempted a line of argument that threatens to degenerate into those very "debates and fretting jealousies" that he laments in "Church-rents and schismes" (*W,* 140, l. 16), Herbert strikes out in a favorite, and a more positive, direction:

> True Christians should be glad of an occasion
> To use their temperance, seeking no evasion,
> When good is seasonable; . . .
> (ll. 13–15)

This is the attitude probably most typical of Herbert's personal piety, and an argument that he has used more than once to persuade the reluctant that authority has done them a great service by prescribing forms and set-times. He makes this appeal when defending the "churching of women" and when discussing the parson's own practice of additional fasting. In the same way, he says here that if a man's heart is full of that fruit of the spirit, self-control, he will fast all the more willingly when the church provides him with special opportunities to do so. And, if this "true Christian" has been immoderate in his appetites, the season will compel him to remember his need for self-discipline. The "true Christian" will not seek theological "evasions" by forcing texts about "scandal" and "freedom in Christ"; instead, he will return to seek the face of the Lord with the fasting church. If a Puritan or separatist were to raise the objection that there can be no time when "good" is not "seasonable," Herbert would agree but ask why they would refuse to do what they admit to be good, when obedience to divinely appointed authority makes the act even better.

The Constitutionalist Parenthesis

In fact, Herbert can think of only one case in which the Puritan or separatist's objection would stand. He could not, as a "true Christian," join in their "evasion"

> Unlesse Authoritie, which should increase
> The obligation in us, make it lesse,
> And Power it self disable.
> (ll. 16–18)

Suddenly, into the midst of what was becoming a neatly authoritarian sermon, Herbert inserts a parenthesis that probably would shock his contemporary readers back to full attention with its allusions and implications. Herbert has admitted the one exception, the formula by which all the earthly powers and principalities, the bishops and the Parliament and the Supreme Governor himself, could be reduced, legally and spiritually, to nothing: that authority which sets out to destroy, destroys itself—"Power it self disable[s]." We have seen how deeply embedded this principle was in the foundations of the Elizabethan Settlement.

In the specific case of Lent, authority's violation of its purpose and limits might consist in decreasing, not our "obligation" to external fasting, but "the obligation *in* us" to internal fasting—the spiritual repentance that leads to salvation and sanctification. As Cranmer writes in the *Homilies,* the purpose of all civil laws should be "to bring men the better to keepe GODS Lawes" (*BH* 1:35). Thus the anonymous homilist on fasting distinguishes carefully between two fasts, "the one *outward,* pertaining to the body, the other *inward,* in the heart and mind. . . . For when men feele in themselues the heauie burden of sinne, see damnation to be the rewarde of it, and behold with the eye of their minde the horrour of hell, they are inwardly touched . . . and they call vnto [God] for mercy" (*BH* 2: 82–83, emphases mine). Furthermore, the homilist specifies that the outward fast does not cause this repentance, but rather reveals and expresses it. For the penitent who has been "inwardly touched" by God's grace and "convicted" of sin, "all desire of meate and drinke is layd apart, . . . so that nothing then liketh them more, then to weepe, to lament, to mourne . . . both with wordes and behaviour of body" (*BH* 2:83). Repentance—the inward fast—leads to and is made visible by outward fasting.

So in these difficult lines Herbert probably is arguing that the authorities could wrongly decrease "the obligation *in* us" by sins of commission or omission. On the one hand, those in power could decree, against the true purpose of Lent, "that our fasting, and our good works, can make us perfect and iuste men, and finally, bring vs to heauen" (*BH* 2:85). On the other hand, the authorities could so fail to preach and teach God's sovereign grace that the people would fall back into "superstitious" ideas about "good works" like fasting. The first claim is impossible to make about the church authorities under whom Herbert wrote; the second can be made with some certainty.

We have observed Laud's program to curtail Calvinist preaching, and we should note Herbert's close connections with episcopal Calvinist holdovers from James's reign. John Williams, James's former Lord Keeper and Bishop of Lincoln, though a man of flexible principles, was more of a Calvinist than anything else, and he was Laud's arch-rival for two decades. It was Williams who saw Herbert appointed to the diaconate. John Davenant, Bishop of Salisbury and a leading English delegate to the Synod of Dordt, ordained Herbert to the priesthood in 1629. Two years later, Bishop Davenant was called before the Privy Council for preaching on predestination in a Lenten sermon before the king at Whitehall.[11] William Abbot, Laud's predecessor at Canterbury, was a staunch though politically ineffectual Calvinist. At Oxford in 1630, Williams and Abbot united their influence with a number of Calvinist faculty behind the candidate who unsuccessfully challenged Laud for the Chancellorship, which had been left vacant by the death of Herbert's cousin William Herbert, Third Earl of Pembroke—who himself had been a Calvinist inclined to Puritanism. The candidate was Philip, the Fourth Earl, William Herbert's brother and the poet's cousin. Laud's election at Oxford was hailed as a great victory for Arminian doctrine and practice.

These persons and events provide a strongly suggestive context for Herbert's lines on authority's undoing of itself. Of course Charles's and Laud's claims to rule above any earthly law in themselves constitute a clear violation of "the bounds of power" as defined by Hooker in the last years of Elizabeth. Quite apart from Puritan threats, this fact alone argues that the principle of the church for which Hooker argued was already moribund.[12]

Evasion and Fragmentation

At this crucial juncture in the poem, Herbert's inner dilemma over authority begins to fragment his argument. For despite the provoca-

11. Amy M. Charles, *A Life of George Herbert,* 113, 147; *DNB,* "Davenant," 551.
12. Trevor-Roper, *Laud,* 113–15.

tive implications of lines 16–18, he is not willing to claim, at least explicitly, that the rising regime is disabling itself. Instead, having voiced such an alarming concession to himself and to his hearers—especially alarming if his hearers are Puritans—he retreats from his constitutionalist parenthesis as suddenly as he turned to it. In so doing, he turns from the unruly to the intemperate in his audience, and he takes another new tack:

> Besides the cleannesse of sweet abstinence,
> Quick thoughts and motions at a small expense,
> A face not fearing light: . . .
> (ll. 19–21)

"Besides" refers elliptically to lines 13–14, before the parenthesis, and presents the carnal with some very physical reasons to "be glad of an occasion / To use their temperance."

Lines 19–21 bring Herbert back to politically safer ground, echoing his translation of Cornaro and his discussion of fasting in chapter 9 of *The Countrey Parson*. In the latter, temperance and prayer are said to keep the parson's body "tame, serviceable, and healthfull; and his soul fervent, active, young, and lusty as an eagle" (*W*, 237). In a similar vein Becon quotes Basil the Great: "[F]asting maketh lawyers witty."[13] And, says Herbert, not only that, but a man can also have these "quick thoughts and motions at a small expense"—fasting, after all, is a bargain.

The next verses further divert the reader from the troubling issue of authority by defining what is meant by "a face not fearing light":

> Whereas in fulnesse there are sluttish fumes,
> Sowre exhalations, and dishonest rheumes,
> Revenging the delight.
> (ll. 22–24)

After the "delight" of Shrove Tuesday and other excessive (and impious) feasting, the body takes its inevitable "revenge"—indigestion.

13. *Early Works,* 104.

Here again Herbert echoes Becon, who writes that "with fasting the flame of the burning Etna is extinguished, and the furnace of the flammivomous Vulcan, quenched within," although when taken in context Becon's vulcanism refers to flaming lust, while Herbert's is more earthily, and onomatopoeically, concerned with flatus.[14]

Thus far Herbert has described the benefits of fasting, and the liability of not fasting, in commonsense, almost entirely physical terms that sidestep the question of institutional authority. Next he turns to consider the spiritual gains "[t]hen" to be had, as

> those same pendant profits, which the spring
> And Easter intimate, enlarge the thing
> And goodnesse of the deed.
> (ll. 25–27)

Maintaining his stress on profit-minded prudence, he slips into the language of witty spiritual paradox, speaking of "pendant profits," the strange "spring" fruit of the final resurrection and glorification of the body. This "profit" is "intimated" by the change of season and by Christ's own Easter resurrection. To portray the relationship between fasting and these "profits," Herbert employs a grammatical pun, by which the "pendant profits" both intransitively "enlarge" while the penitent fasts and transitively "enlarge the thing / And goodnesse of the deed." Thus if Lenten fasting is practiced to express an inner conviction of true repentance, and a desire for holiness, it will bear great fruit at the final resurrection. Self-discipline and its rewards are intertwined; temperance leading to future glory, and future glory encouraging temperance now.

In addition these verses assert the role of tradition, for they tie Lent closely to the spring and the Easter season. So although, according to Herbert, the national church can declare fasts whenever it sees fit, it would make little sense, symbolically, for authority to proclaim Lent in August. In so doing, the authorities would obscure the edifying connection in the faster's mind between his own spiritual wintering and the coming "spring" of eternal life.

14. Ibid.

Since the "constitutionalist" parenthesis of lines 16–18, Herbert's argument has moved from one case to another with little logical transition as he continues to avoid the primary objection against Laudian authority—that it is disabling itself. Now he moves on yet again, almost as an afterthought, to refute specious attempts made by Puritan opponents to impute guilt to Lent by association:

> Neither ought other mens abuse of Lent
> Spoil the good use; lest by that argument
>   We forfeit all our Creed.
>   (ll. 28–30)

In the same way, he has written in the *Musae Responsoriae* (*W,* 390, Epigram 13),

> All things should not be rashly thrown away only because the Popes once breathed on them with their poisonous breath. If all that evil use had polluted were removed, neither the body nor the soul would remain to us.

> (Non quia Pontificum sunt olim afflata veneno,
>   Omnia sunt temere proijcienda foras.
> Tollantur si cuncta malus quae polluit vsus,
>   Non remanent nobis corpora, non animae.)

While the Conformist judiciously "pares the apple" of tradition, the Puritan pursues an impossible (and prodigiously wasteful) ideal; for in a contingent world everything and everyone is "guilty" by association, even "our Creed," the very words of the gospel.

The next two stanzas make still another new departure, and they are tied together by the single image of the road that the fasting pilgrim follows. Herbert develops this image in response to yet another, apparently Puritan, complaint, this one aimed at the Prayer Book claim that the forty-day Lenten fast imitates Christ's forty days of temptation in the wilderness:[15]

---

15. Church of England, *The Book of Common Prayer,* 109.

> It's true, we cannot reach Christ's forti'th day;
>   Yet to go part of that religious way
>   Is better then to rest: . . .
>   (ll. 31–33)

Herbert begins by conceding his opponent's most obvious claim (the truth of which no Conformist ever seriously doubted), and then commences to turn the tables with his characteristic emphasis on additionary devotion, on going "better" and beyond rather than "resting" at minimums. By the next three lines he has in fact turned their logic entirely back upon them, so as to make them, at least potentially, contradict Christ himself:

> We cannot reach our Saviour's puritie;
>   Yet are we bid, *Be holy ev'n as he.*
>   In both let's do our best.
>   (ll. 34–36)

Herbert would explain that the authorities do not ask the impossible. The church's teaching is that fasting is not a justifying work, which we must complete perfectly in order for it to benefit us; it is instead an outward act to show the divinely induced inward state of repentance. Thus the person who blames the church for promoting works-righteousness by instituting Lent would make the same charge against Jesus Christ for commanding his disciples, "Be ye therefore perfect, even as your Father which is in heaven is perfect" (Matt. 5:48).

The hominess of the stanza's final line—"In both let's do our best" —leads into the Bunyanesque development of the next stanza:

> Who goeth in the way which Christ hath gone,
>   Is much more sure to meet with him, then one
>   That travelleth by-wayes:
> Perhaps my God, though he be farre before,
>   May turn, and take me by the hand, and more
>   May strengthen my decayes.
>   (ll. 37–42)

To the man who would treat religious devotion as a thoroughly private matter, Herbert proclaims the legitimacy of the church's corporate path, yet in interestingly personal terms. To "do our best" by going "part" of "that religious way" in which "Christ hath gone"—in other words, to eat less on fasting days, and to eat not flesh but rather fish, as authority commands—is not to be viewed as a half-hearted attempt at ascetic self-justification.[16] Rather, it shows one's desire to enter the pilgrim pathway and thus to meet with Christ, who has gone by the same road. No doubt, Christ is "farre before"; it must be so, since through his fasting and temptation he has, as the Scripture says, "fulfilled all righteousness" in our behalf (Matt. 4:15). However, if we arrogantly choose to travel "by-wayes," those shortcuts that ignore the commands of scripture and authority to fast, we may end in a miserable condition like that of Bunyan's Christian, who took the easy way through "Bypass Meadow" and found himself far from Christ in spiritual darkness and bondage.

Herbert acknowledges that even for the humblest wayfaring Christian a meeting with the Savior depends entirely on God's condescension and grace. But having been met personally by Jesus before—Christ is, after all, "my God"—he knows the Lord's mercy and is therefore "much more sure" of meeting with him now. Herbert's image of such a meeting is reminiscent of the Prodigal Son's return, in which the young man's halting steps on the road home bring the father running "from a great way off" (Luke 15:20). "Perhaps," Herbert likewise hopes, Christ will compassionately "turn" and return to "take me by the hand, and more / May strengthen my decayes." The focus in this stanza, as Vendler rightly notes, is on the believer's personal relationship with Christ; but for Herbert it is the established form of Lenten observance that returns the wanderer to the right path.[17] The church does not claim the power to make fasting efficacious. Yet, in the economy of grace that the church preaches, to begin well and humbly on the way is to meet God, who will himself bring us to the end.

But what, exactly, is that end? Having answered so many disparate objections to Lent, is Herbert suggesting after all that the physical "decayes" worked by fasting really lead in some mystical way to spiritual

---

16. Herbert discusses the church's particular rules for fasting in chapter 10 of *The Countrey Parson,* "The Parson in His House," *W,* 242.
17. *Poetry of George Herbert,* 151.

"strength"? If so, then he would seem to be half-hearted in actual practice, since both the official rules of fasting and Herbert's discussion of them in *The Countrey Parson* call for moderation and plainness in diet, not abstinence. Indeed, Herbert there seems even more concerned with qualifying the rules than with keeping them: "[I]f a peece of dry flesh at my table be more unpleasant to me, then some fish there, certainly to eat the flesh, and not the fish, is to keep the fasting day naturally . . . [Also, if the Parson's] body be weak and obstructed, as most Students are, he cannot keep the last obligation [of eating no flesh], nor suffer others in his house that are so, to keep it. . . . For meat was made for man, not man for meat" (*W,* 242). We see again how Herbert would use personal discretion by a scriptural rule to set aside the letter of authority's decree in favor of what he "naturally" assumes to be its spirit—that is, leading the believer to the threshold of repentance, not into poor health. But if private calculation is to be the final court of appeal, what becomes of the official rule? Every food is "unpleasant" to someone, and "most" students' bodies are, after all, "weak" (if not "obstructed" [!]). Furthermore, if the true end of fasting is, in Herbert's words, "an afflicting of our souls," how is this interior purpose to be made visible in the world?

So the pressing questions raised by the church's coercive authority again emerge near the poem's end. Yet the final stanza, rather than resolving these questions, raises more by laying the closing emphasis in yet another unexpected direction. In these last six lines the constant tension between the enforceable minimum and the spiritual maximum comes to the fore. Herbert has evaded the question of a "disabled" authority for most of the lyric, yet his final words appear to undercut, and perhaps even contradict, authority's commands.

Herbert begins this last fragment of the poem by turning away from his original hearers in order to address Christ himself. "Yet Lord," he begins,

> instruct us to improve our fast
> By starving sinne and taking such repast
> As may our faults controll: . . .
>
> (ll. 43–45)

This prayer agrees with Herbert's desire, expressed in the third stanza, to go beyond the mere letter of Lenten obligation. He asks that Christ personally drive home the lesson that, in Becon's words, he "that abstaineth from meat, and not from evil works, he appeareth to fast, but yet he fasteth not indeed . . . I call fasting abstinence from vices."[18] "[S]tarving sinne," agrees Herbert, is the way to "improve our fast." His meaning seems clearly in line with Conformist teaching that the outward fast is futile if the inward motion is lacking. Furthermore, his additional means of "improvement"—"taking such repast / As may our faults controll"—also seems to agree with the church's order that outward fasting should consist of a reduced and meatless diet rather than no diet at all. After all, the practical Conformist might argue, some "repast" is necessary to moderate the faster's hunger and thus keep him from the "fault" of rebounding in excess.

So, in a strictly doctrinal sense, the poem could end here. Herbert has defended (though quite disconnectedly) the legitimacy both of Lent and of authority's right to prescribe Christian behavior in such matters. He has appealed to the better nature of his hearers, trying to move them to obedience and temperance more by love than by fear. Because he views the fast as an opportunity to join his private devotion with that of the whole church, and in so doing to encounter Christ personally, he exhorts others to go beyond the mere letter of the canonical requirements by keeping the only kind of fast that truly pleases God, the heart's fast from sin.

Conclusion: The Divine Right of Human Need

But the poem does not end here, and in the three lines that follow, the leaven of Herbert's love for spiritual "excess" seems finally to burst the bounds that he has so conscientiously defended in the previous stanzas. For it appears after all that the "repast" that will "improve our fast" is no mere cautionary morsel taken in private to keep off the hunger pangs, but rather a public act of the most extravagant and festive charity:

---

18. *Early Works*, 104.

> That ev'ry man may revell at his doore,
> Not in his parlour; banquetting the poore,
> And among those his soul.
> (ll. 46–48)

All pleading and quibbling have ceased, and the poem's previous concerns about mere compliance and prudent moderation have dropped entirely from view. They are supplanted by a scene from Isaiah—a scene, and a prophecy, that calls authority's decent and indifferent orders into serious question:

Is it such a fast that I have chosen? . . . a day for a man to afflict his soul? Is it to bow his head as a bulrush, and to spread sack-cloth and ashes under him? . . . Is not this the fast that I have chosen? To loose the bands of wickedness, to undo the heavy burdens, and to let the oppressed go free, and that ye break every yoke? Is it not to deal thy bread to the hungry, and that thou bring the poor that are cast out to thy house?" (58:5–7)

The acceptable fast, says the Lord to Isaiah, is not a literal fast at all. It does not consist in posture, or formal prayers, or even in "afflicting one's soul" by withholding food. A true fast is simply true repentance, shown not by ascetic or ritual acts but by practical acts of mercy and justice. Other writers who relate this passage to Lent, including Chrysostom, Augustine, Becon, and the homilist on fasting (*BH* 2:93), take it to mean that ultimately, the best kind of fast is that which enables the faster to give food to the hungry poor.[19] For them, ascetic motives have little to do with Lent. The proper way to show one's sorrow for sin and love for God is not to starve oneself for atonement, but to feed others out of gratitude.

Herbert, who almost certainly derives his ideas from one or more of these men, amplifies their meaning, and the meaning of the Isaiah passage, by portraying the penitent's act of mercy as a joyous "revell." The gladly repentant man holds this revel "[n]ot in his parlour," the figurative space where libertines indulge their appetites in private feasting, but rather "at his doore," that figurative place where he has a view of the needy world and can call out to "the poor, the maimed,

---

19. All quoted in Becon, *Early Works*, 104–5.

the lame, the blind" as they pass by. From there he can even go out, like the persistent host in Christ's parable, and compel them to come into his house and feast (Luke 14:12–24). But for Herbert, this reveling is itself no mere figure; it is a literal affair of knives and trenchers, meat and drink; for *The Countrey Parson*'s chapters 9 and 10, which deal with fasting, are followed immediately by "The Parson's Courtesy," which directs the parson to have the poor to his table often, and to set them "close by him," where he can "carve" for them himself (*W*, 243). Then, once the needy are seated and are enjoying their meal, the host can look around the table and find "among those," in a stunning recognition, "his soul"—possibly the happiest reveler of them all, for the whole literal "banquet" is its spiritual food.

Thus this poem, which begins by judiciously defending the Lenten fast, ends by calling for a literal Lenten *feast*. So also the initial emphasis on affliction of soul yields by the end to a joyous spiritual banquet. What, finally, has become of Lent, and of the authority by which Lent is enjoined and enforced?

The answer seems to be that, by the end of this lyric in its defense, Lent remains as a name and little more. Herbert has qualified, redefined, and even overturned so much of the traditional ascetic ideal that this supposed aid to the spiritual life seems to have been crowded out by the burgeoning spiritual life itself. And authority, "which should increase the obligation in us" to repentance and good works, has had little to do with this central transformation. Indeed, Herbert's call for "ev'ry man" to "banquet the poore . . . at his doore" seems to contradict the spirit of the Poor Law Act (1601), which declares that none "may be suffered to take reliefe at any mans doore, vnlesse it be by the order of the Ouerseers."[20] This law treats the door-to-door beggar merely as an inconvenience and a public nuisance, while stressing the overseer's authority. Herbert acknowledges this authority, but he immediately qualifies the law, recommending that the parson allow "his Charity some blindnesse" to the beggar's offense, since "we are more injoyned to be charitable, then wise," and since "evident miseries have a naturall priviledge, and exemption from all law" (*W*, 245). In the last analysis, Herbert's attitude toward the poor derives more

20. Dalton, *Countrey Ivstice*, 85.

from the transcendent imperative of Isaiah than from his desire to perpetuate the social hierarchy. It is not magistrates, bishops, or even kings who are "exempt from all law," but hungry poor people. Herbert attributes a kind of divine right to human need.

Thus authority's decrees, when viewed from the "doore" of "ev'ry man," seem to miss the spiritual point entirely. If "every door" should serve at Lent as a portal to the needy for their spiritual and economic improvement, then at its best authority seems little better than harmless, an indulgent watchman who sets standards low and vague enough for the vast majority to pass. Moreover, at its worst, authority can become its own reason for being, expanding its influence by placing greater and greater emphasis on the externals that it controls, while growing ever more jealous of that small internal space yet left to everyone, the conscience.

From this viewpoint, the tenure of James I as Supreme Governor of the church was of the more "harmless" type, the tenure of his son and Laud quite otherwise. Herbert grew to maturity under the one, and entered the priesthood under the other; but his spirit was typical of neither regime. James led a church that was tolerant by default, while the Arminians made one that was unyieldingly and swiftly coercive. Neither had much use for conscience. In contrast, Herbert was a man of great inner spaces whose spiritual experience produced a mind at once highly principled, humbly practical, and deeply respectful of that region called the heart, near the conscience, where no one but God has the prerogative or the power to move.

Thus Herbert could coexist with the Jacobeans, whose neglect he was probably able to call benign because they maintained the old Calvinist orthodoxy of God's sovereign grace, which sanctified the church's forms and covered a multitude of other evils. However, if Herbert had lived, one wonders if he could have coexisted with the Arminians, even if they would have let him. For their theological assertions and negations struck at the foundations of the Old Conformity. To silence the preaching of predestinarian "free grace," as Laud hoped to do, was to remove the one great check against a flood of "superstition" and works-righteousness; to proclaim the absolute divine right of both kings and bishops, as Charles and Laud did in grave earnest, was to lay an axe to the roots of the Elizabethan Settlement as defined by Hooker.

So we should not be surprised if "Lent" reveals Herbert as genuinely at odds with himself and his subject, unable to conjure his contraries into a resolution. As a well-evidenced lover of "Authoritie," he had lived to see the day when authority, as he knew it, was about to disable itself. Herbert fails here in his defense of the establishment because, even on its own terms, the establishment is becoming indefensible. But to say that "Lent" is a failed Conformist poem is not to call its composer a failed Conformist, or a Puritan manqué. George Herbert, the man, lived and died a young Conformist of the old school, his ultimate loyalties never to be tested by the Civil War. Yet in the flawed stanzas of "Lent" he has left us, less than intentionally, a psychological monument to the failure of Conformity itself.

4

"Showing Holy"

Herbert and the Power of the Pulpit

> Would you have me
> False to my nature? Rather say I play
> The man I am.
>
> —*Coriolanus* (3.2.13–15)

Herbert entered the ministry under a transitional regime increasingly determined to enforce the unconditional submission of its subjects—a determination that, I have argued, made him profoundly uneasy. So it is worth noting that in chapter 7 of *The Countrey Parson*, he discusses particular ways for a preacher to maintain the attention, fervor, and submission of his rural congregation. The onetime University Orator of Cambridge warns, not without a note of frustration, that "[c]ountrey people are thick, and heavy, and hard to raise to a poynt of Zeal, and fervency, and need a mountaine of fire to kindle them" (*W*, 233). To spark them he suggests a variety of effective apostrophes, exclamations, and scattered "irradiations," concluding with a sampler of dazzling perorations. Having spread these gems before the reader, he steps back, like a jeweler, to a professional distance. "Such discourses," he adds, "shew very Holy" (*W*, 234).

By this point in *The Countrey Parson*, we have already heard a good deal about "showing holy." In the previous chapter, "The Parson Praying," the minister when leading worship "composeth himselfe to all possible reverence; lifting up his heart and hands, and eyes, and using all other gestures which may expresse a hearty, and unfeyned devotion" (*W*, 231). To promote such unfeigned expressions Herbert gives some notably histrionic advice: the parson's praying voice should be "humble, his words treatable, and slow; yet not so slow neither, as to let the fervency of the supplicant hang and dy between speaking, but with a grave livelinesse, between fear and zeal, pausing yet pressing, he performes his duty." From his parishioners the parson expects the same consciousness of role: he "exacts of them all possible reverence . . . causing them, when they sit, or stand, or kneel, to do all in a straight and steady posture . . . answering aloud both Amen, and all other answers, which are the Clerks and peoples part."

Such spiritual histrionics have never been without their moral dangers, as any number of recent, well-publicized ministerial scandals have reminded us. Religious discourse, when appropriated by skilled and unscrupulous performers, can convincingly whiten the sepulcher. And Renaissance writers were keenly aware that the self-effacing language of piety can be both self-justifying and self-authorizing: Molière's Tartuffe abhors his flesh in public so that, unimpeded, he can gratify it in private; Shakespeare's Richard III steals "old ends out of holy writ" and, prayer book in hand, seeks the even darker satisfactions of sheer dominion. It is a story at least as old as that of Cain's false sacrifice.

To mention notorious religious hypocrites, real or imagined, in connection with "the holy Mr. Herbert" is unpalatable. Certainly not the slightest innuendo of sensuality will stick to him; this country preacher was no Elmer Gantry. Yet the deeper question of Herbert's sincerity should not be dismissed out of hand. By his own account he was a naturally ambitious man, even fiercely so, yet in courtly terms he was a major failure; thus it would be hard to overestimate the resentment that a might-have-been privy councillor could feel while ebbing out his days in vanishingly obscure Bemerton. Nor should we underestimate the role that Herbert's former courtliness played in shaping his ideals of the pastoral office. Indeed, noting his courtly past seems crucial to comprehending him, both as priest and as poet. Cristina Malcolmson suggests that "Herbert may have understood his transition from urban gentleman to country parson as primarily a shift from a social to an ecclesiastical elite"; thus, she argues, *The Countrey Parson* is a kind of courtesy book for clergy that also "provides an alternate reading of Herbert's life in which 'failure' is redefined as a willing renunciation."[1]

1. "George Herbert's *Country Parson* and the Character of Social Identity," 253, 247.

Michael C. Schoenfeldt claims further that the rhetorical self-consciousness of courtly language is fundamental to Herbert's poetry. His poems "reveal the glimmers of aggression and manipulation couched in the most apparently humble and benign social maneuvers. The fact that God is the audience . . . amplifies rather than silences the echoes of persuasion and resistance."[2] Herbert left a great deal behind in going from court to country, but he seems to have brought a good deal with him as well.

Elitist, aggressive, manipulative, maneuvering—all of these terms cast a worrisome shadow on *The Countrey Parson,* with its frequent emphasis on pastoral surveillance and control over the parish. In "The Parson in Circuit," "The Parson in Sentinell," "The Parson's Eye," and "The Parson's Surveys," the ideal pastor is virtually ubiquitous, discovering "vicious persons," rebuking idlers, and compelling participation in parish activities. In fact, Herbert recommends that in most cases the parson come upon his people unexpected, so that he will find them "naturally as they are, wallowing in the midst of their affairs, whereas on Sundays it is easie for them to compose themselves to order" (*W,* 247). One can imagine a surprised and discomposed parishioner renaming any of these chapters "The Parson Prying." Is it possible to see a link between the parson's "showing holy" and his omnipresence in others' affairs? The pulpit, Herbert says, is the parson's "joy and throne" (*W,* 232); is it also his stage and his observation platform?[3] Does he dazzle and bully these "thick and heavy" country people by orchestrating his motions, expressions, voice, and words like so many players? Does he do so to wring from them the guilt, self-immolation, gratitude, and sweet acquiescence that he, "in God's stead," so relishes?

I would argue that Herbert is more compelling as man and poet for

---

Malcolmson argues that Herbert's main concern is for the parson, in both his preaching and his life, to make visible and legible this inner quality of holiness. It is this holiness, says Malcolmson, that enables the parson to circumvent the class system by establishing his hierarchical authority on spiritual grounds. I agree with her, but I lay much greater emphasis on Herbert's probable debt as a pastoral theorist to the moderate Elizabethan Puritan William Perkins.

2. *Prayer and Power: George Herbert and Renaissance Courtship,* 4.

3. Stanley Fish advances such an argument in an as-yet-unpublished paper entitled "Herbert's Hypocrisy," delivered at Chicago's Newberry Library in 1989.

having known such temptations intimately, and for sometimes having succumbed. His stuff was, after all, "flesh, not brasse." Yet to read Herbert as a high-order hypocrite would be, in the end, profoundly misleading, for two reasons. First, the element of truth to be winnowed from such a view—that Herbert knew and loved the histrionic ways of power—should not obscure the fact that throughout both *The Temple* and *The Countrey Parson,* such ways are usually presented in order to be criticized, undermined, or overthrown. Second, all that Herbert has to say about "showing holy" identifies him with a preaching tradition—exemplified by William Perkins's *Arte of Prophecying*—that sought the clearest and simplest signs for communicating the preacher's inner life to his hearers. This tradition assumed that inner reality preceded outward "show" and militated against pulpit hypocrisy by insisting that words be matched by everyday deeds. Furthermore, the preacher, according to both Perkins and Herbert, is not only watcher, but watched: he is under the people's, and God's, surveillance—in and out of church. If the parson is acting a role, it is the most rigorous kind of "method" acting imaginable; he must immerse himself in the part twenty-four hours a day, day after day, for the rest of his life.

The Humiliation of Eloquence

Herbert's natural love for the ostentatious show of "great place" is well documented in a letter to his stepfather, Sir John Danvers, written in September 1619, about his desire for appointment as University Orator:

> The Orator's place . . . is the finest in the University, though not the gain-fullest; . . . for the Orator writes all the University Letters, makes all the Orations, be it to King, Prince, or whatever comes to the University; to requite these pains, he takes place next the Doctors, is at all their Assemblies and Meetings, and sits above the Proctors, . . . and such like Gaynesses, which will please a young man well. (*W,* 369–70)

As F. E. Hutchinson notes, the Oratorship was, because of its visibility, generally regarded as a stepping-stone to courtly power as secretary of state (*W,* xxvii).

That the poetry of *The Temple* is permeated by references to courtly show and power relations has been amply demonstrated by Schoenfeldt.[4] These secular performance strategies are frequently invoked not only in the shrewd and prudential "Church-porch" but also in the devotional lyrics of "The Church." The speaker of "The Pearl. Matt. xiii.45" (*W,* 88)—reasonably identifiable with Herbert himself—claims to know

> the ways of Honour, what maintains
> The quick returns of courtesie and wit:
> In vies of favours whether partie gains,
> When glorie swells the heart, and moldeth it
> To all expressions both of hand and eye . . .
> (ll. 11–15)

He is at pains to tell us that his love for God is not the product of naïveté; he understands as well as anyone the high stakes involved when wits exchange ripostes in the presence of their betters, and how to keep score by observing the sinuous and minute interplay of pun, glance, and gesture. Yet he also knows what most gallants do not: that he has become lost in the worldly maze. In this spiritual labyrinth, his serpentine wisdom is useless, merely "groveling wit"; only divine grace, in the form of the "silk twist let down" from the heavenly court, can guide him out (ll. 37–40).

Herbert repeats this rejection of theatrical courtly wit in "The Quidditie" and "The Posie" (*W,* 69, 182), relying instead on biblical terseness; and in "The Quip" (*W,* 110) he movingly dramatizes the consolations of scripture in the wake of his failed career. This latter poem presents a parade of cavalier tormenters so vividly that the sympathetic reader naturally casts around for the retaliatory barb, only to be brought up short by each stanza's psalmic refrain—*"But thou shalt answer, Lord, for me"*—and, at the end, by the apparent blandness of the "quip" sought from Christ—"say, I am thine" (l. 23). If we had hoped for the retort courteous, what we get is language stripped of all

---

4. In addition to *Prayer and Power,* see "Standing on Ceremony" and "'Subject to Ev'ry Mounters Bended Knee.'"

ornament and display, relying fully for its power on the identity of the One to whom it refers.

"The Answer" (*W*, 169), like "The Quip," is set in circumstances of courtly failure, as the speaker again builds expectation of a flamboyant reply that will shut the mouths of his detractors—who claim, significantly, that he brags without real "prosecution." This expectation of a quip is heightened by the English sonnet form, with its concluding lines often reserved for ironic reversal. But the couplet falls flat; instead of the anticipated arch rejoinder, we get an admission of ignorance: "to all, that so / Show me, and set me, I have one reply, / Which they that know the rest, know more then I"—to paraphrase, "if others have information about my future, I wish they would tell *me*." The speaker's dishevelment is palpable. The possibility of a pun on "the rest"—as not only "the remainder of my life," but also as a spiritual quietude—reintroduces a note of cleverness, but it does not compensate for the reader's raised and then disappointed anticipation.

Yet Herbert's criticism of rhetorical ostentation goes beyond such explicit rejections of courtly wordplay. He is even more frequently concerned with the ways that the human will to power conspires with or is cloaked by specifically religious language. At times this criticism takes the relatively mild—and often noted—form of pointing to the limitations of all language in the presence of God. So in "Prayer" (I) (*W*, 51), Herbert circles the looming immensity of this spiritual experience in an ascending spiral of metaphors, all of them as remarkable for their brilliant particularity as for their bewildering diversity. Then, with the imageless generality of "something understood," he comments ironically on the preceding struggle at definition. Without rejecting the attempt, he implies that even at its dazzling best, this process can only bring us to know our ignorance, and to rely on God's omniscience. Prayer is not incidentally, but essentially, "something understood"; indeed it is the only kind of communication that truly is understood, since the divine Understander knows immediately, without the creaturely need for analogies. Similarly, the speaker in "Easter" (*W*, 41), having gathered his poetical garlands to meet the rising Christ, finds that Jesus, like the sun, "wast up by break of day, / And brought'st thy sweets along with thee"—that Christ needs no praise to celebrate his triumphs, but contains his own self-sufficient glory, to which the awed worshiper may hope to be admitted. Thus in both poems, Herbert revels in language while pointing emphatically beyond it.

Often, however, Herbert thematizes linguistic limitation more violently, pruning and even killing his flowers of devotion. "Jordan" (I) and "Jordan" (II) (*W,* 56, 102) present his best-known disavowals of "false hair" and "trim invention" when speaking to and about God. The latter poem addresses more directly the issue of "showing holy." Here he pillories the religious poet's continual nemesis: the preening self-absorption that weaves its way like flame into the fabric of his verse, consuming that which it had seemed to ornament. The sonnet by Sidney that Herbert parodies—"Loving in truth, and fain in verse my love to show"—rejects the laboriously rhetorical self as merely silly; Herbert works the greatest of his changes on the original by portraying this rhetorical self as insidiously corrupting. By the end, the poet's initial intentions are so fully compromised that the poem must itself be taken over in the last lines by the remedial voice of the plain-speaking "friend," whose presence banishes "all this long pretence."

This attack on devotional eloquence is yet more emphatic elsewhere. In "Deniall" (*W,* 79), it intrudes deeply into the very fabric of the poem. "When my devotions could not pierce / Thy silent eares," begins the speaker, complaining of God's unresponsiveness in relatively smooth iambics, "Then was my heart broken, as was my verse." This third line enacts brokenness, stumbling from trochee to iamb to trochee before the caesura. As we read on, we find that within each stanza, no two lines are the same length, and few of the final lines rhyme, either with preceding lines or with each other—although "But no hearing" receives monotonous repetition at the ends of stanzas 3 and 4. The ultimate "chiming" of the last two lines in rhyme, expressing as they do hope for restored harmony with God, depend for their effect on the demonstrable disharmony that precedes them.

In "Grief" (*W,* 164), the speaker furthers this attack on pious display, questioning the sincerity of any person whose anguish "allows him music and a rhyme" (l. 17). This speaker himself had begun histrionically by calling, like Lear on the heath, for "all the watry things" of earth—springs, clouds, rain, rivers—to supply his eyes with tears. However, he has found his own eloquent outpouring in verse to be "too wise / For my rough sorrows: cease, be dumbe and mute," he commands, seeking a formlessness of expression that "excludes both measure, tune, and rhyme." The final fragment of a line provides what amounts to an alternate, "sincere," unpoetic poem—"Alas, my God!" Like Colin Clout in Spenser's first eclogue, this speaker has deliberately shattered his pipes.

But Herbert most profoundly subverts the language of conventional piety in those poems that leave their zealously religious speakers either sputtering or wordless. Among these are some of Herbert's most-discussed lyrics: "The Thanksgiving," "The Holdfast," and "Love" (III). Richard Strier has written that each of these poems is about God's *agape* love violating human reason and decorum;[5] and all of these violations are evidenced, in one way or another, by the breakdown of language. In "The Thanksgiving" (*W*, 35), the speaker's calculating, self-assertive devotion leads him to seek ways of paying back Christ's many unsolicited gifts. Like the persona of "Jordan" (II), his brain runs with ideas, and these flow freely along the well-worn channels of traditional asceticism—voluntary poverty, celibacy, endowment of chapel and "spittle," hostility to "the world." But his logorrhea is twice dammed—and damned—by the measureless obstacle of Christ's passion. At first, the persona manages to skirt the monolith—"But of that anon, / When with the other I have done" (ll. 29–30)—yet only temporarily. After the further euphoric rush of lines 31–48, his fluency is brought to a final, dead stop: "Then for thy passion—I will do for that— / Alas my God, I know not what." It is left to the succeeding poem, "The Reprisall" (*W*, 36), to break the silence and state the lesson, that "there is no dealing with thy mighty passion" (l. 2).

The speaker of "The Holdfast" (*W*, 143) learns a similar lesson about "dealing," and is silenced by it as well. He too is ostentatiously serious about his religious duties, and given to self-assured speech acts—he threatens, trusts, and confesses vociferously in the first two quatrains as if his words were meritorious works. But his assertions are repeatedly interrupted by a "friend" with an ever more confounding message: not only do all religious deeds lack saving merit, but even the words of faith are useless in themselves. "But to have nought is ours,"

5. See *Love Known*, 49–54 for "The Thanksgiving," 65–74 for "The Holdfast," and 73–83 for "Love" (III).

says the friend, "not to confesse / That we have nought" (ll. 9–10). All of his avenues of action blocked, the persona stands dumbfounded, "amaz'd at this, / Much troubled." It is at this nadir of silence that the sonnet turns; the speaker becomes a hearer, and for the first time hears the Good News as good news: that "all things"—both the words and deeds of faith—are "more ours by being his [Christ's]" (l. 12). To be "in Christ" is to speak and act, not out of anxious ambition, but out of grateful security.

Herbert dramatizes this lesson most famously in "Love" (III) (W, 188). As in "The Holdfast," the speaker threatens to be more strict with himself than God would be, repeatedly (and amusingly) voicing his scrupulous objections to being allowed into the heavenly banquet. However, here his interlocutor is not a schoolmasterish (albeit benevolent) "friend," but Love himself, urgent with sweet hospitality. The "guiltie" speaker is even witty at his own expense; when Love asks if he "lacks any thing," he replies with a kind of synecdoche, treating the whole as if it were the part: "A guest, I answer'd, worthy to be here" (ll. 5–6). "I don't have a lack—I am a lack," he says. But although he repeatedly refuses grace with such obstinate self-abnegation, grace is finally as irresistible as a host who refuses to take no for an answer. When the guest finally falls silent to "sit and eat," the silence is neither apoplectic nor befuddled; it is the silence of a hungry man at a feast.

The Preacher: Observer and Observed

So the lyrics of *The Temple* treat in abundant and diverse ways the humiliation of eloquence, and of language itself, in the presence of the divine Word. However, "The Parson Preaching" is not about standing silent in the pulpit, but rather about performing impressively from it. The parson "procures attention by all possible art," says Herbert, "both by earnestnesse of speech . . . and by a diligent, and busy cast of eye on his auditors" (W, 232–33). Everything that he says and does is carefully calculated to affect his hearers and to observe that effect. Even in Herbert's poetry his sudden silences and fragmented sentences can be classified as rhetorical devices with their own Greek names: *aporia, aposiopesis, parenthesis, anacoluthon.* All can be prescribed, like drugs, to produce particular results. What, after all, are we to make of this studied plainness?

Herbert was certainly not alone in his concern for "showing holy." In fact, the phrase itself, and nearly everything that he has to say about homiletics, strongly suggests a direct debt to Elizabethan England's master preacher, William Perkins. In *The Arte of Prophecying* (1592), Perkins writes that for sermonizing "two things are required: the hiding of human wisdom and the demonstration or showing of the Spirit."[6] "This demonstration," he goes on to say, "is either in speech or in gesture." On the one hand, the preacher's speech must be "spiritual and gracious . . . simple and perspicuous." Although extensive reading and careful exegesis are necessary preparation for preaching, nevertheless "neither the words of arts, nor Greek and Latin phrases and quirks must be intermingled in the sermon . . . it is also a point of art to conceal art." In other words, as Herbert writes, the parson preaching "is not witty, or learned, or eloquent, but Holy" (*W*, 233).

On the other hand, Perkins's "showing of the Spirit" also means mastering the language of gesture. As if he were blocking a scene in a play, Perkins directs the posture and movements of God's would-be "grave messenger": "It is fit . . . that the trunk or stalk of the body being erect and quiet, all the other parts, as the arm, the hand, the face and eyes, have such motions as may express and (as it were) utter the godly affections of the heart."[7] Since motions and expressions can "utter" truth, Perkins even provides a brief lexicon of gesture: "The lifting up of the eye and hand signifieth confidence, the casting down of the eyes signifieth sorrow and heaviness." So, both in word and in

---

6. In *The Workes of . . . William Perkins* (1626), 2:670. Translated by Thomas Tuke, the original Latin *Ars Praedicandi* was published in 1592 and became almost immediately the definitive homiletic manual by an English Protestant. Perkins was, as we have seen, a standard-bearer of English Calvinism and a moderate Puritan who sought reform within the established church, largely by promoting the sort of plain, "godly" preaching that his treatise defines. Despite Herbert's probable dissent from William Perkins's neo-Calvinist handling of election, he sounds a great deal like Perkins when discussing homiletics and hermeneutics. It is almost certain that Herbert would have read Perkins's Latin works while a divinity student at Cambridge in Trinity College, then a Calvinist center. He also may have read Tuke's translation while ministering at Bemerton. Either possibility would account for the remarkable similarities not only in thought, but also in wording.

7. *Workes* (1626), 2:672.

action, he defines what Herbert was later to call a new rhetorical "Character of Holiness"—a character, writes Herbert, "that *Hermogenes* never dream'd of, and therefore he could give no precepts thereof" (*W*, 233).

But by supplying this lack with such abundant attention to externals and pragmatics, Perkins and Herbert would seem to create great potential for abuse—especially when we consider their insistence on pastoral authority. Protestants frequently derided Roman Catholic priests as mere "players," yet we see how easily the charge of histrionics might double back on the accusers: Beware the speaker, we may well think, who produces a prepared text, puts it aside as if on impulse, and promises to speak from the heart.[8] Perkins, and Herbert after him, perceived this dangerous space between action and intention where hypocrisies breed and grow. Indeed, they were preoccupied, if not obsessed by it, because their theory of preaching, for all of its concern about performance, was profoundly expressionist. Before "showing holy," writes Herbert, parsons must prepare "by dipping all our words and sentences in our hearts, before they come into our mouths, truly affecting, and cordially expressing all that we say; so that the auditors may plainly perceive that every word is hart-deep" (*W*, 233). Perkins writes similarly: "Wood that is capable of fire doth not burn unless fire be put to it: and he must first be godly affected himself who would stir up godly affections in other men."[9] Thus the charlatan who masters the words and gestures of holiness in order to cover his sins receives Perkins's harsh and solemn condemnation: it is "execrable in the sight of God that godly speech should be conjoined with an ungodly life"; the secretly or openly wicked minister "is not worthy to stand before the face of the most holy and the almighty God."

It is hardly surprising to find sincerity praised and hypocrisy denounced in a pastoral manual; no doubt duplicity is more effectively practiced than preached. The remarkable fact about Perkins's, and especially Herbert's, treatments of hypocrisy is that for them, the hyp-

---

8. See Jonas Barish, *The Anti-Theatrical Prejudice,* 162. See also Philip Edwards et al., eds., *The Revels History of Drama in English,* vol. 4, *1613–1660,* 64.

9. *Workes* (1626), 2:671.

ocrite's problem is not too *much* attention to outward performance, but too *little*. This fact may seem strange given their concern for "hart-deep" devotion, but it becomes intelligible as part of their larger faith that, sooner or later, a tree will be known by its fruit. The bad clerical apple may shine for a time, but the worms will out. It is probably because of this belief that Herbert portrays in harrowing detail God's chosen engine against aspiring impostors: the stifling, busybody country parish.

If, as has been suggested, the parson's office is a kind of observation platform from which he surveys his people, Herbert would make him fully aware that the lines of sight run in both directions—and that the Argus-eyed gaze from the pew can be withering. If a man wishes to master the role, he must first be "an absolute Master and commander of himself," especially "in those things which are most apt to scandalize his Parish" (*W,* 227), for the congregation's eyes are everywhere. When he is counting his tithes, they are there: "Countrey people live hardly . . . and consequently knowing the price of mony, are offended much with any, who by hard usage increase their travell [travail]"; therefore "the Countrey Parson is very circumspect in avoiding all covetousnesse." When he is considering whether to marry, they are there: he would rather be single for devotion's sake, but "as the temper of his Parish may be, where he may have occasion to converse with women, and that among suspicious men, . . . he is rather married" (*W,* 237). When he is drawing up a guest list for dinner, they are there, or want to be: "Having then invited some of his Parish, hee taketh his times to do the like to the rest, . . . because countrey people are very observant of such things, and will not be perswaded, but being not invited, they are hated" (*W,* 243). They are there when he is arbitrating disputes, so he calls in other wise heads to give their opinions first, and thus make things pass "with more authority, and lesse envy" (*W,* 260). They are there when he is joking, so he seldom jokes, except as a "key to do good"; they are there when he is thinking of a drink, so he avoids this "most popular vice; into which if he come . . . he disableth himself of authority to reprove them" (*W,* 268, 227). The congregational eyes—as well as its fingers and nose—are upon him even when he dresses in the morning: since "disorders" of apparel are "very manifest," his clothing must be "plaine, but reverend, and clean, without spots or dust, or smell" (*W,* 228). There is much of the courtier's sensibility in Herbert's awareness that public people have no real privacy, that everything they do is cause for comment. The parson must run a virtually epic gauntlet of scrutiny. Only a deceiver of equally epic endurance could hold up under such a communal inquisition, and by doing so probably would win sympathy, if not admiration, from the hypocrite in us all.

Yet by multiplying these examples—of which I have cited not the half—Herbert drives home the point that ultimately the parson's authority depends not on his official status, but on his personal integrity; and in the enforced intimacy of a rural village, integrity cannot be put on with the preacher's robes. Country people may be "thick, and heavy"—and petty—but they are shrewd; if the parson is not honest, says Herbert, "he wil quickly be discovered, and disregarded: neither will they beleeve him in the pulpit, whom they cannot trust in his Conversation" (*W,* 228). "Conversation," in its richer archaic sense, joins words and deeds. Similarly, in "The Windows" (*W,* 67–68),

> Doctrine and life, colors and light, in one
>   When they combine and mingle, bring
> A strong regard and aw: but speech alone
>   Doth vanish like a flaring thing,
>   And in the eare, not conscience ring.
>   (ll. 11–15)

Every preacher should know that his auditors can hear more convivial and less demanding liars at the alehouse.

So for all of Herbert's apparent commitment to the elite status of the pastor's office, he nevertheless knows that the parson's actual power in the parish is constituted by an implicit but exacting social contract.[10] Like a usurping king, he "disableth himself of his authority" when he breaks this contract through his sins, which, he says, "make all equall, whom they finde together" (*W,* 227). In such straitened circumstances, under so much surveillance, the satisfactions of lording it over the likes of Bemerton would seem meager indeed.

10. See chapter 8, below.

Divine Surveillance

That *The Countrey Parson* raises so many hedges against clerical duplicity and arrogance argues that Herbert was himself well acquainted with these temptations. There is a psychologically suggestive pattern observable throughout the book, but particularly in "The Parson's Surveys": Herbert was a "younger son" of the nobility, and he inveighs against "loose" younger sons; he for years lacked "employment," and he attacks the great national sin of "Idlenesse"; he had been a finely dressing gentlemen, and he scolds ostentatious "Gallants"; he had been an ambitious courtier, and he calls the court a place of eminent ill (*W,* 277, 274, 275, 277). It is of course axiomatic that hypocrites cry out against their favorite sins; however, it is also true that converts, religious or otherwise, often feel the most vehemence against former sins—more even than seasoned veterans, because converts have the bitterness of direct experience in their mouths. So it may be that when Herbert seems most the busybody, he is preaching as much to himself as to the people. To use a medical analogy implied in the curate's title, it is as if, having survived a disease, he sets out to heal his parish.

Such an analogy is appropriate, because in his emphasis on vigilance, Herbert is imagining the country parson not as a prison warden, but as a parent and spiritual physician. "When any sinns, he hateth him not as an officer, but pityes him as a Father" (*W,* 250), for sin afflicts the sinner. Significantly, one of the manual's longest chapters (besides "The Parson's Surveys") is "The Parson's Dexterity in Applying of Remedies" (*W,* 280–83). Here, having surveyed the people, the parson diagnoses their most common distempers of soul—complacency, atheism, and despair—and administers their particular cures. As in "The Parson Preaching," Herbert's prescriptions take the form of suggested speeches: the comfortable he would afflict with an exhortation to judge themselves, lest they be judged; and those afflicted with atheism he would comfort with friendly observations about God's marvelous providence. With those near despair, the parson acts strikingly like the Host of "Love" (III): his quick and comprehensive eye takes in the parishioners' spiritual conditions, but he refuses either to minimize their sinfulness or acquiesce in their self-contempt. Instead, he shows them, in effect, that the God who sees their sins has borne the blame.

So for Herbert the mutual surveillance of parson and people is redeemed by a kind of gracious divine surveillance. God's quick, all-seeing eye is a loving eye, and a powerful eye as well, capable not only of penetrating but also of regenerating with a glance, and, in the end, of "look[ing] us out of pain" ("The Glance," *W,* 171–72, l. 21). Herbert believed that, under God, it is the parson's omnipresent diligence that spreads spiritual healing, regeneration, and compassion among his normally inquisitorial flock. Their natural watchfulness will always exist as a sobering check against pastoral malpractice, but when transformed by grace it will express itself as shrewd charity—the sort that discerns between sins and foibles, confronting the former, and winking at the latter. Because it is the parson's work that produces this change, Herbert's entire pastoral theory finally stands or falls on the parson's regenerate state. If he is not himself "hart-deep," he cannot hope to mediate such a communal transformation. Introducing *The Countrey Parson,* Herbert thanks God "who giveth mee my Desires and Performances" (*W,* 224); but throughout, the book teaches that if the parson lacks true desires, his performances are unlikely to stir anything but amusement, pity, or contempt.

It is possible to hear in Herbert's aside about "showing holy" the voice of the cynical rhetorical manipulator, just as it is possible to hear in his remarks about "thick and heavy" country folk an elitist sneer. However, given Herbert's oratorical training, his relatively great birth, and his former courtly ambitions, what seems truly remarkable is not that he was to some degree a manipulator and a snob—what would we expect?—but that he came so far and so deliberately toward humility.

And, at least in Herbert's remarks about homiletic technique, it is not necessary to hear any note of hypocrisy at all. The primary imagined audience of this chapter is probably the exact opposite of a hypocrite: that is, the earnest novice in his first pulpit, sincere of heart but tied of tongue. To such a struggling young preacher, groping for clear words and gestures to express his inner zeal and kindle others to it,

Herbert—like Perkins before him—gives a wealth of hearteningly specific advice. "They listened to this. They understood this. They responded to this." It is as if he were to say, "Be true to your new nature: play the man you are—or rather, the man whom God is making you."

5

"Doctrine and Life"

Herbert's Protestant Priesthood

> The Countrey Parson . . . [has] three points of . . . duty, the one, to infuse a competent knowledge of salvation in every one of his Flock; the other, to multiply, and build up this knowledge to a spirituall Temple; and third, to inflame this knowledge, to presse, and drive it to practice, turning it to reformation of life . . .
>
> —*The Countrey Parson* (*W*, 256–57)

When George Abbot died in August 1633, George Herbert was already five months in his grave. With the old Calvinist archbishop's death and Laud's elevation to the primacy, the delicate and unsteady balances of the Elizabethan Settlement collapsed, and Laud vigorously set about clearing the rubble to make room for his own ecclesiastical machinery. Years of waiting had clarified his goals: he would shut Calvin's "new-fangled" doctrines of predestination and "parity of ministers" out of all pulpits, tightly control or silence all lecturers, end lay bestowal of livings, exalt royal and episcopal power, and strictly enforce conformity.[1] His diary entry for September 19 is that of a

---

1. A. Tindal Hart, *The Country Clergy, 1558–1660*, 86–92. It is incorrect to view Laud's exaltation of royal power as a subordination of episcopal power. Instead, he poised two "divine right" claims, royal and episcopal, in a new balance. In fact, William Lamont argues that the real ecclesiastical power of the Caroline-Laudian regime was episcopal, since Charles willingly yielded both practical and formal control over the church to the bishops. See Lamont, *Godly Rule*, 57, 62–63.

man in a hurry: "Thursday, I was translated to the Arch-Bishopric of Canterbury. The Lord make me able, etc."[2]

Against this Laudian background, Herbert begins to look almost "Puritanical," with his Calvinist connections, his belief in a monarchy limited by common law, and his emphasis in *The Countrey Parson* on plain-style preaching, practicality, and the reformation of particular lives. Nevertheless, we should not conclude from these elements of the pastoral manual that Herbert was somehow a Puritan at heart, as if only Presbyterians (or crypto-Presbyterians) possessed a zeal for "experimental religion." Rather, by writing his pastoral, Herbert attempts something new and different in the English church, yet different in degree rather than in kind. He calls his country parson to bring the church's reformed doctrines of divine grace to bear on every aspect of parish life and practice in a manner consistent with the "fit array" of the church's established canonical order. In other words, Herbert calls on his fellow ministers to accomplish the further reformation of England, one person at a time, within the bounds of the Elizabethan Settlement.

In retrospect, we must see this collapse of the "Old Conformity" at Laud's accession as final, for the Restoration brought nothing like the Elizabethan Settlement. This settlement had combined evangelical and Catholic elements: on the one hand, outspoken scripturalism, strongly Protestant doctrine and preaching, and increased lay participation; on the other hand, a reformed Catholic liturgy administered by a limited but powerful episcopacy, all under a supreme yet not absolute monarch. This unique combination was not re-created by Charles II, his bishops, or the Restoration Parliament. However, looking ahead in the late 1620s and early 1630s, Herbert saw the old establishment's institutions as seriously threatened, yet still intact. For Herbert, this model provided the plan for a fit structure within which a country parson could nurture the spiritual life of his people. It is after this pattern that the parson must build, rebuild, and expand. To delineate it more clearly for himself and other pastors, Herbert wrote *The Countrey Parson*.

The mere existence of this book is important. Completed by Her-

2. *Works of Laud* 3:219.

bert sometime in 1632 and published twenty years later with his literary remains (*W*, 556), it is the first attempt by a Protestant English churchman of any party at a practical, and especially a thorough, pastoral manual.[3] Of the reams of divinity and sermons that had been published in England since the Reformation, most were doctrinal and controversial. Those writings that did deal specifically with the pastor's office were either too parochial and administrative or too unsystematic to be called manuals.[4] Thus the English clergy lacked an adequate exposition of both the principles and the particular duties of their office, and they needed concrete suggestions for the whole work. Herbert sought to fill these needs.

This is not to say that *The Countrey Parson* departs from ninety years of English Protestant theology. On the contrary, Herbert extends and develops that tradition in a way profoundly consistent with its first principles of *sola scriptura, sola gratia,* and *sola fide.* He attempts to detail for the parson the means of "driving . . . their generall Schoole rules ever to the smallest actions of life" (*W*, 265–66). From the Reformation on, England's theological writers insist on the practical outworking of faith as its necessary demonstration. The *Articles of Religion* speak of good works as the fruit of faith. Such acts

3. While it is possible that Herbert knew of patristic and medieval pastoral manuals, it is unlikely that these served in any substantial way as models for his work. Not surprisingly, Herbert shares their emphases on teaching by example as well as by precept, and on heartfelt concern for parishioners, but his book differs fundamentally in both theology and form. By the late patristic era, the pastor's "cure of souls" had come to focus on the administration of confession and penance, a tendency that only increased in medieval times. For example, John Myrc's *Instructions for Parish Priests* (c. 1440, in English) deals briefly with homilies, the Lord's Prayer, and the Creed, but it is patterned mainly on the order of the seven deadly sins and the seven sacraments, with special attention to the confessional. See John McNeill, *A History of the Cure of Souls,* 93–94, 156–57. Cristina Malcolmson suggests a much more likely model for the form of *The Countrey Parson*—the Tudor-Stuart courtesy book. She argues that Herbert's manual "replaces the 'court-stile' and courtier with the unambitious patriotic country minister, a 'character of holiness,' translated in language and social identity." See Malcolmson, "Society and Self-Definition," 9.

4. For important examples of Protestant pastoral concern before Herbert, see John Bradford's letters in Miles Coverdale, ed., *Letters of the Martyrs,* 251–489, 650–52; Bishop Hooper's *Visitation Articles* in Charles Nevinson, ed., *The Later Writings of Bishop Hooper;* and the abundant pastoral references in *The Sermons of John Donne.* Indispensible for perusing Donne's sermons is Troy D. Reeves, ed., *Index to the Sermons of John Donne.*

are "pleasing and acceptable to God in Christ, and do spring out necessarily of a true and lively Faith; insomuch that by them a lively Faith may be evidently known, as a tree discerned by the fruit" (Article 12).

All the major divines under Elizabeth and James share this same concern for "fruit"—Bernard Gilpin's sermon on pastoral shortcomings before the Bishop of Durham, Thomas Cartwright's controversial writings on church government, William Perkins's pioneering works on preaching and casuistry, Richard Bernard's on preaching, Bishop Joseph Hall's on casuistry—all call for the individual's conscious conversion to Christ and for the edification of each believer in Christ through scriptural preaching, catechizing, and counseling.[5] Furthermore, all hold a Calvinist view of election, and, except for Hall, all are inclined toward, if not actually committed to, something like the Genevan model of church discipline.

In contrast, no member of the church's Arminian party, with the exception of Lancelot Andrewes, had produced any work of practical divinity by the time that Herbert wrote his pastoral.[6] The visitation articles of archbishops Bancroft and Laud, and of Arminian bishops like William Pierce, Richard Montague, Augustine Lindsell, and Robert Skinner, are fundamentally administrative documents. Their articles treat the pastor's "cure of souls" as mainly a matter of communicating and enforcing episcopal policy—especially the limitation of preaching and the turning of communion tables "altar-wise"—and make uniformity rather than individual edification their primary goal. Although the Laudians spoke often of "edification"—and indeed Laud's diaries sometimes display minute spiritual self-examination—they saw

5. For a relevant excerpt of Gilpin's sermon, see Hart, *Country Clergy,* 138; for Cartwright on church government, see especially *The Second Replie. . . Agaynst. . . Whitgift;* for Perkins on preaching, see *The Arte of Prophesying,* in William Perkins, *Workes* (1626), 2:643–73; for Perkins on casuistry, see *A Discourse of Conscience* and *The Whole Treatise of Conscience,* in *Workes* (1612). For Bernard, see *The Faithfull Shepheard.* For Hall, see *Resolutions and Cases of Conscience,* in *Works.* Other major practical divines, such as William Ames, Robert Sanderson, and Jeremy Taylor, did not publish in Herbert's lifetime.

6. Andrewes's *Patterne of Catechisticall Doctrine* grew out of lectures that he delivered in the late 1570s, very early in his career, when he was Catechist of Emmanuel College, Cambridge. Significantly, during this period of his life, Andrewes appears to have been influenced by Emmanuel's Puritan atmosphere. See Paul A. Welsby, *Lancelot Andrewes, 1555–1626,* 20–22.

individual spiritual health as resulting inevitably from the uniform obedience and "peace of the church."[7]

Yet while Herbert's emphases lie in strikingly different directions from those of Laud, Herbert's ambitious plans for reforming England house by house and person by person suggest a degree of "thorough" perhaps analogous to Laud's, raising questions about his own exaltation of pastoral power. If his goal, like St. Paul's, is "the perfecting of the saints, for the work of ministry, for the edifying of the body of Christ" (Eph. 4:12), then to what extent is the parson deliberately undermining his own position? How much authority is Herbert willing to delegate to "godly laymen"—to church wardens, vestrymen, and heads of households—whose lives show sufficient "reformation" to be trusted with the edification of others? To what extent is the pastor a member of the body of Christ, with only a special leadership function, and to what extent does he belong to a separate priestly order, possessing a special metaphysical status in the parish?

The answers to these questions help to distinguish Herbert from the *jure divino* episcopacy of Laud and the Arminians on the one hand and the nonhierarchical ministry of the Presbyterian model on the other. In *The Countrey Parson,* and in the lyrics that touch on the pastor's office, Herbert walks the Old Conformist "middle way," between the deeply antagonistic "New Conformists" and the "Non-Conformists." Like the 1559 Prayer Book, he retains the title of "priest," yet he redefines *priesthood* primarily as the ministry of the word. The "priest's" preeminence in the parish and his administration of the sacraments serve this scripturalist mission.

Still, while Herbert's emphasis on the pervasive "edification" of his parish moves him at times toward the idea of a shared ministry, *The Countrey Parson* never fundamentally questions the distinction between clergy and laity. The manual places definite limits on lay ministry by stressing the parson's central position in the spiritual life of the parish. On this and other points we may compare Herbert to his Puritan admirer Richard Baxter, the most prominent seventeenth-century advocate of a "godly ministry" by sincerely converted, "heart-deep" men. Baxter's *Reformed Pastor,* published in 1656, only four years

---

7. Charles Carlton, *Archbishop William Laud,* 12.

after *The Countrey Parson,* uses Herbert's language of a Protestant "priesthood," while amplifying Herbert's zeal for preaching, catechizing, and discipline; unlike Herbert, he rejects the outward forms of the Elizabethan church and more of "priesthood's" hierarchical privilege in English country life.

So an overview of Herbert's pastoral theory (since we know so little of his actual practice at Bemerton) distinguishes him even further from the Laudians than do the Hookerian political notions discussed in chapters 2 and 3, above. King James's Calvinism notwithstanding, it remains true that before 1650, both divine-right monarchy and divine-right episcopacy were increasingly opposed and supplanted by the leaven of Calvinist doctrine. Calvin's theology of an absolute monarch of heaven and earth was more and more taken to preclude any absolute human ruler. This leaven might have pervaded the commonwealth if more parsons had worked out Herbert's vision for the practical ministry of the word, reaching out of the church building into the fields and homes of each parish.

The Protestant Priesthood

Herbert begins his manual of pastoral practice by defining the office. "A Pastor," he writes, "is the Deputy of Christ for the reducing of Man to the Obedience of God. This definition is evident," he continues,

> and containes the direct steps of Pastorall Duty and Auctority. For first, man fell from God by disobedience. Secondly, Christ is the glorious instrument for the revoking [calling back] of Man. Thirdly, Christ being not to continue on earth, but after hee had fulfilled the work of Reconciliation, to be received up into heaven, he constituted Deputies in his place, and these are Priests. . . . Wherein is contained the complete definition of a Minister. (*W,* 225)

One striking characteristic of Herbert's definition is the freedom with which he uses different terms to designate the office: a pastor is a deputy, a priest, a minister, even, a few sentences later, a "Vicegerent" of Christ. In multiplying titles, Herbert follows the Prayer Book, which retains, along with the comfortably Protestant terms *pastor* and *minister,* other terms more suspect in Geneva: *prelate, bishop, curate, vicar,* and most questionable of all to Protestants, *priest*.[8] Does Herbert's "priesthood" call his strong Protestantism into doubt?

This question requires us to distinguish carefully between the reformed English "priesthood" and the sacerdotal "sacrificing priesthood" of the medieval and Roman church. The *Oxford English Dictionary*'s definition of *priest* notes that much confusion results because this one word is used to translate two different sets of terms. In one sense it is "a synonyme for [Greek and Latin] *presbyter* or elder, and designates the minister who presides over and instructs a Christian congregation; in the other it is equivalent to the Latin *sacerdos*, the Greek *hiereus*, or the Hebrew *koh'n*, the offerer of sacrifices, who also performs other mediatorial offices between God and man."[9] Significantly, the Latin text of Herbert's subscription at his ordination (September 19, 1630) refers to him not as *sacerdos*, but as *"presbuterus."*[10]

Once this distinction is drawn, Herbert's reformed faith is no more doubtful for his "priesthood" than that of the Prayer Book itself. The rubrics may speak of "priests," but the *Articles of Religion* make it clear that these "priests" do not claim to offer a mystical sacrifice on the altar. We have already seen that the *Articles* on the Lord's Supper explicitly reject Roman transubstantiation and Lutheran consubstantiation for Calvin's "receptionist" doctrine of Christ's "Real Presence," and that Herbert's Communion poems prominently incorporate Calvin's imagery of "ascent." So it would seem that Herbert believed in Christ's unique, "eternal priesthood" as fully as did Calvin or any Puritan. Jesus, Herbert says, having *"fulfilled the work of Reconciliation,"* and "being not to continue on earth . . . constituted Deputies in his place, and these are Priests" (*W*, 225, emphasis mine). The priest stands in Christ's place and, empowered by Christ, applies this reconciliation to individual lives, to return men "to the obedience of God." Thus the term *priest* is conspicuously absent from the one chapter

8. While Herbert's discourse prudently "ariseth not to the Reverend"—and increasingly controversial—"Prelates of the Church" (*W*, 225), he more than once notes the "priestly" nature of the parson's office. His parson is to "give like a priest" (*W*, 245) and gladly pronounce "a priest's blessing" (*W*, 377); and he condemns flattering chaplains whose self-service "wrongs the Priesthood" (*W*, 226).

9. *OED* quotes Lightfoot's commentary on Philippians (1869, 2d ed., 184), which says that "the word 'priest' has two different senses."

10. Charles, *Life of George Herbert*, 153.

in *The Countrey Parson* where a Roman Catholic or Anglo-Catholic might expect it most: "The Parson in Sacraments." Instead, the chapter stresses that only an experiential knowledge of biblical doctrine and of God's grace will make the Communion efficacious (*W,* 257–59). Just as significantly, this chapter comes more than halfway into the manual, after Herbert has laid down the foundational early chapters on the parson's chief means for accomplishing his priestly work of reconciliation: imitating Christ in both "Doctrine and Life" (*W,* 225). The "true priest" must work out his evangelical faith in practice if he hopes to earn the "strong regard and awe" essential to an effective ministry.

Preaching

We have already noted the remarkable correspondences between Herbert's beliefs about "the art of prophesying" and those of the Elizabethan Puritan William Perkins.[11] It now remains to compare Herbert's recommended style to that of the two most famous preachers in Herbert's own day, John Donne and Lancelot Andrewes. While Donne is not to be classed as a disciple of Andrewes—he was idiosyncratic rather than fully Arminian in theology, nor was he exclusively a court preacher, nor devoted to wordplay and minute grammatical analysis —he was devoted to aureate pulpit eloquence.[12]

---

11. In *The Arte of Prophesying* (1592), Perkins writes, "[T]here are two parts of prophecy: preaching of the word and conceiving of prayers" (*Workes* [1626], 2:646). Herbert makes the same connection by treating "The Parson Praying" (chapter 6) just before "The Parson Preaching" (chapter 7). Furthermore, Herbert ends *The Countrey Parson* with "The Authour's Prayer before Sermon" and "A Prayer after Sermon," both of which, significantly, he composed himself. This linking of prayer to preaching is explained by another Calvinist homiletician, Richard Bernard, in *The Faithfull Shepheard* (1607):

> Praier must be the Proeme; it is the Lord that both giues wisedome to vnderstand, and the words of vtterance. . . . The Disciples might not goe out before they had received the spirit; neither may wee goe vp and speake without it. It is not by the instrument that men are converted; neither in the words lieth the power to saue: But it is the Lords blessing thereupon, who thereby addeth to the Church such as are ordained to be saued. (13)

For Bernard, whose book shows an obvious debt to Perkins's, it is the Lord who enables communication and who elects people to salvation. Yet this knowledge does not make the humble preacher fatalistic; rather, it gives him hope of real success; the One who inspired the Word can inspire the hearers to understand it.

12. See Charles H. George and Katherine George, *The Protestant Mind of the English*

Of course, as Barbara Lewalski tells us, Donne (like Herbert) grounded his style in "the scripture itself as the epitome of eloquence, and proposes it to the preacher's imitation as the model and sanction for his most exquisite art." However, she adds, "Donne's conception of 'imitation' . . . admits of a very creative relationship to that model . . . Donne is able to fuse the biblical emphasis with [his] expectation of art precisely because he takes the scriptures to be the most witty and most eloquent of texts."[13] Thus Donne says in a sermon of November 1628 that "for the purity and elegancy, for the force and power, for the largenesse and extention of the words, . . . there are not so exquisite, so elegant Books in the World, as the Scriptures."[14] In *Devotions upon Emergent Occasions,* he writes that God is "a metaphoricall God. . . . A God in whose words there is such a height of figures, such voyages . . . to fetch remote and precious metaphors . . . as all prophane Authors, seeme of the seed of the Serpent, that creeps; thou art the dove, that flies."[15] In contrast, Lewalski points out that for Herbert, imitation of scriptural plain style means not "fetching remote and precious metaphors," but rather "using similes and illustrations drawn from homely things—'a plough, a hatchet, a bushell, leaven, boyes piping and dancing . . .' especially for a rural congregation."[16]

Certainly we must note the vast differences in the audiences to which a country parson and a cathedral dean had to adapt their messages. Donne was acutely aware of the various capacities among his auditors. In fact, in a sermon before the king during the Lenten season of 1630, he declares that in preaching "it is a good art, to deliver deepe points in a holy plainnesse, and plaine points in a holy delightfulnesse: for, many times, one part of our auditory understands us not, when we

---

Reformation, 1570–1640, 68–70, and W. Fraser Mitchell, *English Pulpit Oratory from Andrewes to Tillotson,* 187–89. *DNB* notes that in 1619 Donne received from the Dutch States-General a gold medal struck to commemorate the Synod of Dordt, at which English bishops sent by King James had helped to formulate the so-called "five points of Calvinism." The fact that Donne preached before the States-General at the time of the award suggests that while he was no Calvinist, he was no fully committed Arminian, either. See *DNB,* "Donne," 1134a.

13. *Protestant Poetics,* 220–21.
14. *Sermons* 8:273.
15. *Devotions upon Emergent Occasions,* Anthony Raspa, ed., 99–100.
16. *Protestant Poetics,* 222, quoting *Countrey Parson* 21, *W,* 257.

have done, and so they are weary; and another part understands us before we begun, and so they are weary." Donne admits the simplicity of Christ's language, which used "none of this battery of eloquence," and would limit his display of reading and ornament to the "Auditories, acquainted with such learnings."[17] Furthermore, we should not forget Herbert's earlier Latin eloquence—and his flattery of king and prince—as University Orator at Cambridge. Conversely, "thicke, and heavy" country people were unlikely to be touched by erudite references and comparisons, so Herbert probably did not begrudge Donne some of his "precious metaphors," at least in London.

In any case, Herbert's differences with Donne seem minor in comparison with Herbert's criticism of the style that characterized Andrewes's Laudian imitators, and at times Andrewes himself. Fundamentally Herbert's homiletics differ with the Laudians' because he differs from their methods of scriptural exegesis, particularly as practiced by Andrewes. Walton is right in telling us that Herbert knew and admired Andrewes personally,[18] but Herbert clearly disagreed with Andrewes hermeneutically, writing that

> [t]he Parsons Method in handling of a text consists of two parts; first, a plain and evident declaration of the meaning of the text; and secondly, some choyce Observations drawn out of the whole text, as it lies entire, and unbroken in the Scripture it self. This he thinks naturall, and sweet, and grave. Whereas the other way of crumbling a text into small parts, as, the Person speaking, or spoken to, the subject, the object and the like, hath neither in it sweetnesse, nor gravity, nor variety, since the words apart are not Scripture, but a dictionary, and may be considered alike in all the Scripture. (*W,* 234–35)

The preacher treats the text simply, directly, and most significantly, "entire, and unbroken . . . as it lies" in its whole context.

In contrast, Andrewes treats minute grammatical and etymological analysis as the substance of preaching. Expanding on the word *Immanuel* in his Ninth Sermon on the Nativity, he not only examines the "words apart," but also literally takes the words themselves apart. He tells us that the name

17. *Sermons* 9:215; ibid., 10:147–48.
18. *Lives,* 273.

is compounded, and to be taken in peeces. First, into *Immanu* and *El* of which, *El,* (the latter) is the more principall by farr: for, *El,* is GOD. . . . For the other, *Immanu:* though *El* be the more principall, yet, I cannot tell, whether it, or *Immanu,* do more concerne us. For, as, in *El,* is might: So, in *Immanu,* is our right, to His might. . . . This *Immanu* is a Compound againe: we may take it, in sunder, into *Nobis,* and *cum:* And so then we have three peeces. 1. *El,* the mighty GOD: 2. and *Anu,* we, poore we . . . ; 3. And *Im,* which is *cum,* And that *cum,* in the midst betweene *nobis* and *Deus,* GOD and Vs; to couple GOD and us. [I]f we have Him; and GOD, by Him, we need no more: *Immanu-el,* and *Immanu-all.*[19]

By thus displaying the marvelously complex scaffolding of his exegesis for all to see, Andrewes sometimes achieves stunning effects, some of which movingly dramatize the doctrine that he proclaims, like his excursus on *venimus* and the "cold comming" of the wise men, made famous in this century by inclusion in T. S. Eliot's "Journey of the Magi."[20] However, these effects often have little to do with the larger context of the word or the sentence analyzed, and in extreme cases, like the "crumbling" of *Immanuel,* they degenerate (at least from Herbert's viewpoint) into reverberating wordplay. Andrewes handles the "pieces" of language much like precious gems to be cut, and he delights in the dazzling colors to be revealed as new facets are broken open and held up to light.

However, some of Andrewes's hearers who recognized that he treated words almost as tactile objects described his practice in different terms. A Scots laird who heard Andrewes told James that the preacher "did play with his text as a jackanapes does, who takes up a thing and tosses and plays with it, and then takes up another and plays a little with it. Here's a pretty thing and there's a pretty thing."[21] To the laird, almost certainly a Calvinist, Andrewes's delight in the "pretty things" of the text marked him as self-absorbed, random, and childish. Herbert is more charitable, but his dominant metaphor treats the "words apart" not as gems, but crumbs.[22]

In addition to style and method, the country parson's preaching

19. *XCVI Sermons,* 75–76.
20. Ibid., 143; Eliot, *Complete Poems and Plays, 1909–1950,* 68–69, ll. 1–5.
21. Welsby, *Andrewes,* 195.
22. According to W. Fraser Mitchell, Herbert's critique of "Arminian exegesis" links him to the "practical" preaching tradition later epitomized by Baxter (*English Pulpit,* 364).

differs from that of the Arminians in its content, or at least in its emphasis. Laud writes in his preface to the 1629 edition of Andrewes's *XCVI Sermons,* "[A]fter the building up of the Faith of Christ, [the preacher's] chief work should be, to beat down those Strong Holdes, which any sinnes have built up in the hearts of men." The chief sins of these "evill days," says Laud, are "all hatred, contention, variance, all sedition and disobedience to Lawfull Authoritie." Therefore, he continues, "all Preachers are the Iawes of the Church, and the sinnes of the people are, as it were, to be ground *inter Maxillas,* between these Iawes, before the People themselves can be made fit to nourish the Church, or the Church them."[23] By means of this grisly metaphysical conceit, borrowed from Jerome, Laud asserts that the times demand stern absolutist preaching to crush seditious Genevan ideas of a limited monarchy and the "parity of ministers." He recommends Andrewes, a staunch defender of divine-right monarchy and episcopacy, as a model for such sermons.

However, Herbert's recommendations for sermon material, written in the same "evill days" as Laud's preface, lack any similar exhortation especially to preach up submission to the powers that be. Herbert advises that the parson choose his sermon topics "by way of expounding the Church Catechisme, to which all divinity may easily be reduced" (*W,* 230). Thus, while expounding the catechism would certainly mean defending obedience to the king's ecclesiastical supremacy over against papal authority, the great bulk of the parson's sermons would treat matters far more basic to Protestant faith and devotion.[24]

Herbert further differs with Laud's stress on absolute uniformity by advising that parsons personally rework or compose sermons of

23. Andrewes, *XCVI Sermons,* iv. This preface was cosigned by Joseph Hall, the Bishop of Ely, and a Calvinist. However, the substance is almost certainly Laud's, since Hall, in his own book defending episcopacy, allowed himself to be ruled, and overruled, by the archbishop. See *DNB,* "Hall," 962a.

24. The five main divisions of the *Short Catechism of 1604* deal with 1) the meaning of the two sacraments, Baptism and Communion, including a denial of transubstantiation and the sacrifice of the Mass; 2) the Apostles' Creed, stressing the finished work of Christ and the sovereign grace of God; 3) the Ten Commandments, with strong condemnations of images and idolatry; 4) the Lord's Prayer, as a pattern for prayer rather than as a rote form; and 5) the definition of Scripture as the only rule of faith and life, with emphasis on the vital role of preaching. See John Mayer, *The English Catechism Explained.*

their own. Herbert's parson may borrow freely from the sermons of others, including, surely, the *Book of Homilies,* but he presents them "diversely clothed, illustrated, and inlarged." For "though the world is full of such composures, yet every man's own is fittest, readyest, and most savory to him" (*W,* 230). The parson must preach from personal experience of Christian doctrine, "dipping, and seasoning all our words and sentences in our hearts." Hence original compositions are best.

So in his approach to preaching—in style, exegetical method, doctrinal emphases, and personal composition—Herbert not only differs with the Laudians, but also agrees with Perkins and the tradition that Perkins defined.[25] In short, while Herbert's ideas on the "art of prophesying" do not make him a Puritan, they reveal his profound oneness of mind with other practitioners of reformed homiletics, on the subject that concerned the Puritans most.

Catechizing

However, while Herbert vigorously recommends preaching as essential to "inflame" the knowledge of salvation and "drive it to practice," he admits that even preaching has its limits, for "at Sermons, and Prayers, men may sleep or wander." The antidote to sluggishness in the pews, says Herbert, is the well-aimed catechistical question. For "when one is asked a question, he must discover what he is" (*W,* 256–57). Indeed, Herbert writes, successful preaching depends on thorough catechizing. "Catechizing," he says, "is the first point" of a parson's duty, "and but by catechizing, the other [i.e. edification and reformation through preaching] cannot be attained" (*W,* 255). Consequently, Herbert is careful to define catechizing as more than mere recitation of the prescribed orthodox answers. When he returns to the subject

---

25. Herbert and Perkins appear to diverge over the use of stories; Herbert recommends them, while Perkins forbids the "telling of tales." However, on closer examination we see that by "tales" Perkins means "all profane and ridiculous speeches," and that Herbert would use stories to aid the people's memory, and only "according as his text invites him." Furthermore, Perkins allows for the use of "allegories" so long as they are used "for the instruction of the life and not to prove any point of faith" (*W,* 233; Perkins, *Workes* [1626], 670, 677).

while discussing the sacraments in the following chapter (22), he stresses that "the saying of the Catechism is necessary, but not enough; because an answer in form may still admit ignorance: but the Questions must be propounded loosely and wildely," for then, he reiterates, "the Answerer will discover what hee is." Otherwise the respondents will only speak "by rote, as parrats, without ever piercing to the sense" (*W*, 259, 256).

The essential importance of this kind of "discovery" was expressed twenty-four years later by Richard Baxter from his own experience:

> I am daily forced to wonder how lamentably ignorant many of our people are, who have seemed diligent hearers of me these ten or twelve years, while I spoke as plainly as I was able to speak. Some know not that each person in the Trinity is God; nor that Christ is God and man; nor that he took his human nature to heaven; nor what they must trust to for pardon and salvation; nor many similar important principles of our faith.[26]

Even the plainest preacher (and Baxter was certainly among the plainest) cannot know from the looks and nods of his congregation that they understand the plain truth. Therefore, Herbert writes, if the parson informs his people through individual catechizing, his sermons will better inflame this knowledge.

Moreover, says Herbert, not only the people but also the parsons themselves benefit from catechizing; this work makes the clergy more aware of their membership in the parish, and of their own sinfulness. While it is good, he writes, that "in Sermons there is a kinde of state," yet this elevated position creates a spiritual danger for the parson, who might forget his own humanity and set himself above the people's problems. In contrast, he continues, "in Catechizing there is an humblenesse very suteable to Christian regeneration, which exceedingly delights [the parson] . . . by way of preaching to himself, for the advancing of his own mortification; for in preaching to others, he forgets not himself, but is first a Sermon to himself, and then to others; growing with the growth of his parish" (*W*, 255). The parson has

---

26. *The Reformed Pastor*, 212.

not "arrived." Like all of his parishioners, he needs both mortification of sin and growth in spiritual life. Only by growing with them can he remain qualified to minister to their spiritual needs.

Baxter expands on the importance of the humility and fellowship produced by the pastor's personal instruction of the people:

> [Catechizing] will do much to subdue our own corruptions, and to exercise and increase our graces. . . . All the austerities of monks and hermits, . . . who think to save themselves by neglecting to show compassion to others, will not do near so much in the true work of mortification. . . . [Furthermore], by distance and unacquaintedness, abundance of mistakes between ministers and people are fomented; while, on the other hand, familiarity will tend to beget those affections which may open their ears to further instruction.[27]

For Baxter, as for Herbert, even the humility and sense of community brought by catechizing are not ends in themselves, but means to the higher end of further edification.

Besides informing the people and "inflaming" himself, a third benefit derived from catechizing is the parson's knowledge of individuals' spiritual health, especially when examining potential recipients of the Lord's Supper. Thus Herbert devotes much of his chapter on the sacraments (22) to preliminary questioning. In the weeks before a Communion Sunday, the parson "looks into the ignorance, or carelesness of his flock, and accordingly applies himselfe with Catechizings, and lively exhortations" (*W,* 258). Furthermore, since for Herbert it is the communicant's experiential knowledge that enables him or her to "receive" Christ in the sacrament, he specifies that "[t]he time of every ones first receiving is not so much by yeers, as by understanding," a principle that would include some younger children and exclude some adults. Baxter recommends catechizing for the same reason.[28] Both Herbert and Baxter claim that only by personal questioning can the pastor get past the appearances of maturity to discover the true convert.

In *The Living Temple,* Stanley Fish has fruitfully analyzed Herbert's unusually Socratic method of questioning. Socrates, says Herbert,

27. Ibid., 187, 177.
28. Ibid., 178.

held that the seeds of all truths lay in every body, and accordingly by questions well ordered he found Philosophy in silly Trades-men. That position will not hold in Christianity, because it contains things above nature: but after that the Catechisme is once learn'd, that which nature is towards Philosophy, the Catechism is towards Divinity. To this purpose, some dialogues in Plato are worth the reading, where the singular dexterity of Socrates . . . may be . . . imitated. (*W,* 256)

When Herbert catechizes, says Fish, his typical question is "one whose purpose it is to set the listener's mind to working." Furthermore, Fish is right that "by including the catechist among the beneficiaries [of catechizing, Herbert] . . . suggests a view of the transaction considerably more dynamic than that held by his predecessors and contemporaries." Most importantly, Fish sheds considerable light on the "catechistical strategy" of *The Temple* as a whole. This strategy, Fish says, repeatedly invites the reader

> to a premature interpretive conclusion, which is first challenged, and then rein-stated, but in such a way as to make it the vehicle of a deeper understanding; . . . the reader [of the poems] plays the role assigned in *A Priest To the Temple* to the catechized, moving by stages and in response to questions (overt or implied) to that which he knows not by means of that which he knows. . . . What is crucial is not the dialogue in [a] poem, but the dialogue [a] poem is in, and that, in turn, is a function of the way these poems characteristically engage their readers.[29]

Thus Fish goes a long way toward explaining the provisional and "surprising" quality of *The Temple,* and particularly of "The Church"—its frequent reversals, apparent equivocation, and restlessness—as didactic strategies.

However, Fish seems to overstate his point when he claims that the goal of this strategy, both in catechizing and in *The Temple,* is "the *self-discovery* of the respondent" (emphasis mine).[30] The problem may lie in Fish's imprecise use of "self," for in the same passage he admits that Herbert's parson has a predetermined doctrinal "marke" in view, and that he questions the respondent "loosely and wildely" to give him the "'delight' of working things out for himself."[31] Still, Fish unduly im-

29. *The Living Temple: George Herbert and Catechizing,* 21, 15, 35.
30. Ibid., 24.
31. Ibid., 25.

poses his own philosophical and theological predilections when he claims that "order and surprise," "assurance and restlessness" essentially contradict one another, and therefore that they never find resolution in Herbert's mind.

On the contrary, Herbert, like Calvin, Perkins, or Baxter, works to drive doctrine to a consistent experience and practice, not to encourage the unending free play of "self-discovery." Unfortunately, while Fish acknowledges that Herbert carefully limits the range of his Socratic questioning, he misses the import of a central metaphor in Herbert's discussion: "Socrates," says Herbert, "held that the *seeds* of all truths lay in every body, . . . but that which nature is towards Philosophy, the Catechism is towards Divinity" (emphasis mine). For Herbert, the catechism is the seed of the gospel, a pattern made to grow and be fulfilled. Order and spontaneity come together in this scriptural metaphor, which points to the exfoliation of a preordained pattern that is experienced subjectively as "surprise." Though the gospel seed requires the parson's planting and cultivation, it possesses a power and life of its own.

In discussing the parson's actual procedure for individual instruction, Herbert directs him to catechize every Sunday afternoon and on holy days, as required by the church canons.[32] The parson examines the "younger sort" publicly, by rote, so that all may perceive "the authority of the work," and reexamine themselves as they listen; he questions the "elder sort" privately, "giving age honour," requiring of them not "the very words," but "the substance." He goes about this work gently, "helping and cherishing the Answerer, by making the question very plaine with comparisons, and making much even of a word of truth from him" (*W,* 255–56). This method, says Herbert, if skillfully practiced, "will draw out of ignorant and silly souls, even the dark and deep points of Religion."

Herbert is so committed to this kind of personal instruction that he would not confine it to the church building on Sundays, nor to the parson's supervision alone. In fact, the parson ensures that fathers and masters catechize their own children and servants at home (see *W,* 248, 255). In doing so the parson is not acting as a "Puritan" but

32. Church of England, *Canons,* Canon 59.

as a Calvinist. Christopher Hill notes that "[d]omestic catechizing, by fathers and masters in their families, was one of the things insisted on by the divines at the Synod of Dordt."[33] We have yet to examine the larger implications of such spiritual delegation by the pastor, but it is clear that for Herbert, driving doctrine to "reformation of life" means quite literally driving it *home*.

Cases of Conscience

Closely related to catechizing, both in purpose and in practice, is the parson's work as spiritual physician, his applying of remedies to particular "cases of conscience"—those gray areas of thought and behavior not touched by the explicit rules of the Bible and the creeds. Camille Wells Slights defines case divinity as "the branch of theology that attempts to provide the perplexed human conscience with a means of reconciling the obligations of religious faith with the demands of particular human situations."[34] No method could better suit Herbert's purpose of building up every member of his flock than private conferences on particular problems. These conferences combined the advantages of catechizing with those of preaching: a question-and-answer "discovery" of "what a man is," and a miniature sermon tailored by the parson to the man himself. "[I]ndeed," he writes, "herein is the greatest ability of a Parson to lead his people exactly in the ways of Truth, so that they may neither decline to the right hand, nor to the left" (*W,* 230). Significantly, this "middle way" is again the exact way, not merely a convenient compromise between competing extremes.

The Countrey Parson abounds in casuistry. Herbert gives as examples such questions as: when does one cross the line from pleasure in God's gifts of food, drink, sleep, and sex into "gluttony, drunkenness,

33. *Society and Puritanism in Pre-Revolutionary England,* 454. This emphasis is of course Lutheran as well.

34. *The Casuistical Tradition in Shakespeare, Donne, Herbert, and Milton,* 3. The Protestant casuistical works available to Herbert in 1632 were Calvinistic in theology. Most notable are Perkins's *Discourse of Conscience* and *The Whole Treatise of the Cases of Conscience,* published in the *Workes* of 1612–1613. As noted above, the works of the great "Anglican" casuists Robert Sanderson and Jeremy Taylor did not appear until after Herbert's death, nor did those of the Puritans William Ames and Richard Baxter. See Slights, *Casuistical Tradition,* 10 n. 13.

sloath, [and] lust"? When does natural desire "for increase of means" become "a sin of covetousnes"? When is it "a fault to discover anothers fault, or when not"? (*W,* 230). In seeking to resolve these and other dilemmas, the parson must understand scriptural truth not just generally, but specifically and circumstantially. He "hath throughly canvassed al the particulars of humane actions," for, he says, "[i]f the Parson were ashamed of particularizing in these things, hee were not fit to be a Parson: but he holds the Rule, that Nothing is little in Gods service" (*W,* 248–49).

Of all the lyrics in "The Church," the two that deal most explicitly with particular "cases of conscience" are "Lent" and "To All Angels and Saints." "Lent," as I have argued above, fails to justify the Lenten fast coherently—and therefore fails as casuistry—because Herbert seems inwardly at odds with the authoritarian principle that he defends. He cannot convince the Puritan to obey unquestioningly the Arminian authorities because he is not entirely convinced that he can himself.

However, "To All Angels and Saints" (*W,* 136–37) works better as casuistry. Richard Strier has argued that Herbert's rhetorical strategy in the poem is to "separat[e] out warmth of need and desire from 'true religion'" in order to refute the Roman Catholic charge that Protestants refuse to invoke the Virgin, angels, and saints out of envy.[35] According to Strier, Herbert accomplishes this separation by dividing the poem into two parts: "the opening vision" of the first three stanzas, with their reverent "rush of feeling" for the heavenly beings; and the "sober reality" of the last three stanzas, in which the speaker exposes those feelings as "irresponsible" by reminding himself and his hearers that "we dare not from [God's] garland steal / To make a posie for inferiour power" (ll. 24–25). Thus the first half of the poem engages the attention and feelings of the conscience-troubled reader in language that echoes his own fear of being "stingy" toward the angels and saints. After this engagement of sympathy and interest, the second half resolves these fears by assuring the reader that the heavenly host, as fellow creatures and servants of God, do not desire human "vows" and prayers. Instead they, like the earthly Christian, "never

35. "'To All Angels and Saints': Herbert's Puritan Poem," 145.

move a wing" unless "any one our Masters hand can show" (ll. 21, 30). In "To All Angels and Saints," Herbert succeeds casuistically (and catechistically) by single-mindedly driving the reader to the doctrinal "mark." Though the poem's strategy is indirect, its logic, in retrospect, is internally consistent.

Looking beyond such explicitly casuistical lyrics, Slights, like Fish, argues that "The Church" as a whole is unified by a didactic strategy. Its poems, she says, are didactic not in tone and precept, like "The Church-porch," but rather because they present "a mind in the process of resolving the problematical." Like Fish, she affirms that in the lyrics we participate in Herbert's "characteristic concern with experiences of doubt." However, unlike Fish, she affirms that Herbert writes from a stable center of assurance and pastoral concern. In the lyrics, Herbert shepherds the reader on the necessary path through the bewildering specifics of human sin and doubt, leading toward mature resolution.[36]

Therefore, even the most dissonantly "anti-casuistical" moments of poems like "The Collar," in which the speaker's rebellious soul dares him to "leave thy cold dispute / Of what is fit, and not" (*W*, 153, ll. 20–21), are framed by and resolved into the lyric's (and "The Church"'s) larger purpose: reconciling the reader to the law and love of God. If we can believe Walton, Herbert sent the poems to Ferrar with the condition that he publish them only if they would "turn to the advantage of any dejected poor soul."[37] Like every other pastoral duty or action, Herbert apparently intended his poetry to be concretely useful and practical. In a special way, the lyrics of "The Church" allow the details of the parson's life to preach.

Visitation

We have already noted the remarkable extent to which Herbert's parson is to involve himself personally with his people, catching them "as they are, wallowing in the midst of their affairs" (*W*, 247–48). In fact, while *The Canons of 1604* require parsons to visit no one but the

---

36. *Casuistical Tradition,* 186, 194–95, 186–87.
37. *Lives,* 314.

sick, and then only when the sick are "dangerously" near death, Herbert's parson ministers in practically every setting of country life.[38] Sundays, after public prayers, preaching, and catechizing, he spends out about the parish, "either in reconciling neighbors that are at variance, or in visiting the sick, or in exhortations to some of his flock by themselves, whom his Sermons cannot, or doe not reach" (W, 236).[39] And the parson, sharing Herbert's horror of idleness expressed in the "Employment" poems, exhorts men of all ranks and conditions "either to have a Calling, or prepare for it," serving as a kind of employment counselor (W, 248). The parish and village merge as this command to edify overcomes distinctions between the sacred and secular, not by "secularizing" formerly religious activities, but by raising mundane activities to a sacred status. As we will see in Chapter 8, Herbert regards everyday affairs as better than a curse, indeed, as divinely endorsed. Draining an unhealthy marsh becomes an act of spiritual charity toward one's neighbors; ordering one's own household well is a preparation for giving to the poor and for training one's children in godliness.

This last concern—for home catechizing by fathers and masters—is shared by Thomas Taylor, a Puritan contemporary. He enjoins "every master of a family [to] see to what he is called, namely, to make his house a little church, to instruct every one of his family in the fear of God, to contain every one of them under holy discipline, to pray with them and for them."[40] The house as "a little church" implies that the father or master is rightly a kind of pastor himself. Thus in his "circuits" and "surveys" the parson works to multiply his pastoral functions in every home. Fathers, by the very nature of their "office," possess major spiritual responsibilities. In order to drive the word to practice, Herbert's parson seems to multiply ministers.

38. Church of England, Canons, Canon 67.

39. Conspicuously absent from Herbert's list of Sunday activities are the "lawfull sports" so vigorously protected and encouraged by Charles and Laud. At the time when The Countrey Parson was being written, 1630–1632, the controversy over sports and Sunday observance was coming to a head, and Herbert's failure to defend or recommend "harmless Sunday recreations"—church-ales, Whitsun-ales, Maypole and Morris dancing, "leaping and vaulting"—suggests a lack of sympathy with this policy of the king and future archbishop. See Hart, Country Clergy, 72–73, 96–97.

40. Works, 190; quoted in Hill, Society and Puritanism, 455.

Church Discipline

In addition to these mainly positive means of doctrinal and practical edification—preaching, catechizing, casuistical counseling, and thorough visitation—Herbert requires that the parson use negative inducements to godliness as the need arises, namely "church-discipline" in various forms, including excommunication. Yet we have noted how reluctant Herbert is to coerce by "calling in Authority" from outside the parish. If we briefly examine how church-discipline was practiced under Elizabeth, James, and especially under Charles and Laud, we will better understand Herbert's reluctance.

In the period between Elizabeth's accession and the civil war, excommunication from the national church was officially a spiritual penalty for spiritual offenses, and it meant exclusion from the Holy Communion and the other services of the parish church.[41] However, many, especially the Puritans, commonly complained that the authorities deliberately confused civil punishment and church discipline, exacting harsh civil penalties for spiritual offenses and imposing spiritual penalties like excommunication for often petty civil and political offenses.[42] Indeed, as Hill writes,

[t]he system had been under attack at least since the days of Wyclif. Luther had said that bishops who excommunicated over money matters should not be obeyed. Archbishop Grindal suggested that excommunication was used too frequently, but found himself opposed by other bishops. . . . Parliament and Puritans alike continuously opposed the use of excommunication for trivial and procedural offences . . . [w]hile under Laud [e]xcommunication was used to enforce unpopular ceremonies; churchwardens were excommunicated for backwardness in railing in communion tables. . . . It was in 1644 that Bishop Hall, wise after the event, admitted that "the dreadful sentence of excommunication hath too frequently and familiarly passed upon light and trivial matters."[43]

41. "5. Eliz. cap. 23 laid it down that excommunication should be valid only for heresy or erroneous doctrine, for refusal to have a child baptized, to receive communion or attend church, or for incontinency, usury, simony, perjury in the ecclesiastical courts, or idolatry." See Hill, *Society and Puritanism,* 360.
42. Ibid., 360–61. Hill notes that such complaints are mentioned in the *Admonition to Parliament* of 1572, the Bishops' letter to Parliament of 1587, the *Constitutions of 1597,* the Millenary Petition of 1604, and in Parliamentary debates of 1606 and 1610.
43. Ibid., 360–62.

Thus for Herbert to "call in Authority" meant that his own pastoral concern could very well be overruled by the venality or the spite of a church or civil official. Though Herbert does not mention such administrative corruption in *The Countrey Parson,* his knowledge of these affairs may have increased his reluctance to bring in the higher powers. This same knowledge may have influenced Donne's similar statement that to be a minister requires "a gentle, a supple, an applicable disposition, . . . That he doe not alwaies, press all things with Authority, with Censures, with Excommunications."[44] So, as we have seen, the parson seeks to keep discipline a local, indeed almost a family matter. "[W]hen any sinns, he hateth him not as an officer, but pityes him as a Father" (*W, 250*), and even when he "proceeds so farre as to call in Authority . . . he forbears not in any wise to use the delinquent as before, . . . [and] esteem[s] him . . . as a brother still."

Furthermore, if this discipline "happily take effect, [the parson] then comes on faster, . . . doubling his regards, and shewing . . . that the delinquents returne is to his advantage" (*W, 263–64*). Thus the parson punishes cautiously, deliberately, and as mildly as duty allows, since his goal is the heartfelt reconciliation of the sinner to God and the church. On these matters, a great distance separates Herbert both from the Arminian bishops and from their Puritan supplanters in the early Commonwealth Parliament, who as spiritual discipline imposed heavy fines and commanded imprisonment and scourging, in addition to their more notorious sentences of cheek-branding, nostril-slitting, ear-cropping, and tongue-boring.[45]

Preacher, catechist, physician of souls, employment and family counselor, administrator of public charity, disciplinarian—not to mention universal example and gazing-stock—the parson cannot shoulder these burdens without preparatory struggle; he cannot think "that when they have read the Fathers, or the Schoolmen, a minister is made, and the thing done" (*W, 226*). As Baxter writes, "Alas! it is the common danger and calamity of the Church, to have unregenerate and inexperienced pastors, and to have so many men become preachers before they are Christians; who are sanctified by dedication *to the altar as*

44. *Sermons* 8:42.
45. Hart, *Country Clergy,* 102–6.

the priests of God, before they are sanctified by hearty dedication as the disciples of Christ" (emphasis mine).[46] Since the Protestant priest's main work is to preach the saving knowledge of God—and note how willingly even the Puritan Baxter uses the language of "priesthood" here—the preacher's work will be hypocritical, if not utterly worthless, unless he has this knowledge himself, and lives it out. It is the terrifying possibility of such unreadiness, and the divine wrath that it might bring, which Herbert dramatizes in "The Priesthood," to which we now turn.

46. *Reformed Pastor,* 56.

6

Slowly to the Flame
"The Priesthood" and Herbert's Hesitation

The [pastor's] greatest and hardest preparation is within: For, *Unto the ungodly, saith God, Why dost thou preach my Laws, and takest my Covenant in thy mouth? Psal. 50.16.*
— *The Countrey Parson* (*W*, 226)

Any conscientious seventeenth-century aspirant to the ministry, upon reading these stern words of Herbert's, with their stinging divine question, might well tremble on the verge of ordination. After all, he might ask, how can any sinner—and all are sinners—presume to stand in as Christ's "Vicegerent"? According to the Twenty-Fifth Article of Religion, holy orders are not a sacrament, but rather a "state of life," because ordination lacks "any visible sign or ceremony ordained of God."[1] What then does ordination accomplish or signify? If reformed "priests" make no claim to offer sacrifices for their people, what do they offer? What, spiritually, distinguishes the priest from the people? Most of all, how can he be worthy? Herbert wrestles these questions in his lyric "The Priesthood" (*W*, 160–61).

Critics have almost completely ignored this poem, perhaps because, like "Lent," its title seems to fit it into the "high-church" persona constructed for Herbert by Walton and augmented by the Oxford Movement. In fact, Walton apparently borrows key phrases and images from "The Priesthood" to color his account of Herbert's actual ordination.

1. Compare this statement with the title of chapter 9 of *The Countrey Parson*, "The Parson's State of Life" (*W*, 236).

We can hardly blame Walton for capitalizing on the poem's biograph-
ical references, which are clearer than those of nearly any other lyric
in "The Church": "The Priesthood" is almost certainly Herbert's apol-
ogy for delaying his ordination.

That Herbert hesitated on the threshold of the priesthood for an
unusually long time is a fact that has exercised his biographers from
the first. Walton allows for an interval of more than four years between
Herbert's proceeding deacon in July 1626 and his ordination as a priest
in September 1630. Most recently, Amy Charles's biography has added
almost two years to Herbert's hesitation by providing evidence that he
had decided to seek the diaconate by late 1624. Walton's enormously
influential version portrays Herbert vacillating between the carnal and
ascetic poles of conventional hagiography, wondering "[w]hether he
should return to the painted pleasures of Court-life, or . . . enter into
Sacred Orders? . . . for ambitious Desires, and the outward Glory of
this World, are not easily laid aside." Amy Charles offers no such
global explanation for Herbert's six-year wait, but she ascribes it in-
stead to a combination of self-doubt, frustrated ambitions for secular
and ecclesiastical preferment, and "his own admitted tendency toward
delay."[2] However, while all of these factors, particularly Herbert's
struggle with ambition, may enter into any account of his long indeci-
sion, neither Walton nor Charles gives any real attention to the expla-
nation that Herbert himself offers in "The Priesthood": that he dared
not take holy orders until he was certain of an enabling divine call.

Walton's neglect of Herbert's explanation is not surprising, since
the poem reveals an idea of ordination, and of the Order, which would
hardly please a Laudian apologist. For while Herbert's confessions of
unworthiness exalt the power and holiness of the priesthood, his con-
ception of the office is strongly Protestant, inclining even toward the
Puritan notion of a "godly ministry": he repeatedly asserts that only

---

2. Walton writes that Herbert, after fasting and praying for not less than a month,
"had some resolutions to decline both the Priesthood, and that Living." Yet according to
Walton, Herbert changed his mind and "changed his sword and silk Cloaths into a Ca-
nonical Coat" and lay "prostrate on the ground before the Altar" in private dedication.
For Walton's discussion of Herbert's delay, see *Lives,* 277–78, 287–89, 291–94. For
Charles's evidence of Herbert's earlier entrance into the diaconate, see *A Life of George
Herbert,* 112–13. For her various explanations of Herbert's delay, see 114, 118, 138, 149,
respectively.

those who have directly experienced God's saving and sanctifying grace may safely preach and administer the sacraments. Thus Herbert delays in taking holy orders precisely because his theology compels him to distinguish between the apparent call of the office—however urgent, natural, and worthy that call may seem—and the direct, unmediated call of God.

Unworthy Preacher: The Word

Herbert begins his apology with a direct address to the priesthood itself:

> Blest Order, which in power dost so excell,
> That with th'one hand thou liftest to the sky,
> And with the other throwest down to hell
> In thy just censures; fain would I draw nigh,
> Fain put thee on, exchanging my lay-sword
>   For that of th'holy Word.
>   (ll. 1–6)

From the first, Herbert speaks in answer to the implicit question of why he is waiting so long. He takes special pains at the outset to dismiss the notion that he is delaying out of contempt for priestly power or dignity. On the contrary, he is so far from adding to "the generall ignominy which is cast upon the profession" (*W,* 268) that he describes the Order's power in awestruck terms that usually refer to the power of God himself. In "The Flower," Herbert praises the "Lord of power" for His sovereign "wonders" of "bringing down to hell / And up to heaven in an houre" (*W,* 166, ll. 15–17); here the "power" that "with th'one hand . . . liftest to the sky, / And with the other throwest down to hell" is the priesthood itself. Furthermore, the priesthood's acts of excommunication are not merely arbitrary decrees but "just censures." As an office, the Order is both mighty and holy, an eminently worthy object for a man seeking honor and influence. Thus, he protests, he does not delay because of any residual courtly or secular ambitions. "Fain would I draw nigh, fain put thee on, exchanging my lay-sword" —and its inferior power—for "that of th'holy Word." Herbert would have the Order—and perhaps his own accusing conscience—understand that he is neither a scoffer nor a fool. He knows real might and dignity when he sees it, and he knows that the greatest might comes from the sword of Scripture.

This prominent reference to the Bible might raise questions—if we had assumed that "priests" deal primarily with sacrifices and sacraments. The stanza's emphasis on the "power of the keys" would seem to confirm sacerdotalist expectations but for this stress on the "Word." Yet even as the suitor expresses his desire for this priestly power, his repetition of "fain" sets up his retreat. He recognizes the terrible stakes of even addressing an Order that raises and dashes men with such objectivity, like the arms of a scale.[3] He might at any moment be weighed and found wanting.

The second stanza elaborates on Herbert's fears. He would approach the Order,

> But thou art fire, sacred and hallow'd fire;
> And I but earth and clay: should I presume
> To wear thy habit, the severe attire
> My slender compositions might consume.
> I am both foul and brittle; most unfit
>   To deal in holy Writ.
>   (ll. 7–12)

As Herbert has led us to expect in the first stanza, he does not actually "draw nigh" but rather keeps his distance, overawed by the prospect of being himself the burnt offering consumed on the priestly altar. Furthermore, while Herbert had indeed struggled with courtly ambitions, we see here that he does not view such ambitions as his basic problem. Rather, they only manifest his more fundamental human corruption: he is "but earth and clay . . . both foul and brittle," a born sinner. Although in mentioning his corruption he does not actu-

---

3. Compare the speaker's terror of God's justice in "Justice" (II), (W, 141):

> The dishes of the ballance seem'd to gape,
> Like two great pits;
> The beam and scape
> Did like some torturing engine show . . .
>   (ll. 7–10)

ally deny his own regenerate state, he does fear that should he "presume" to lay hold of the spiritual authority symbolized by the priestly "habit," he will suffer severe judgment. His "slender compositions"—his unsanctified nature—might be tested beyond their limits by the Order's "sacred and hallowed fire."

His fear of the priesthood's spiritual fire here differs notably from his eager prayer to God in "Love" (II) (*W*, 54):

> Immortal Heat, O let thy greater flame . . .
>   kindle in our hearts such true desires,
>   As may consume our lusts, and make thee way.
>   (ll. 1, 4–5)

Donne's "I am a little world" concludes with a similar plea. Although "the fire of lust and envy" have heretofore "burnt" the speaker's "world" —his physical and spiritual being—he prays that God would

>   let their flame retire
>   And burn me O Lord, with a fiery zeal
>   Of thee and thy house, which doth in eating heal.
>   (ll. 10–14)[4]

In contrast to these flames, the fire of the priestly office frightens Herbert because instead of consuming his lust or healing him it might reveal that his "foul and brittle" self is all dross and consume the whole of him with just judgment. We see the distance traveled from the salad days of Herbert's spiritual journey, when "my sudden soul caught at the place, / And made her youth and fiercenesse seek [God's] face" ("Affliction" [I], *W*, 46, ll. 17–18).

Herbert again characterizes this office by one activity, "deal[ing] in holy Writ." As in the last line of the first stanza, Herbert passes over the sacramental duties of the priest in favor of exegetical duties. In retrospect, we can even see a pun on the "compositions" of line 10; this term may refer not only to the speaker's fallen nature, but also to his woefully inadequate sermons. In this light the "fire" that so awes

4. *The Complete English Poems*, 31.

Herbert begins to take on associations with the flaming tongues which descended at Pentecost on the apostles and transformed them into mighty preachers of the Word (Acts 2:1–4).

The emphasis on the Bible and on preaching in the final lines of the first two stanzas echoes "The Windows": "Lord, how can man preach thy eternall word? / He is a brittle crazie glasse" (*W*, 67, ll. 1–2). As we have already observed in chapter 4 above, every man's deeply flawed nature—not to mention the unsparing gaze of a whole parish—should dissuade the ambitious from forcing their way into the pulpit. The "slender compositions" of an unholy preacher "show watrish, bleak, and thin." As St. James warns, "My brethren, be not many masters [teachers], knowing that we shall receive the greater condemnation" (James 3:1). "Sermons are dangerous things" to their hearers, Herbert says in *The Countrey Parson* (*W*, 233); how much more to the preacher? Preaching brings greater accountability, and accountability means condemnation for "foul and brittle" man, apart from grace. In this context of preaching, we can better understand Herbert's fear.

However, just when his double stress on his unworthiness seems to have closed his case against himself, Herbert turns and considers an earthly, and earthy, analogy to his situation. This analogy suggests another possibility for advancement to the priesthood:

> Yet have I often seen, by cunning hand
> And force of fire, what curious things are made
> Of wretched earth. Where once I scorn'd to stand,
> That earth is fitted by the fire and trade
> Of skilfull artists, for the boards of those
>   Who make the bravest shows.
>   (ll. 13–18)

Herbert realizes that at least in the physical realm the "cunning hand[s]" of skillful artists "often" transform the basest of materials—"wretched earth"—into vessels beautiful and acceptable to men, fit even for "the boards of those / Who make the bravest shows." In the same way, Herbert implies, his skillful self-presentation might make possible a "brave show" of holiness. Yet as soon as this possibility of spiritual self-fashioning presents itself, he dismisses it. Beautiful and "curious" vessels may please the "great ones" at table,

> But since these great ones, be they ne're so great,
> Come from the earth, from whence these vessels come;
> So that at once both feeder, dish, and meat
> Have one beginning and one finall summe:
> I do not greatly wonder at the sight,
>   If earth in earth delight.
>
>   (ll. 19–24)

The very earthiness of the analogy proves to be its intrinsic flaw. The "fire and trade" of skillful human artists may be able to change the form of the "wretched earth," but they cannot change its substance. Earth is still earth. Neither can such well-formed vessels ultimately raise the "feeders" above their mortal "earth and clay." Since "both feeder, dish, and meat / Have one beginning," all must share "one finall summe." This "feeding" is inevitably a case of earth to earth, dust to dust, no matter how "brave" the table service.

Herbert must reject the false hope offered by this analogy. As he and Perkins and Bernard warn in their respective treatises, the most cunning human "art" amounts to deadly presumption when equated with preparation for the ministry; that is, when the would-be priest perfects his outward speech and actions without "the greatest and hardest preparation . . . within"—by God's grace. Herbert attributes an ironically stifling and doomed quality to this self-empowering priesthood. Sermons given and deeds done by unregenerate or unsanctified ministers will fail to transcend the "foul" limits of merely human ingenuity. Their trajectory is circular, leading the pastor and perhaps his people back to "wretched earth."

Unholy Hands: The Eucharist

Having rejected any quick elevation by refashioning himself, Herbert further emphasizes his point by contrasting such merely earthen "vessels" with the Lord's true priests:

> But th'holy men of God such vessels are,
> As serve him up, who all the world commands:
> When God vouchsafeth to become our fare,
> Their hands convey him, who conveys their hands.

> O what pure things, most pure must those things be,
> Who bring my God to me!
>   (ll. 25–30)

With this stanza Herbert extends his call for priestly purity beyond the need for "heart-deep" preaching and behavior to the necessity of a truly holy Communion. We have seen that for Herbert, as for the *Articles of Religion* and for Calvin, Christ's "Real Presence" in the eucharist is spiritual rather than physical, and the Lord's Supper is efficacious only when taken by one who understands and trusts in the divine grace "which *with*"—not "*in*"—"these elements comes" ("The H. Communion," *W*, 52, l. 19, emphasis mine). In this stanza of "The Priesthood" Herbert is personalizing this doctrine. Since Herbert is himself one of the regenerate—God is "my God"—the Lord "vouchsafeth to become our fare," specifically, Herbert's fare. The Protestant priest can truly "bring my God to me," if God is truly "my God" in the first place.[5]

However, this stanza does not deal primarily with the "worthiness" of the receiver, but of the priest. Herbert's passionate exclamation— "O what pure things, most pure must those things be!"—expresses not only his awe at taking Communion, but also his deep anxiety about administering it. The practical purity required of priests to "serve up God," like that required of preachers to proclaim God's grace, is apparently greater than the purity required to receive that grace. With the authority comes the possibility of "greater condemnation." This realization brings Herbert's claims of unworthiness near their climax. The truly holy man, unlike either Herbert himself or the artfully fashioned "vessels" of the previous stanzas, must be unalloyed, without "foul" admixture, especially his "hands." In keeping with Elizabethan eucharistic doctrine, Herbert feels anxiety not mainly for the people to whom he might minister, but for himself, since the faithful parishioner will not suffer for the pastor's impurity, but the

5. For this reason, as I have already noted in my first and fifth chapters, Herbert's discussion of communion in chapter 22 of *The Countrey Parson* follows chapter 21 on catechizing. In addition, Herbert devotes much of the chapter on the sacraments to the parson's insuring that none take Communion in doctrinal or experiential "ignorance" of salvation.

pastor may. Article 26 states, "[B]ecause of Christ's institution and promise . . . the unworthiness of the Ministers . . . hinders not the effect of the Sacraments. . . . Nevertheless . . . enquiry [is to] be made of evil Ministers, . . . and finally being found guilty, by just judgment [they are to] be deposed." Yet as we have already seen, Herbert fears more than earthly judgment.

The Shaking Ark: Resisting Duty's Natural Call

"Wherefore," he begins the sixth stanza,

> I dare not, I, put forth my hand
> To hold the Ark, although it seem to shake
> Through th'old sinnes and new doctrines of our land.
>   (ll. 31–33)

This "wherefore" signals the turn of his argument from the particular reasons of the first five stanzas to a summation. His case for his delay has been a case for a holy priesthood and against himself. His own "hand" is too impure to take hold of priestly duty. These lines cast this duty as analogous to that of the Levitical priests in the Old Testament who guarded the ark of the covenant. Herbert refers here to the death of Uzzah, who in II Sam. 6:6–7 rashly "put forth his hand to the ark of God, and took hold of it, for the oxen [carrying it] shook it. And the anger of the Lord was kindled against Uzzah, and God smote him there for his error." Uzzah presumed to lay hands on the ark and steady it although, as a priest, he should have known that God's power could protect the ark, as it did against the priests of Dagon (I Sam. 5:1–6) and the men of Beth-shemesh (I Sam. 6:19). The reference to Uzzah brings into clearer focus the specific offense that Herbert "dares not" commit, and that his waiting prevents. The source of all the foulness that Herbert sees in his own nature lies not in his having a self as such (which would make mere existence a sin), but rather in his asserting that self according to his own interests and insights, not according to God's.

So Herbert repeats the "I" in line 31 to stress that the one who "dares not" move is the "I" of self-centered action. This is the same kind of

"I" who in "The Holdfast" "threatned to observe the strict decree / Of my deare God with all my power & might . . ." (*W,* 143, ll. 1–2) and, in "The Thanksgiving," seeks ways to "revenge me on thy love, / And try who shall victorious prove" (*W,* 35, ll. 17–18). This "I" makes the utterly "natural"—and culpable—error of assuming that he can empower himself for spiritual action. Ironically, he begins his pursuit of holiness full of zeal, but runs in exactly the wrong direction. The speakers of "The Holdfast" and "The Thanksgiving" can make real progress only when they recognize that all of their efforts (even at repentance) are futile without divine grace.

In this light we can appreciate Herbert's allusion to Uzzah and "the Ark," which was primarily a repository of Scripture (Exod. 25:16, Deut. 31:26). Yet because the ark also contained the manna (Heb. 9:4) it carries certain eucharistic associations. In reaching out to steady the ark, Uzzah trusted his own perceptions more than God's power, and he sought to remedy the problem that he saw by expedient human means. In contrast, Herbert refuses to grasp rashly at the "Ark" of the priesthood, an order which exists to protect and perpetuate biblical preaching and the proper use of the sacraments. By postponing his ordination he refuses to trust his own insight, which tells him that the priesthood urgently needs pious and learned men like himself; for the ark "seem[s] to shake / Through th'old sinnes and new doctrines of our land."

Which "new doctrines" Herbert means we cannot say with absolute certainty, since all sides in major theological debates regularly accused each other of "innovation" and promoted their own way as that of the "primitive church." Separatism may be intended (although by this time it was hardly "new"); however, we have already seen that in the late 1620s by far the "newest" doctrines in the land were the Arminianism and episcopal absolutism of Laud and his bishops. In any case, in these uncertain circumstances, what could be more natural for a loyal churchman than to put one's able hand to the unsteady ark by taking holy orders as soon as possible?

Yet Herbert resists the temptation to do the "natural" thing. His apparent inaction amounts to resisting the call of the Order itself, or rather, the call that he perceives from the Order. He has in fact been resisting this call throughout the poem. Herbert's Calvinism compels him to distinguish between his perception of the need and the call of God himself. The Order's needs may be urgent and worthy, but he does not heed this call because it is finally too "common-sensical" and expedient. In Herbert's view, to preach and administer God's grace without a direct divine warrant of one's own is to court spiritual disaster, at least for the preacher.

So, humanly speaking, Herbert has refuted all the possibilities for his becoming worthy of the Order. He sees and feels the church's pressing need for a "godly ministry" but knows that no earthly power, whether his own or even the priesthood's, can purify his "wretched earth" for heavenly service. One possibility alone remains open to him, the one which he seems to have had in mind all along:

> Onely, since God doth often vessels make
> Of lowly matter for high uses meet,
> I throw me at his feet.
> (ll. 34–36)

Having ruled out the proud and dangerous self-assertion of "laying hands on" the priesthood, the volitional Herbert ("I") casts his objectified self ("me") at God's feet, hoping to be raised up after being remade. He is sure that his earthiness presents no problems to the Almighty. Unlike the "skilfull artists" of stanzas 3 and 4, God "often" and effectively tranforms "lowly matter" into "vessels" truly fit and worthy for divine service. God can renew Herbert's inward substance, not merely his outward form.

Walton's Version: A Caroline Tableau

Herbert's "prostration" at God's feet is the pivotal moment in "The Priesthood." It is for him the first and only "move" that the would-be priest can legitimately and safely make. It is also the point at which Walton's account begins to diverge most sharply from the poem, both in biographical detail and in theology. Walton claims that Herbert, after his induction to the living of Bemerton on April 26, 1630, "did lie prostrate on the ground before the Altar: at which time and place (as he after told Mr. Woodnot) he set some Rules to himself," rules, says Walton, which eventually grew into his pastoral manual.[6]

Although it is not completely unlikely that Arthur Woodnoth actually saw Herbert pray facedown in St. Andrew's church, this story is more probably Walton's attempt to weave the imagery of the poem into his version of Herbert's spiritual transformation and to add the glow of "priestly" inspiration to *The Countrey Parson*. Significantly, prostration was not included in Elizabethan or Jacobean ordination rites, nor does Herbert anywhere refer to the Communion table as an "altar."[7] However, regardless of whether Herbert literally prostrated himself that day at Bemerton, in "The Priesthood" he throws "me" at *God's* "feet," indicating a state of heart rather than a particular physical place or position. Walton's emphasis differs strikingly.

Walton diverges even further from the intent of Herbert's seventh and final stanza. By the end of stanza 6, Herbert has answered the questions of why he delays his ordination and what action he can take to ready himself for it. Yet the most obvious question remains: when will he know that he is ready? Walton's answer to this question perfectly suits his purpose of eulogizing the Laudian establishment. According to Walton, Herbert resolved his doubts about entering the priesthood by conferring with Laud himself.

In this version of events, Philip Herbert, Fourth Earl of Pembroke, petitioned King Charles early in 1630 to bestow the living of Bemerton on his cousin George, and the king said, "Most willingly . . . if it be worth his acceptance." However, says Walton, Herbert was much troubled by spiritual conflicts and resolved "to decline both the Priesthood, and that Living." Yet Herbert's persistent friend Woodnoth took him in late April on

---

6. *Lives,* 289, 294.
7. For ordination rites, see Paul F. Bradshaw, *The Anglican Ordinal,* 22–23, table. However, given Herbert's love of the Old Testament, he may have been inclined generally to pray in a prostrate position, like Abraham or the Hebrews as a whole (see e.g. Gen. 17:3, I Kings 18:39).
   As to the "altar," his few uses of the word (seven altogether) are spiritual and metaphorical, and refer either to the "altar" of the believer's heart or to God's heavenly altar. See Mario DiCesare and Rigo Mignani, *A Concordance to the Complete Writings of George Herbert,* under "altar."

a Journey to Wilton, the famous seat of the Earls of Pembroke at which time, the King, the Earl, and the whole Court were there, or at Salisbury, which is near to it . . . but that Night, the Earl acquainted Dr. Laud, then Bishop of London, and after Archbishop of Canterbury, with his kinsmans irresolution. And the Bishop did the same day so convince Mr. Herbert, That the refusal of it was a sin that a Taylor was sent for . . . to take measure, and make him Canonical Cloaths, against next day . . . and Mr. Herbert being so habited, went with his presentation to the learned Dr. Davenant, who was then Bishop of Salisbury, and he gave him Institution immediately.[8]

As presented by Walton, Laud's resolution of Herbert's dilemma is definite, immediate, and final. However, it is almost certainly fiction.

Actually, on April 25–26, 1630, the king and court were neither at Wilton nor at Salisbury, and Laud was very probably at Oxford waiting to be sworn in as Chancellor on the 28th.[9] Ironically, in the bitter election for the Oxford Chancellorship, the Arminian Laud had just defeated the leading Calvinist Philip Herbert, the same man whom Walton presents as Laud's host and confidant that month at Wilton.[10] Walton's fabrication of the scene at Wilton provides him with an ideal Caroline tableau. He presents the martyred king and archbishop, whose combined calls amount to a divine call for Herbert, the mirror for royalist clergymen. For a man so learned and pious to ignore so clear a summons is not merely a mistake but a "sin."

"Then Is My Time": Awaiting God's Supernatural Call

In contrast to Walton's account, the last stanza of "The Priesthood" presents Herbert waiting not on king or bishop, but on God alone. Having thrown himself at God's feet, he vows

> There will I lie, untill my Maker seek
> For some mean stuffe whereon to show his skill:
> Then is my time. The distance of the meek
> Doth flatter power. Lest good come short of ill

8. Walton, *Lives,* 287–88.
9. Charles, *A Life of George Herbert,* 146–47; Laud, *Works* 3:211.
10. Trevor-Roper, *Laud,* 114.

> In praising might, the poore do by submission
> What pride by opposition.
>
> (ll. 37–42)

Herbert knows that God can transform his "mean stuffe" into something "fit" and "meet" for the priesthood, if only He will. When is God's affair, but whenever God seeks him, "Then is my time." That time is a mystery, yet Herbert seems strangely hopeful, since he has a prior claim on God's attention: the divine Maker is, in the first place, "my Maker." As his Creator, God knows Herbert better than Herbert knows himself, and He may mend what Herbert has marred.

This sense of relationship is further expressed by the new, easier tone of mock cynicism that characterizes these last, highly compressed lines. "The distance of the meek / Doth flatter power" is as tart a Baconian aphorism as any courtier could utter. Yet it is sweet for Herbert. By resisting the urgent "call" of the "Blest Order"—a call that seems eminently worthy and reasonable—he has refused to flatter an inferior power. The "godly" members of the Order certainly would not desire such "flattery" since they do not claim to make a man, even a religious and educated one, into a priest. Rather, under the Old Conformity, episcopal ordinators only recognize the work that God has done within him. Because the priesthood is God's gift, not man's, Herbert hopes to "flatter" the supreme Power by keeping his distance and not grasping at the gift. Herbert can safely claim that it is impossible to "flatter" or "praise might" too much, since God is not only true "might," but also "good." Thus, while Schoenfeldt is illuminating when he finds the anxious language of courtly ambition not only here but throughout *The Temple,* it is not necessary to imply, as he seems to, that Herbert presents God as somehow actually susceptible to flattery of the kind that he had heaped on King James as University Orator at Cambridge.[11] "Flattery" is flattery only when the giver of praise does not believe it and the object of praise does not deserve it.

Indeed, Herbert concludes "The Priesthood" by contrasting his own ironically sincere "flattery" with that of the "ill" and the proud, who foolishly confuse means and ends, while divorcing power from real

---

11. *Prayer and Power,* 183–84.

goodness. Such proud place-seekers miss the Almighty's ethical purpose and admire only his "might," grasping at power by forceful "opposition." In the case of Uzzah the priest, this "opposition" masked itself as piety but was instantly revealed as fatal presumption. Conversely, the godly "poore"—the "poor in spirit"—submit themselves to God's will and wait patiently. If God chooses to exalt them, that is God's business.

So Herbert's apology for delay becomes at last a statement of faith and aspiration. Yet it ends without an actual resolution of his predicament. This time-serving "flatterer" in the heavenly court is, after all, still waiting; his "time" is clearly in the future. He will not presume to "lay hands on" the preaching office or the Holy Communion, but he must wait until his Maker "lays hands on" him to remake him. Strangely, at least in an episcopalian context, Herbert here presents the necessity of direct divine "ordination" to the ministry by spiritual re-creation. Institutional ordination by bishops drops from view, its vestments and gestures—habits, imposition of hands, prostration—transformed into metaphors for repentance and regeneration.

"Aaron": True Priest, True Christian

Such a doctrine of immediate divine "calling to the ministry" through "re-formation of life" had radical implications. Paul writes, "[I]f any man be in Christ, *he is a new creature*" (II Cor. 5:17, emphasis mine). If, as "The Priesthood" seems to claim, the main qualification of a true "priest" is a "new creation" lived out in action, then some episcopally ordained priests would seem to be disqualified, and many godly laymen included. This doctrine of regeneration as the primary requirement for ministry is the theme of Herbert's other lyric about preparation for priestly service. "Aaron" (*W*, 174) comes fifteen poems later in "The Church" and begins with its priestly speaker ordained but once again doubting his call. His resolution of these renewed doubts sheds light back on the all-important moment between the end of "The Priesthood" and the beginning of "Aaron" when Herbert's "time" arrived and he decided to enter the "Blest Order."

Strier interprets "Aaron" as "an exposition and celebration of how the Christian attains holiness or righteousness," since "the subject of

'Aaron' is the nature of the true or good priest" and "the main characteristic of the true priest is holiness." Indeed, he argues that "Herbert is very much in line with the Reformation tradition in presenting the conditions for being a 'true priest' as basically identical with those for being a true Christian."[12] Thus the poem's initial description of Aaron's priestly garments pretends to be literal, but from the beginning "hover[s] on the border of allegory." So by the end of the third stanza it is Christ who has become the true "garment of righteousness," for only *"in him* [am I] well drest" (l. 15, emphasis mine). In stanza 2 the priest confronts his own deeply felt "profanenesse," "defects," "darknesse," and "passions," but rejoices in stanzas 4 and 5 that Christ has struck this "old man . . . ev'n dead," wrapped him in righteousness, and "tun'd" his doctrine for preaching. By the poem's final line, the priest has achieved the sense of "fitness" for ministry sought throughout "The Priesthood": "Come people," he calls out, "Aaron's drest" (l. 25). Having reaffirmed that he is new in Christ, he is ready to preach.

We ought to note especially that "Aaron" dramatizes a reaffirmation of saving grace and priestly vows, rather than the original experiences of either conversion or calling to the ministry. The priest of this poem—and we may as well identify him with Herbert—speaks as a regenerate Christian engaged in the ongoing struggle with the "old man," his remaining sinful nature. His being a priest preparing to deliver his Sunday sermon only makes him more painfully aware of his unworthiness; again he fears the "greater condemnation." In this fear it would seem that he has not advanced much beyond the preordination Herbert of "The Priesthood." However, Herbert's spiritual state in "Aaron" differs from his state in "The Priesthood" in one important way. In "Aaron" he knows that despite all of his defects he is a priest.

To say this is not merely tautological. In line 10 he might have called himself "no priest" and given up in despair. Instead, he judges himself a "poore priest" and turns hopefully to Jesus, the high priest for reassurance and sanctification. By not abandoning his "priesthood," Herbert displays a sustaining confidence in his priestly calling that is analogous to his persevering confidence in his Christian calling. As one of

---

12. *Love Known,* 127. Please see 127–33 for Strier's full discussion of the poem.

those elected by God to salvation, he knows that Christ keeps him. Similarly, as a man subsequently "elected" by God to the priesthood, he knows that his vestigial "defects" and "passions" within do not invalidate his vocation. The old, rebellious "me" having been struck "dead" (l. 18) at conversion, his new "I" can "rest" (l. 19) in Christ and get on with priestly duties. It is this foundational assurance beneath his spiritual turmoil that turns him to Christ, and eventually back to his congregation.

Biographically speaking, we do not know when or how Herbert arrived at this foundational sense of calling to the priesthood. Unlike Bunyan, he left no spiritual autobiography aside from his poetry. However, based on these two lyrics we can guess that Herbert looked within for the evidence of God's call—a greater sorrow for sin, a fuller awareness of his own weakness, a deeper reliance upon God's power and mercy. Perhaps Herbert also observed his outward actions, almost as those of another man, and found patterns of increasing discipline, charity, and good "temper." In any case, after his long delay Herbert came to the conviction that God had indeed "laid hands on" him. Therefore, Herbert sought to confirm this calling publicly at the hands of Bishop Davenant. In Herbert's view, it was God who had made him a priest; the bishop recognized God's work. Yet Herbert did not believe that God's "second call" suddenly transformed him into a perfect man. He wrote "The Priesthood" to enact the profound anxiety of purification, a process begun at conversion that, he believed, must be well advanced before a man dare take the Word and sacraments in his hands. He wrote "Aaron" to show that God's call to ministry means not an end to this struggle for purity, but its continuation on a higher plane of responsibility. The victory is assured, but the fight is no less hot.

Lay Priesthood and Its Limits

Strier recognizes that "'Aaron,' with its delineation of the purely spiritual 'vestments' of the 'true Aaron,' could have been written by an antivestiarian."[13] Is it also true that if every "true priest" is converted,

---

13. Ibid., 150.

every converted Christian is a kind of priest? "Aaron" implies just
that. If read on its own, apart from Herbert's known loyalty to the
episcopal establishment, the poem could be taken as the work of a
Presbyterian. It presents the essential attribute of "priesthood" as the
conversion common to all Christians. The church leader, or "pres-
byter" (and recall that Herbert received this Greco-Latin title at ordi-
nation), is an "elder" who is simply further along the road of sancti-
fication that all true Christians walk. As the "priest" achieves holiness
in Christ, he leads others to the same holiness, and the same experi-
ence of "life and rest" (l. 4). It would seem that the sheep eventually
become shepherds.

Baxter powerfully expresses this vision of Christian ministry as
organic and self-replicating. In his view the minister succeeds only
if he reproduces his own spiritual life in the lives of others who can
in turn carry on and expand the work. Only then will the leaven of
holiness work its own way through England, causing the "increase of
the body unto the edifying of itself in love" (Eph. 4:16). Writing to
an assembly of pastors in 1656—four years after the publication of
Herbert's *Countrey Parson*—Baxter argues that their duty of personal
instruction

> will exceedingly facilitate the ministerial work in succeeding generations. . . .
> It is like to be a work that will reach over the whole land, and not stop with us
> that have now engaged in it. . . . I will not be so uncharitable as to doubt,
> whether *all that are godly* throughout the land (or at least the generality of
> them) will gladly join with us. And oh, what a happy thing it will be to see
> such *a general combination for Christ* and to see all England so seriously
> called upon, . . . and set in so fair way to heaven! Methinks the consideration
> of it should make our hearts rejoice within us, to see *so many faithful servants
> of Christ all over the land,* addressing every particular sinner with such im-
> portunity, as men that will hardly take a denial. (emphases mine)

Indeed, in the case of Baxter's Kidderminster parish, this "work of the
ministry" was carried on long after he had left the scene. J. I. Packer
writes that when "in December 1743, George Whitefield visited Kid-
derminster he wrote to a friend: 'I was greatly refreshed to find what a
sweet savour of good Mr. Baxter's doctrine, works, and discipline

remained to this day.'"[14] Throughout *The Reformed Pastor,* Baxter stresses this kind of cooperative, shared, and spreading ministry.

However, Baxter, like most Puritans, is not anticlerical. He never forgets the difference between "us"—the pastors—and "them"—the people. He introduces his book with an exhortation to his fellow clergymen that "we teach one another, as brethren in office, as well as in faith." If "the people of our charge must teach and admonish and exhort each other daily," no doubt teachers may do it to one another, "without any super-eminancy of power or degree."[15] Even as he dismisses the "super-eminancy" of bishops and endorses the competence of laymen to teach each other, he maintains the special teaching authority that he shares only with his "brethren in office." Indeed Baxter, like Calvin, reserves some of his sharpest criticism for Anabaptists and others (like Quakers) who deny the ordained and "learned" ministry altogether.[16]

In Herbert's case, we find strong evidence in *The Countrey Parson* that he would perpetuate the church hierarchy that he seems to question. This evidence helps to explain why his internalizing and leveling impulses are usually penned (in both senses) within the bounds of his devotional lyrics. First and foremost, he preserves throughout *The Countrey Parson* a stronger distinction between the clergy and the laity than does Baxter. For example, while St. Paul seems to intend that all Christians exercise their differing spiritual gifts in the church "according to the grace that is given to us, whether prophecy, . . . or ministry, . . . or . . . teaching" (Rom. 12:6), Herbert applies this passage to pastors alone (*W,* 226). Fellow priests are "his Brethren" (*W,* 253), while others are almost always "the people." Furthermore, the parson works to establish himself as central to the life of his parish; he "desires to be all" to them (*W,* 259). As "a Father" he "professeth himselfe thoroughly of the opinion, carrying it about with him as fully, as if he had begot his whole Parish," considering each offender "as a child" (*W,* 250). We have seen that, standing "in God's stead," he

14. Baxter, *Reformed Pastor,* 185, 188–89, 12.
15. Ibid., 51.
16. For Baxter's condemnation of anticlericalism, see e.g. his critique of the "Separatists, Anabaptists, and Antinomians" in the New Model Army in A. S. P. Woodhouse, *Puritanism and Liberty,* 387–89. For Calvin on ministerial authority, see *ICR* 4.4.1–4.

embraces an awesome role and responsibility, "discharg[ing] God what he can of [H]is promises" (*W,* 254). He defends the efficacy of the priestly blessing, claiming that "even ill Priests may blesse," demonstrating from the case of Eli and Hannah (I Sam. 1:18) that "it [is] not the person, but Priesthood, that blesse[s]" (*W,* 285).

So Herbert's parson is not training his replacements, but rather, his assistants. He seeks to maintain, and indeed advance, the priesthood as a privileged institution in country life. While he is not *sacerdos,* the sacrificer, nor *pontifex,* the bridge between God and man, he is a "Vicegerent," triply stamped with the image of God, first in his creation, second in his regeneration, and third in his special calling. The first stamp is applied by God without human involvement. The final stamp of the priesthood, like the second stamp of salvation, is God's work from first to last, yet it also involves human means. God does not need the seals of the king and the church to make "priests," but in Herbert's view God chooses to include those seals under his own. Man's approval gives no spiritual power, but it gives a legal dignity and privilege to the God-ordained role of spiritual leader, thereby integrating him into the social hierarchy of the commonwealth. Herbert would carry his privilege benevolently, but he would carry it, nonetheless.

Thus we have reached the limits of Herbert's vision for reforming the British church and her clergy. Cristina Malcolmson helps us to understand these limits:

> [The parson's] sacred identity may put to rights injustices, errors, and impurities of social roles, but it does not provide for Herbert the means of visualizing new cultural or individual possibilities. . . . His poems on aristocratic identity equal Ben Jonson's plays in their ability to evoke and destroy illusions of grandeur; . . . [b]ut what is a potential radicalism is held in religious suspension, never reaching political or social articulation, and, one feels, only rendered safe to consider through its proximity to a vividly clear submission to God.[17]

Malcolmson articulates an important historical tension in Herbert. It is fair to ask why Herbert's egalitarianism is muted and even trun-

---

17. "Society and Self-Definition," 205–6.

cated in *The Countrey Parson;* indeed, my final chapter will pursue this question in more detail. However, it seems even fairer to ask why this egalitarianism is present at all, and present in ways that would work it into the fabric of daily parish life.

If Herbert and Laud had anything in common, it was that both believed in being "thorough." Indeed, if James's and Charles's country clergy had practiced Herbertian "thorough" with half the energy recommended by Herbert himself, the leaven of established Protestant doctrine would very likely have permeated the kingdom, probably reducing the Puritan pressure that led in large part to the civil war. We observed in chapter 3 that the doctrine of God's absolute sovereignty tends to subvert any doctrine of absolute monarchy or "divine right" episcopacy. By embracing Laud's Arminianism, James's son found a truer theological home, and set up the inevitable confrontation with the Calvinist Parliament. A more pervasively reformed city, court, and country would have had much less about which to fight.

So, however much Herbert labored to focus his pastoral attention on local and "spiritual" matters, both the theology and the thoroughness of his agenda give *The Countrey Parson* a definite political edge, distinguishing him sharply from the hierarchical autocracy of both the Caroline court and the Laudian church. He may have been aware of his dangerous differences, and caution may have constrained him while writing the book. However, while working in the genre of religious verse Herbert seems to have felt more freedom from social and political constraints, perhaps because such verse was commonly viewed as private expression. It is ironic that there, especially in the lyrics, we find his most "Puritanical" statements on public issues—particularly statements, like "The Priesthood" and "Aaron," that make every man, at least potentially, his own priest.

Here again we confront the unsatisfying options of seeing Herbert as either a failed Conformist or a would-be Puritan, and again we must reject both options. Probably Baxter was more consistent and effective in working out the principle of *sola scriptura* in everyday parish life, driving doctrine to practice. Thus Baxter's *Reformed Pastor* is, in many ways, the "compleat Pastorall" that, in "The Authour to the Reader," Herbert prayed *The Countrey Parson* would eventually become (*W,* 224). When compared to Baxter's trenchant, zealous

plea for continuing reform, Herbert's seems somewhat complacent—
bounded and hindered, it appears, by the forms, customs, and cere-
monies of the establishment.

However, such judgments of value are a matter of chronological
and ecclesiastical perspective. When *The Countrey Parson* was com-
pleted in 1632, it constituted the avant-garde of reformed pastoral
theology in England, and, like "The Church Militant," it might have
caused a considerable stir if published at that time. Yet as the next
chapter will show, Herbert did not see his church's externals of form,
custom, and ceremony as hindrances to scripturally edifying the peo-
ple, but rather as an integral part of that edification. For Herbert, the
"exact middle way" of the Elizabethan Settlement was defined not
merely against the extremes of Laudianism and Puritanism, but by its
own internal consistency.

7

The Church Legible

Herbert and the Externals of Worship

Christ's gospel is not a ceremonial law, as much of Moses' law was, but it is a religion to serve God, not in bondage of the figure or shadow, but in the freedom of spirit, being content only with those ceremonies which do serve to a decent order and godly discipline, and such as be apt to stir up the dull mind of man to the remembrance of his duty to God by some notable and special signification whereby he might be edified.
—*The Book of Common Prayer,* 1559 ([Thomas Cranmer], "Of Ceremonies, Why Some Be Abolished and Some Retained," 19)

Aside from Walton's *Life of Herbert,* few statements have more influenced readers of *The Temple* than Herbert's own lyric "The British Church" (*W,* 109–10). This poem, placed exactly midway in the lyrics of "The Church," confidently celebrates the British "middle way":

> I joy, deare Mother, when I view
> Thy perfect lineaments and hue
>   Both sweet and bright
> . . . .
> Outlandish looks may not compare:
> For all they either painted are,
>   Or else undrest
> . . . .
> But, dearest Mother, what those miss,
> The mean, thy praise and glorie is,

149

> And long may be.
> Blessed be God, whose love it was
> To double-moat thee with his grace,
> And none but thee.
> (ll. 1–3, 10–12, 25–30)

These lines, with their patriotic insistence on the unique blessedness of the British church, are the glass through which Herbert's poetry, and Herbert himself, have long been seen as paradigms of Anglo-Catholicism. Hutchinson says of this poem, "[T]he *via media* of the Anglican Church, between Rome and Geneva, *both in doctrine and in worship,* is often commended by Herbert" (*W,* 515, emphasis mine).[1]

Yet how could the most quoted celebrant of the *via media*'s beauties have declare to God that "all this glorie, all this pomp and state,"

> Did not affect thee much, was not thy aim
>
> . . . .
> For all thy frame and fabrick is within
>
> . . . .
> All Solomons sea of brasse and world of stone
> Is not so deare to thee as one good grone.
> ("Sion," *W,* 106, ll. 7–8, 12, 17–18)

Do "The British Church" and "Sion" reveal the self-contradictions of a man of two minds? Or can these seemingly opposed statements, one praising and the other denigrating external "glorie," be reconciled by placement in a larger theological context? Reconciliation is indeed possible if we refer Herbert's various treatments of visible ecclesiastical structures to the idea of "notable and special signification" enunciated in the Prayer Book's prefatory statement "Of Ceremonies": that English Christians should serve God *only* with those outward things that "edify" by being necessary and clearly understandable. Cranmer insists that England has been reformed according to the written Word, and that its reformed church must, like that Word, be

1. Thomas Wood speaks representatively in the introduction to his pastoral anthology when he compares the "moderate Calvinist" Perkins to Herbert, who "belonged to the school of Andrewes and Laud," which emphasized Catholic continuity over Protestant distinctiveness (*Five Pastorals,* 1). Indeed, E. C. E. Bourne, one of Laud's more recent advocates, employs "The British Church" as the epigraph to his entire book. See *The Anglicanism of William Laud,* vi.

legible. The stress laid on this "legibility" by the Prayer Book and by Herbert reveals their surprising common ground with the establishment's Puritan critics—surprising, that is, if we had assumed that an appreciation of outward "decency" necessarily implied a hostility to Calvinist theology.

Such an assumption seems to have led many modern literary critics to join the ecclesiastics by placing Herbert in a "high-church" context. Some of Herbert's most influential readers—Rosemond Tuve, Louis Martz, Patrick Grant, and more recently, Stanley Stewart—have treated him mainly as a liturgical poet, a cheerful celebrant of the established church's outward forms.[2] This classification is partially understandable. Even if we were completely to disregard Walton's account of Herbert as a devoted ritualist and restorer of parish sanctuaries, the poems of *The Temple* and especially of "The Church" are permeated with references to the externals of English worship—the church's sacraments, ceremonies, architecture, vestments, liturgy, and calendar.[3]

However, we have already observed much in Herbert's theology, his attitude toward royal and episcopal authority, and his pastoral practice that distinguishes him profoundly from the school of Andrewes and Laud. In fact, as we have already noted, Herbert's only anti-Puritan work, *Musae Responsoriae,* engages the Puritan Andrew Melville in controversy over "sacred ritual" and other externals only after agreeing with Melville's basic Calvinist theology.

2. Tuve, *A Reading of George Herbert;* Martz, *Poetry of Meditation;* Grant, *The Transformation of Sin;* and Stewart, *George Herbert.*

3. "The Church" is entered from "The Church-porch" through the portals under the "Superliminare" dedication. The titles of the first nine poems in "The Church" promise meditation on Christ's passion—"The Altar," "The Sacrifice," "The Thanksgiving," "The Reprisall," "The Agonie," "The Sinner," "Good Friday," "Redemption," and "Sepulchre" (*W,* 26–41). Most of the last eleven lyrics deal with the eucharistic feast and three of the Four Last Things—"The Invitation," "The Banquet," "Death," "Dooms-day," "Judgement," "Heaven," and "Love" (III) (*W,* 179–89). Poems named for most of the major feast-days in the Catholic tradition are interspersed in canonical order throughout the work—"Good Friday," "Easter," "Whitsunday," "Trinitie Sunday," "Sunday," "To all Angels and Saints," "Christmas," and "Lent." Thus the nineteenth-century Anglo-Catholic John Keble often has been seen as following both spiritually and poetically in Herbert's steps by composing *The Christian Year,* a cycle of devotional poems meditating upon each of the rubrics in the Prayer Book (Brian W. Martin, *John Keble: Priest, Professor, and Poet,* 28–29). See also Elbert N. S. Thompson, "*The Temple* and *The Christian Year.*"

Acknowledging such evidence, other scholars during the past decade have been more willing to address Herbert's Protestant inwardness and even to stress it in order to balance the traditional view of him as a ritualist enamored of outward forms. Indeed, Herbert's broad popularity in his own century, especially among Puritans, casts further doubt on the Laudian Walton's proprietary claims. Ilona Bell writes, "Everyone seemed to love Herbert's poetry, and many claimed him as a posthumous ally. Herbert was no less an inspiration for the Puritan expatriate Edward Taylor than for the Anglican Henry Vaughan, and many devout English Puritans embraced him. When Richard Baxter praised *The Temple* in the preface to his *Poetical Fragments* (1681), he admired 'Heart-work and Heaven-work,' spiritual inwardness, not ceremonial richness."[4] So Herbert's treatment of the church's visible "aray" in *The Temple* seems more complex and more explicitly Protestant than is suggested by Walton, Walton's Anglo-Catholic successors, or even the apparently complacent accolades of "The British Church."

Yet these complexities and apparent contradictions fall away when we set Herbert's ecclesiastical poetry alongside Cranmer's Tudor Protestant principles, and a new consistency among the poems emerges. From this juxtaposition we also understand better why the supposedly "Anglo-Catholic" Herbert sounds positively "Puritan" in places. The "Old Conformity" that he inherited was itself relatively "Puritan" in rejecting institutional forms that threatened to obscure or to crowd out Reformation spiritual experience. He shared Cranmer's idea of a "legible" church, celebrated it in his verse, and sought to revive it through his pastoral manual and practice.

Legibility

All reformed Christians of the sixteenth and earlier seventeenth centuries agreed that Baptism and Holy Communion, the two sacraments retained in their churches, were the ceremonies with the most explicit warrants from Christ in the New Testament. We have seen

---

4. "'Setting Foot into Divinity,'" 220–21.

that the Thirty-Nine Articles interpreted these sacraments in terms entirely consistent with Calvin's. However, while no quarrel arose between the mutually Calvinist "Old Conformists" and Puritans over the visibility or meaning of the sacraments, a sharp disagreement did emerge over the church's other accoutrements. What was the role of the external edifice—the vestments, architecture, extra-biblical rites and traditions, music—in edifying the people? Were the things retained at the Reformation an aid to worship or a stumbling block? Significantly, even in the midst of this, the foremost Elizabethan controversy, we still find remarkable agreement between the antagonists. Both parties acknowledge that the ceremonies and other externals established by the monarch in Parliament must be, in the words of the Prayer Book preface, "neither dark nor dumb . . . , but . . . so set forth that every man may understand what they do mean and to what use they do serve." Their "special signification" must be clear so that all "might be edified."

Thus, in condemning former British "superstition," Cranmer laments, "[O]ur excessive multitude of ceremonies was so great and many of them so dark that they did more confound and darken than declare and set forth Christ's benefits unto us."[5] Similarly, Richard Hooker's attack on superstition employs the metaphor of a "creeping, encroaching" rank growth that eventually obscures the clean, clear, and reasonable edifice of the church, resulting in "heapes of rites and customes" (*LEP* 5.3.4). The Puritan Millenary Petition of 1604 uses this common Protestant language of simplicity and intelligibility in calling for changes in the church, now "groaning as under a common burden of human rites and ceremonies." The petition requests of the new king that "superfluous" ceremonies be eliminated, Baptism better explained, Communion administered only after examination and with a sermon, more "edifying" church music provided, and the "uniformity of doctrine prescribed."[6]

Each of these statements—Cranmer's, Hooker's, the Petitioners'—concurs essentially with Calvin's: "Shall no ceremonies then . . . be given to the ignorant to help them in their inexperience? I do not say

5. Church of England, *Book of Common Prayer,* 20, 19.
6. Kenyon, *Stuart Constitution,* 132–33.

that. For I feel that this kind of help is very useful to them." Rather than rejecting ceremonies out of hand, Calvin only contends that the means used "ought to show Christ, not to hide him." Accordingly, he recommends that "to keep that means, it is necessary to keep fewness in number, ease in observance, dignity in representation, which also includes clarity" (*ICR* 4.10.14).

All that Herbert says outside *The Temple* about the institutional edifice of the church aligns him, often markedly, with this emphasis on the "legibility" of externals as signs. When Andrew Melville, like the Millenary Petitioners and most Puritans, attacks many of the human rites retained by the English Church, Herbert responds in his Latin polemic by explaining how these controverted rituals and objects teach biblical lessons.[7] Although Herbert's casuistry in *Musae Responsoriae* is sometimes distractingly ingenious, and sometimes more sarcastic than substantive, the same cannot be said about chapter 35 of *The Countrey Parson,* "The Parson's Condescending."[8] Here a more mature and temperate Herbert invokes the same principle of doctrinal utility to defend some traditional rituals:

> The Countrey Parson is a Lover of old Customes, if they be good, and harm-lesse; and the rather, because Countrey people are much addicted to them. . . . If there be any ill in the custome, that may be severed from the good, he pares the apple, and gives them the clean to feed on. Particularly he loves Procession, and maintains it, because there are contained therein 4 manifest advantages. First, a blessing of God for the fruits of the field: Secondly, justice in the preservation of bounds: Thirdly, Charity in loving walking . . . with reconcil-ing of differences. . . . Fourthly, Mercy in releeving the poor. . . . There is much preaching in this friendliness. (*W,* 283–84)

In chapter 3 above, we considered this passage as it relates to the "old custom" of fasting at Lent. Here Herbert implicitly criticizes Puritan wastefulness in discarding the good with the bad, and he praises the

7. See, respectively, Epigram 9, "De S. Baptismi Ritu," 388–89; 12, "De Purificatione post puerperium," 389–90; 14, "De Superpelliceo," 390; and 26, "De annulo coniugali," 396.

8. We should bear in mind Hutchinson's statement that this polemic is a relatively early and immature work, perhaps even begun by Herbert as a precocious schoolboy and later completed by the ambitious young University Orator. See note in *W,* 587–88.

edifying clarity—indeed the "preaching" power—of the good old customs. Yet Herbert's position is finally utilitarian in its condescension to the simple country folk who are "much addicted" to customs. The parson seeks the lesson or lessons to be taught, not the preservation of old ways per se. He capitalizes on the popular traditions and conforms them to his scripturally informed purposes. In other circumstances, he could just as well use other customs. His stance is that of "adiaphorist" Protestantism; that is, his judgments on "indifferent things" (from the Greek *adiaphora*) depend entirely upon what clearly edifies his flock.

Nowhere is Herbert's commitment to Cranmer's principle of "clear and special signification" clearer than in chapter 13, "The Parson's Church." Beyond keeping the church building clean and repaired, and maintaining the furnishings necessary for preaching, the sacraments, and charity, the parson concerns himself primarily with making the sanctuary "legible" in the most literal way.[9] First, he ensures that "all the books appointed by Authority"—the Bible, *The Book of Homilies,* and the Prayer Book—be there in good condition.[10] Second, and most strikingly, "he takes order . . . [t]hat there be fit, and proper texts of Scripture every where painted, and that all the painting be grave, and reverend, not with light colours, or foolish anticks" (*W,* 246). The very fabric of the church should bear the holy text, thus removing any possible ambiguity about the building's purpose. In light of Herbert's subsequent reputation, it is ironic that *scripture* is the only "ornament" of which Herbert speaks in this chapter. The parson's church is not a house of images, but of biblically focused devotion. Herbert intends the visible edifice to direct the worshiper's mind to heaven, but in a peculiarly Protestant way, and he cautions the parson to keep all of the externals in necessary perspective: "[A]ll this he doth, not as out of necessity, or as putting a holiness in the things, but as desiring to keep the middle way between superstition, and slovenlinesse, and as following the Apostles two great and admirable Rules in things of this nature: The first whereof is, *Let all things*

9. This furniture includes "the Pulpit, and Desk, and Communion Table, and Font, . . . and a Bason for Almes and . . . a Poor-mans Box" (*W,* 246).
10. Church of England, *Canons,* Canon 80.

be done decently, and in order: The second, *Let all things be done to edification, I Cor. 14* [26, 40]." According to Herbert's "exact middle way," there is no holiness in the outward structures. The sanctity that they have, they acquire functionally, by declaring God's holiness in His word and in His people. As Donne says in dedicating Lincoln's Inn Chapel, "These walls are holy, because the Saints of God meet here within these walls to glorifie him."[11] All the better, says Herbert, if the walls themselves preach to the saints.

Herbert, Ferrar, and the Edifying Edifice

However, we cannot ignore Herbert's reputation as an edifier of actual edifices. This reputation rests largely on Walton's account of Herbert's friendship with Nicholas Ferrar, the founder of the liturgically minded community at Little Gidding, and of their cooperation in rebuilding Leighton Ecclesia in Leighton Bromswold nearby. Ferrar's often idealized community appears to have been a truly fascinating place, partly because it defied the religious classifications of that day. Indeed, the ferment of the 1620s and 1630s is well illustrated by the fact that, as we will see, Ferrar and his project were attacked both as Papist and as *Puritan.*[12]

After the Restoration, Barnabas Oley and especially Izaak Walton set about rehabilitating Ferrar, along with Herbert, as Laudian heroes. Walton, referring unabashedly to Ferrar as "Saint Nicholas," holds him up as a perfect example of the beautifying, retiring temperament that typified the Caroline establishment over against the fanatical, ravaging Puritans. The Ferrar family's loyal receptions of Charles I at Little Gidding from 1632 to 1646, known to many modern readers through T. S. Eliot's *Four Quartets,* served to substantiate Walton's royalist hagiography.[13]

However, both the Puritan and the Laudian versions of Ferrar's life

---

11. *Sermons* 4:364.

12. For a description of Ferrar's sumptuously restored church at Little Gidding, see A. L. Maycock, *Nicholas Ferrar of Little Gidding,* 133. For a page reference on Ferrar's being called a "Puritan," see note 14, below.

13. Walton, *Lives,* 309–15; Maycock, *Ferrar,* 128, 140, 148, 276; Eliot, *Complete Poems and Plays,* 138–45.

and work fundamentally misrepresent their subject by overlooking his emphatically Protestant faith and his non-Arminian associations. For example, Ferrar insisted that the pope was Antichrist, which Laud made a point of denying. Ferrar may have been made deacon by Laud and visited by Charles I, but he was much more substantially protected and patronized by John Williams, Bishop of Lincoln and Laud's greatest adversary in the church. In fact, Ferrar's attachment to Williams led him to visit Williams in the Tower in 1636, where Laud's ill will had temporarily confined him. Even more significantly, a visitor to the Little Gidding church in 1634, a year *after* Laud's accession to Canterbury, found the sanctuary arranged in a decidedly non-Laudian manner. The Communion table was not turned "altar-wise," and he saw no stained glass and no crucifix. (Indeed, Ferrar once said that if he knew Mass had been said in a room of his own house, he would have that room pulled down.) What the visitor did see were four brass tablets on the east wall displaying the Lord's Prayer, the Apostles' Creed, and the Ten Commandments. As to the character of Ferrar and his family, a more regular visitor described them as "Orthodox, Regular, *Puritan Protestants*" (emphasis mine), while a Roman Catholic priest who once engaged Ferrar in theological controversy favorably compared the force of Ferrar's arguments to that of Martin Luther's.[14] Whatever Ferrar's "Puritanism" may have been, we see that his love of ornamental and ceremonial richness does not seem to have softened his opposition to Roman Catholic sacramental doctrine or moved him to erect an edifice that he thought inconsistent with the Protestant gospel.

Herbert and Ferrar enjoyed an exceptionally warm, if mainly epistolary, friendship. The two exchanged personal counsel and various theological writings. Ferrar sent Herbert his translation of Juan de Valdes's *Considerations,* to which Herbert responded with his *Briefe Notes* (*W,* 304–20). It was Ferrar who after Herbert's death saw *The Temple* past Laud's censors and through the press at Cambridge (*W,* 546–47). The two men seem to have trusted one another's judgment

14. For Ferrar and Laud on the Pope, see Maycock, *Ferrar,* 239, and Laud, *Works of Laud* 4:308–9. For Ferrar and Williams, see Maycock, *Ferrar,* 236–39. For the non-Laudian furnishings at Little Gidding, see Maycock, *Ferrar,* 132, 138. For Ferrar on the Mass, see Maycock, *Ferrar,* 239. For Ferrar called "Puritan," see B. Blackstone, *The Ferrar Papers,* 74. For Ferrar compared to Luther, see Maycock, *Ferrar,* 240.

completely. Barnabas Oley writes, "[T]hey loved each other most entirely, and their very souls cleaved together most intimately, and drove a large stock of Christian intelligence together long before their deaths."[15] What we have of their correspondence bears out this estimation (*W*, 378–79).

This trust seems to have extended to the reconstruction of the parish church at Leighton Bromswold, in which Herbert played an important but secondary role.[16] The ideal plainness of "The Parson's Church" does not seem perfectly in accord with the sumptuousness of Little Gidding, nor perhaps of Leighton Ecclesia. The difference may be due to money—Little Gidding and Leighton were exceptional in enjoying the wealth of Ferrar and of Herbert's donors—or to taste, since Herbert, who never saw the building at Leighton, may have deferred to Ferrar. However, regardless of the richness displayed, both men seem to have agreed that church furnishing and decoration should act like the marginalia of a judiciously illuminated manuscript: to frame and visibly express the beauty of biblical truth, yet in careful moderation so as not to obscure the "text" itself, the scripture read, preached, and even visibly displayed. Even according to Walton, Herbert on his deathbed put the edification of Leighton Ecclesia in perspective, saying that it was a "good work, if sprinkled with the blood of Christ, and not otherwise."[17] To the last, Herbert was careful not to put "a holiness in the things."

Laud, Andrewes, and Externals

During the ecclesiastical skirmishes of the 1620s, it was the resurgence of belief in the inherent holiness of externals, and the loss of a common appeal to "clarity and simplicity," that ominously widened the old gap between Puritans and the church establishment. As Laud and his bishops consolidated their positions in the church hierarchy, they carried on controversies with the Puritans in terms different from those of their episcopal predecessors, terms which seem designed to

15. In George Herbert, *The Complete Works in Verse and Prose* 3:231.
16. Charles, *A Life of George Herbert*, 121, and Maycock, *Ferrar*, 273–75.
17. *Lives*, 317.

cut off discussion entirely. Ironically, not the activist Laud but the bookish and personally mild Lancelot Andrewes, more than anyone else, provided the new rationale and its vocabulary.

Shortly before his death in 1626, Andrewes composed *A Learned Discourse of Ceremonies Retained and used in Christian Churches,* a seventy-seven-page distillation of his belief that the reformed English church should maintain and restore itself in the "beauty of holiness." While this work was not printed until 1653, it was almost certainly read in manuscript form by his clerical admirers, and by Laud in particular. In any case, the book expresses views that the "Arminians" had held and defended for years. When Andrewes's argument is considered against the Tudor backdrop—Cranmer's Prayer Book preface, the homilies on ceremonies, and Hooker's *Laws*—its omissions are as prominent as any of its positive claims. The older language of ceremonial "clarity" and "utility" practically disappears. Virtually absent, therefore, are any claims that the "ceremonies retained" by the church contribute to the people's spiritual good.

Instead of thus shoring up Cranmer's and Hooker's traditional line of defense against Puritan charges of "popery" and "paganism," Andrewes diverges sharply by conceding—in an anthropologically fascinating twist—that many English rites do in fact derive from paganism, but that this ancestry is no cause in itself for shame. He writes of his purpose to show

> [t]hat of the Ecclesiasticall government and policy observed [by] Brittish and English ancient Pagans, as formerly having their Common-wealth in frame, and beautified with our common Laws, they being converted unto Christianity, many of the Paganish Ceremonies and Usages, not contrary to the Scripture, were still retained in their Christian policy; by means whereof tranquillity and peace was observed, and the alteration in the State lesse dangerous or sensible; For in General Arnobius is true, writing, Nothing was innovated for Christian Religion in *rerum natura.* . . . [O]ur Ancestors being Heathens, when they agreed to receive Christian Religion, that which was established before, and concerned externall policy, they held and kept still with that which was brought off new by their Christian Apostles and Doctors. (*LD,* 2–4)

While dismissing pre-Christian divinity as "superstitious and wicked," Andrewes embraces much of its "externall policy" as natural and reasonable, and he even treats these pagan origins as a major selling point when he concludes a fortiori: "If our Fore fathers which were enlighted onely by naturall reason would have so good Orders in their Temples, at their worshipping of false and superstitious Gods: What great care should Christians have for enjoyning and observing of comely and godly Ordinances in the worshipping of the true and everlasting God!" (*LD*, 77). That the pagans had temples, holy days, bishops, priests, set-prayers, altars, and surplices proves, not that such externals are corrupt and to be rejected, but that they are intrinsic to God's order, the *rerum natura,* and not to be altered.

Andrewes also notes that the derivation of church ceremonies from native British paganism brings with it another distinct advantage by demonstrating more than ever the British church's independence of Rome: "If much of the Christian Policy and Discipline was in practice when the State of the Land was Heathen, the lay-Catholiques are much mistaken in their Petition, where they write, We have all our Feasts and Ceremonies from Austin the Monk: these forget what their Father Bellarmine confesseth, that all Christian Ceremonies were not invented by the Pope" (*LD*, 12–13). Therefore, Andrewes argues, the Puritans cannot attack or reject English ceremonies as "popish," and they must obey their king's command to conform in these "things indifferent." Indeed, he claims, the retention of pagan forms was even an aid to the spread of the gospel, since as Pope Gregory observed, this continuity eases the transition of those "weak in faith" into the church.

An apparent inconsistency emerges in Andrewes's argument when, after defending the English rites as based on the natural reason of indigenous paganism, he seems to base them on revelation, after all. "[T]his pedigree of our Ceremonies," he says, "staineth not our Christian policy; For that all the good Orders of the Heathens came by Tradition, or reading, or seeing the Ceremonies of God commanded among the Jews in the Land of Promise" (*LD*, 9). Andrewes appears to overturn his emphasis on both the naturalness and the Englishness of church ceremonies, making them somehow derivative of the Jewish rites prescribed by God in scripture.

However, if there are knots in Andrewes's argument, they all give way before the cutting edge of royal authority. He consistently praises the benevolent agency of kings and emperors throughout history in discouraging idolatry, preserving temples and good ceremonies, and resolving religious disputes. Even before the advent of Christianity, the prince was "the politique Father of the people [and] made Laws to be observed by the Heathenish Clergy" (*LD*, 69). In particular, the kings and magistrates of the pre-Christian Romans, Germans, Persians, and "Caes" [*sic*] "by speciall Law forbad the worshipping of Images" (*LD*, 29–30). On the other hand, Andrewes would remind iconoclasts that the pious Christian emperors Constantine and Honorius actually forbade their Christian subjects to destroy formerly pagan temples and monuments, and that they instead commanded that these structures be put to Christian uses (*LD*, 32–33). In the warmth of his royalism, Andrewes apparently even praises King Herod the Great for bringing "much of the Romane Heathenish Discipline into [the Jews'] policy," since long before the Romans had adapted these rites (he does not say which) they were "used in the Common-wealth of Jury, wherein God was the Law-giver" (*LD*, 10).

Andrewes illuminates his claims for the church's debt to the pagan past with some odd, disconcerting analogies. He reasons that "if the Spaniards well may glory of their Alphonsus King of Arragon, *Qui per cloacam ingressus subter Muros* [who through a sewer entered under the city walls], [and] won Naples . . . reasonably then cut out of former rags of the Gentiles, the glorious and fair garment of Christianity in times may be woven" (*LD*, 8). Such a blithe, and apparently intentional, association of the church's outward array with filth and rags seems to play directly into Puritan hands, and would no doubt enrage—or perversely delight—Presbyterians like Thomas Cartwright and Andrew Melville.

The Old Conformity, Calvin, the Puritans, and Externals

Such associations also would have set Richard Hooker's teeth on edge. While Hooker writes warmly of the "naturall conveniencie" that stately and sumptuous churches and ceremonies bear to God's glory (*LEP* 5.15.4), he never hints at anything like Andrewes's argument based on pagan origins. Instead, as Cranmer had done, Hooker claims that some of the lawful ceremonies and externals came directly from the Jews, while others originated with the early Christian Fathers and emperors, and are retained for their orderliness and teaching value (*LEP* 5.11, 5.12). Hooker particularly stresses that the stately house of worship serves the believer "as a sensible help to stirre up devotion" (*LEP* 5.16.2).

While Hooker shares his Conformist predecessors' view of externals as auxiliary to devotion, he seems to differ from them over how these outward forms actually help the worshiper. Hooker considers church architecture a sensory aid; when the senses are applied to properly meaningful objects, he believes, one's thoughts will rise to God. In contrast, the writings of the earlier Conformists focus, like Herbert, not on "sensible" richness but on the necessity and utility of the church as a well-kept meeting place where the gospel is clearly proclaimed. So we find the authorized homily on "comely adorning of Churches" (1571) approaching very closely a "Puritan" statement, claiming that in "the cleare light of Christ Jesus . . . all shadowes, figures, and significations are vtterly gone, all vaine and unprofitable ceremonies, both Jewish and Heathenish, fully abolished." Church buildings "are not set up for figures, and significations of Messias . . . to come, but for other godly and necessary purposes," like preaching, prayer, and Communion. The "Church or Temple" is called "holy, yet not of it self," but because of these "godly and necessary" activities (*BH* 2:78–79).

Like Cranmer in his Prayer Book preface, and unlike Hooker, the homilist foregrounds the function of the holy place, stressing what has been "cut away and clean rejected" by the Reformation, and why. He anticipates Herbert, exhorting his readers to keep their sanctuaries well repaired, "honourably adorned, . . . cleane and sweete, to the comfort of the people," and inveighing against "phantasticall adorning and decking" (*BH* 2:77, 80).

Horton Davies has contrasted this quasi-Puritan "functionalism" with the architectural "numinosity" advocated by Andrewes, Laud, and their disciples. Just how far both Hooker and his predecessors would diverge from the Arminian sacralization of architecture appears in Andrewes's prayer consecrating Jesus Chapel, Peartree, Southampton, in 1620. To Andrewes, the building is no mere "sensible help," but fully God's "habitacion," since "above all, in this place, the very gate of heaven upon earth, . . . [we meet] to do the work of heaven" at the altar.[18] For as Laud writes elsewhere, the altar is "greater than the pulpit; . . . there it is 'This is My Body'; but in the pulpit it is at most but. . . . 'This is My Word.' And a greater reverence no doubt is due to the Body than to the Word of our Lord."[19] Thus, as Davies argues, from Hooker to Laud there is a de-emphasis of verbal edification, accompanied by an increase in the claims made for the divine preeminence of the physical edifice. To the Laudians, churches are not merely "convenient" or "didactically valuable," nor only places where "angels joins with humans in worship"; they are the dwelling places of Christ's "Real Presence" *in* the consecrated bread and wine. The place, and its furnishings, become holy in themselves—indeed "numinous."

Much as the earlier Conformists sound surprisingly "Puritan" in comparison to the Arminians, most Puritans were not as iconoclastic as has often been thought. As already noted, Calvin held some ceremonies to be useful "to the ignorant to help them in their inexperience," as long as "the means . . . show Christ, not . . . hide him" (*ICR* 4.10.14). For this reason, as Father Kilian McDonnell writes, Calvin chided John Knox "for being unbending on a matter of ritual, unbending even to the point of disturbing a refugee congregation with Anglican ritualistic leanings." Yet even Knox's own *Booke of Discipline* (1560) orders that all the dilapidated kirks of Scotland be quickly repaired "with such preparation within, *as appertaineth as well to the Majestie of God,* as unto the ease and commodity of the people [l]est the word of God, and the ministration of the Sacraments by unseemlinesse of the place come in contempt" (emphasis mine).[20] Even for the Scots Presbyterians, ecclesiastical architecture must in some way fit God's grandeur.

As to English Puritan attitudes toward liturgy and ceremony, Patrick Collinson writes that under Elizabeth they were at least "willing to enclose their worship in a fixed and invariable order." Collinson cites George Gifford, "the deprived vicar of Maldon and no moderate," as a

18. Davies, *Worship and Theology in England* 2:17; J. W. Legg, *English Orders for Consecrating Churches in the Seventeenth Century* 41:57.

19. *Works of Laud* 6:56–57.

20. McDonnell, *John Calvin, the Church, and the Eucharist,* 129, referring to John Knox, *Works* 4:51–52; Church of Scotland, *The First and Second Booke of Discipline,* 71.

defender of set-prayers and liturgies against the separatist John Green-wood. Gifford speaks for the Puritan mainstream when he writes, "[a]bout . . . commanding a prescript form of prayer to be used, our Church doth agree with all godly churches, yea the reformed churches have and do practice the same. . . . There would sundry inconve-niences grow for want of a liturgy, or prescript form of public prayers." Thus while many Puritan ministers omitted certain collects and cere-monies in their use of the Prayer Book, they still chose to use it rather than the plainer (and forbidden) Puritan alternative, *The Geneva Book,* so that "there might be as much conformity as might be outwardly."[21]

So we see that the Elizabethan Conformists and Puritans agreed that their church needed a "fit aray," but they disagreed over which externals, or how many, best suited God's glory and the clear preach-ing of the gospel. As in their other disputes over "things indifferent," the controversy reduces to two conflicting views of scriptural author-ity. For all their theological common ground, they parted company over whether the church should establish and enforce only those things clearly commanded in the Bible—the Puritan position—or whether the church's prerogative extended to mandating things allowed by, or not contrary to, the Bible—the Conformist position.[22] Yet they share far more in common with each other than with Laud's renewal of devotion to holy places.

Externals and *The Temple*

I turn now to consider the relationship of *The Temple,* and particu-larly the lyrics of "The Church," to the externals of worship. Herbert, as both pastor and poet, is committed to edifying the congregation and the reader within the structures of the British church, so he praises them as necessary, fit, and beautiful. Yet his overall thrust is internal, toward building the altar and temple in the heart. This internalizing impulse carries through poem after poem; so much so that he appar-ently is responding to the attitude, if not to the claim, that mere ob-

---

21. John Greenwood, *The Writings of John Greenwood, 1587–1590,* 57–58, 75; Col-linson, *Elizabethan Puritan Movement,* 363, 361, respectively.
22. Coolidge, *Pauline Renaissance,* 10–11.

servance of the church's outward order can substitute for a deeply felt inward life. Thus the church edifice is for Herbert a kind of three-dimensional emblem-book "to stir up the dull mind of man" toward God. Yet when the sign is set in the scales against the spiritual reality that it signifies, Herbert values "all this pomp and state" as less than "one good grone."

When we consider each of Herbert's many poems that touch directly or indirectly on the church's sacraments, architecture, vestments, ceremonies, liturgy, and calendar, we discover that these entities are seldom literally present to the poem's speaker, and even when literally present to his senses they lead him to specifically Protestant meditations and lessons. However, most of Herbert's poetic references to ecclesiastical externals are clearly metaphorical from the beginning, so that while they reveal a mind favorably disposed to liturgical orderliness, they do not provide models for direct meditation on places and physical objects. Besides these straightforwardly literal or clearly metaphorical references to the visible edifice, there is a third way in which Herbert typically treats outward things, wherein he deliberately misleads us with a "redefining" or "vanishing" motif. In this kind of poem, the speaker either considers a literal entity—a feast day, Christ's Passion, Solomon's temple—only to redefine or devalue it; or he causes the "real" object to vanish by the poem's end. We are left to see the object in retrospect as an emblem of, rather than a numinous aid to, devotion.

The "Literal" Edifice

The great exception to such diminishing treatments of externals would seem to be "The British Church" (*W,* 109–10); Herbert's serene satisfaction here with his "dearest Mother" is all the more notable when compared with Donne's restless questioning in Holy Sonnet XVIII, "Show me dear Christ, thy spouse, so bright and clear."[23]

---

23. *Complete English Poems,* 316. Because of the poem's searching theme, some scholars have placed it before Donne's ordination in 1615; however, as Evelyn Simpson and Helen Gardner have argued, the particular historical references seem to place it in 1620. See ibid., nn. 635–36.

Donne's poem, probably written in 1620, reveals his doubts about the status of not only the continental Catholic and Protestant churches, but also of his own. In contrast, Herbert warmly praises England's unique "middle way," the "mean" that all others miss. However, we should note carefully just what Herbert is, and what he is not, praising. Many have found in these lines a defense of Laudian "finery." Yet a closer look at the first two stanzas reveals that the church's "fineness" is not in her "aray"—presumably the liturgical and material externals—but in her "aspect," her "face," where living personality and rationality are most clearly displayed. Her "lineaments and hue" may be "perfect," her array "fit," but their perfection does not necessarily imply Hooker's, or even Ferrar's, "sumptuousnesse." The church's array is "fit" because it does not distract from the "beautie" of her "face." Ecclesiastical "nakedness"—the Genevan "she" who "nothing wears" (l. 24)—is also to be avoided, for it distracts in an opposite fashion from the church's "fine aspect."

Furthermore, although Herbert portrays the British way as a mean between extremes, he does not portray these extremes as equally dangerous. The painted "wanton" (l. 13) of Rome, with her excessive ornamentation, is a continually seductive threat who "allureth all" to idolatrous worship at her "painted shrines" (l. 16). On the other hand, the nakedness of Geneva "in the valley" is not seductive, but unattractive, and in Herbert's view somewhat absurd. Geneva can be faulted for a strange and inappropriate "shyness" rather than "pride." Hooker had noted that in the days of primitive Christianity, before the advent of Christian kings, the church's plainness "was suteable unto the nakednes of Jesus Christ and the simplicitie of his Gospel" (*LEP* 5.15.1). Hooker makes no similar allowance for Roman excess. Likewise Herbert, in walking his *via media,* is less harsh on Protestant Geneva than on papal Rome.[24]

So the traditional reading—that "The British Church" endorses the "beautifying" policies of emerging Laudianism—cannot be maintained. Even if we disregard the evidence of Herbert's statements about the relatively plain "Parson's Church," this lyric itself will not bear such

24. See Richard Strier, "History, Criticism, and Herbert: A Polemical Note."

a reading. Herbert gives no direct, literal referent for the "fit"—not "fine"—"aray" that he celebrates. We have no warrant to assume that this array includes the railed altars, additional stained glass, and statuary that Laud instituted.

Beyond this poem's appreciation of the church's modesty and decency of dress, such externals very seldom stir the senses of *The Temple*'s poetic speakers as direct aids to devotion. Only "Church-monuments" (*W,* 64–65) among all *The Temple*'s lyrics even suggests the kind of sensory "numinosity" that was to become the model for later "Anglican" meditation—such objects usually being liturgical or physical entities not specified in scripture. This "Anglican" paradigm is adumbrated in Hooker's recommendation of "sensible help[s] to stirre up devotion," developed in such Arminian works as John Cosin's *Private Devotions,* and given its fullest expression two hundred years later in John Keble's *Christian Year.*

However, even "Church-monuments" is problematic as "Anglican" meditation. While the poem's speaker seems to focus visually on the more elaborate indoor genealogical memorial of "Jeat and Marble" —suggested by the "dusty heraldrie and lines" (l. 9) and the repeated play on "birth" and "true descent" (l. 18)—he combines these "sensible" qualities with those of the more common outdoor headstone— suggested by the language of grave "heaps" (l. 16), the windy "blast of death's incessant motion" (l. 4), and even the poem's monolithic shape (there are no stanza breaks in the Williams or Bodleian manuscripts — see *W,* 498–99). This mental blurring of two distinct visual forms makes it difficult to imagine the monument as a discrete object, yet adds to the monument's power as a *memento mori,* a sign of impending death on which we must all read our own names.

Indeed, the monument's lessons, while not uniquely Protestant, are all clearly biblical. The imagery of dusty headstones and grave-heaps draws the speaker to echo Gen. 3:19 ("dust thou art, and unto dust shalt thou return") and Psalm 39:4 ("Lord, make me know mine end, and the measure of my days what it is; that I may know how frail I am"). Reminded of his "true descent," the speaker exhorts his flesh to mortify its lusts and thus "fit thy self against thy fall" (l. 24). Correspondingly, the image of heraldic lineages suggests the irony of celebrating one's family name in a place intended to show that such names are inconsequential.[25] Thus the church monuments, and perhaps even the churches themselves, teach their lessons not by their numinous "sumptuousness" or their intended permanence, but by their ironic and inevitable decay. In the state of mind expressed by this poem, Herbert would behold Laud's grandest sanctuary and think, very probably, of the biblical *vanitas vanitatis*.

In fact, of all Herbert's lyrics, only "The Knell" (*W,* 204), works as "Anglican" meditation. Like Donne in the *Devotions upon Emergent Occasions,* Herbert hears the tolling of the plague-time bell and is led by it to contemplate the impending physical disease as a spiritual remedy, since it draws his mind to impending death.[26] However, while "The Knell" appears in the Williams manuscript, Herbert chose to exclude it from the final version of *The Temple.*

None of Herbert's other poems that deal literally with the church's outward forms can be seen as distinctly "Anglican," since all of these refer to rites and events specified in the New Testament and that all but the most extreme Puritan sects treated as parts of the church's necessary order. The "H. Baptisme" and Communion poems, especially "The H. Communion" and "The Banquet" (*W,* 43–44, 52–53, 181–82), celebrate the Holy Spirit's use of the outward sign to seal its promises and lift the believer to experience heavenly glories. Similarly, "Church-musick" (*W,* 65–66) raises the worshiper in ecstasy to "heavens doore" (l. 12) as St. Paul recommends in Col. 3:16. "Sunday," "Easter," and "Christmas" (*W,* 75–77, 41–42, 80–81) meditate on scriptural events or holy days in terms that Puritans could, and often did, share. "Sunday" in particular would appeal to Sabbatarian sensibilities since it stresses that the Lord's Day is for rest and worship, not for the "burden" (l. 12) or the "vanities" (l. 25) of the "worky-daies" (l. 11)—much in contrast to Laud's controversial defense of Sunday "sports," dances, and church-ales.[27]

---

25. I am indebted to Cristina Malcolmson for this insight.
26. *Devotions upon Emergent Occasions,* Anthony Raspa, ed., 86–87.
27. Such activities were strongly opposed by the Puritans as profaning the Sabbath. See Hart, *Country Clergy,* 72–73, 96–97.

The "Internal" Edifice

While Herbert's literal references to the church's outward forms and structures are surprisingly few, *The Temple* as a whole is permeated with ecclesiastical and liturgical language. However, these ecclesiastical references are, from the beginning, clearly metaphorical or otherwise internalized, representing spiritual realities that come to exist fundamentally *within* the believer. Some of these "internalizing" lyrics display a unique relationship between the title and the body of the poem, a relationship like that exhibited by "The Pulley," "The Collar," and "The Holdfast" with their respective titles. In such cases, the title object never appears within the poem itself, even as a metaphor, yet the title is the key to the poem's unity. After reading the entire poem we return to the title and relate certain key words, images, and motifs to the speaker's inner state, retrospectively discovering the purpose of that governing image or action.

For example, in "Trinitie Sunday" (*W*, 68) the holy day is not named outside of the title, nor are the particular persons of the Trinity named anywhere. However, the overall three-line, three-stanza pattern is implicitly "trinitarian," as is the application to the self of God's saving work:

> Lord, who hast form'd me out of mud,
> > And hast redeem'd me through thy bloud,
> > And sanctifi'd me to do good;
>
> Purge all my sinnes done heretofore:
> > For I confesse my heavie score,
> > And I will strive to sinne no more.
>
> Enrich my heart, mouth, hands in me,
> > With faith, with hope, with charitie;
> > That I may runne, rise, rest with thee.

Each person performs a particular function: God the Father as creator "forms" and "purges," God the Son "redeems" and as priest hears "confession," and God the Holy Spirit "sanctifies" by removing the tendency to sin. The three triads of the third stanza complete the pattern.

Similarly, Herbert's famous "hieroglyph" "Easter-wings" (*W*, 43) mentions Easter nowhere but in the title.[28] The "daye" referred to (l. 18) could and should be every day, according to the lesson of "Easter" (*W*, 42–43):

> Can there be any day but this,
> Though many sunnes to shine endeavor?
> We count three hundred, but we misse:
> There is but one, and that one ever.
> (ll. 27–30)

The believer rises constantly with Christ's Resurrection, and the missing reference to the canonical Easter Sunday in "Easter-wings" reminds us that the Resurrection numbers all our days.[29] Likewise, the title of "The Crosse" (*W*, 164) might lead us to expect a meditation on "the bloudie crosse of my deare Lord" ("Conscience," *W*, 106, l. 23). Instead we find an implicit, extended pun on the "crosse-biassing"—the spiritual frustration—of which Herbert complains in "Affliction" (I) (*W*, 48, l. 53). Herbert's elimination of a literal crucifix is consistent with the Protestant rejection of ascetic mortification. It is the speaker's proud will, not his prison-house of flesh, that causes his misery.

Analogously, the title of "Confession" (*W*, 126) gives its lyric an ironic twist, since this heading introduces not a liturgical confession, but a complaining individual Christian's view of suffering as divine torture, calculated to extract an unwilling admission of guilt:

> No scrue, no piercer can
> Into a piece of timber work and winde,
> As Gods afflictions into man,
> When he a torture hath design'd.
> (ll. 7–10)

Furthermore, the poem's final, non-ironic confession of real "faults and sinnes" (l. 25)—sins like the ingratitude of the earlier lines—is

---

28. See Summers, *George Herbert: His Religion and Art*, 123–46, for a discussion of such "hieroglyphs" as "complete visual emblems."

29. See Strier's account of Herbert's challenge to our reasonable numerical expectations in "Easter" in *Love Known*, 59–60.

expressed in colloquial and arrestingly personal terms not borrowed from any collect:[30]

> I challenge here the brightest day,
> The clearest diamond: let them do their best,
> They shall be thick and cloudie to my breast.
>   (ll. 28–30)

Confession and cleansing take place entirely within the penitent. There is no priest here to pronounce absolution.

"Mattens" and "Even-song" (*W,* 62, 63) display Herbert's internalizing tendency by personalizing the public Prayer Book collects for morning and evening prayer. While the emphasis in "Mattens" on seeing God in his creation (ll. 13–20) echoes the *Benedicite omnia opera Domini Domino* of morning prayer, the emphasis in "Even-song" is notably different from that of the collect for evening prayer.[31] All of the evening collects mention the peril of the night, especially the third, which calls on God to "[l]ighten our darkness . . . and by thy great mercy defend us from all perils and dangers." In contrast, "Even-song" celebrates the night's sheltering, beautiful tranquillity: it is the "ebony box" where "Thou dost inclose us," "th'harbor" from the day's "gale," the "arbour" and the "grove" of restful shade (ll. 21–22, 26–28). Conversely, the "Euen-song" of the Williams manuscript, which repeats the Prayer Book plea for protection, is an entirely different poem that Herbert excludes from the final version of "The Church." Moreover, in none of these three poems—"Mattens," "Even-song" or "Euen-song" —does Herbert speak to, or for, or with a congregation, but rather as an individual "I" to the divine "Thou." The distinctly liturgical quality of *common* prayer that the titles lead us to expect is replaced in the lyrics by a single personal voice.

Distinct from these lyrics, which bear only a retrospective, and sometimes ironic relationship to their metaphorical titles, are those tied together by an extended ecclesiastical analogy, introduced in the title and explicitly invoked more or less throughout the poem. From the

30. Ibid., 50–51.
31. Church of England, *Book of Common Prayer,* 54–56, 64.

beginning, each of these lyrics figuratively uses outward objects to express inward realities. Thus "The Windows" (*W*, 67), one of Herbert's most affecting architectural poems, is not about how stained-glass windows inspire devotion, but about how a preacher is a window. In and of himself the preacher, like all mortals, is only a "brittle crazie glass," which "shows watrish, bleak, & thin"; but through God's grace Christ's life will be "annealed" within his life, so that "[d]octrine and life, colours and light, in one" will "bring / A strong regard and aw" (ll. 11, 13) from his hearers. Another architectural lyric, "Church-lock and key" (*W*, 66), works as allegory. The "church" to which the speaker wishes admittance signifies God's attentive presence, his "eares"; the "lock" that keeps the speaker out is "my sinne"; and the "key" is Christ's shed blood, which wins a hearing from God for the sinner. It means much for "The Church" as a whole cycle of poems that to be inside "the church" means to be heard by God. The space of the sanctuary becomes a metaphor for divine favor.

Herbert's most famous architectural poem, his hieroglyph "The Altar" (*W*, 26), is explicitly metaphorical and internalized from the first, being "[m]ade of a heart, and cemented with teares" (l. 2). Herbert's analogy here is not to a church Communion table turned "altar-wise" in Laudian fashion, but to the Old Testament sacrificial altar made of stones not touched by a "workman's tool" (l. 4; see Deut. 27:5–7). This ancient altar Herbert likens to his heart, which is "such a stone, / As nothing but / Thy pow'r can cut" (ll. 6–8). Thus Herbert points to the finished sacrifice of Christ, and at the same time to the now wholly inward sacrifice of the believer's broken and contrite heart. This prominently metaphorical use of "altar," a politically explosive term in the 1630s, and the absence of a contemporary literal "altar" cut against Laud's and even Hooker's exaltation of visible, physical sumptuousness to focus instead on the hidden core of the self.

The "Redefined" and "Vanishing" Edifice

A third kind of ecclesiastical poem not only counters Hooker and Laud but also seems to place Herbert on the borderline between the "Old Conformist" and Puritan positions. In these poems, Herbert either redefines the external entity in terms more strongly Protestant than he had led us to expect, or he simply makes the literal object disappear. As Ilona Bell has argued, the "Passion cycle" that begins "The Church" shows Herbert's commitment "to the Reformation and Protestantism, to reform and protest" by turning the forms of ascetic devotional poetry back against themselves. "Much as Sidney and Donne raided and exploded the Petrarchan conventions," writes Bell, "Herbert used and doomed the familiar images, postures, and goals of Catholic meditation."[32]

We have already noted in earlier chapters how other Herbert lyrics redefine Catholic externals in Protestant terms. "Lent" (W, 86) initially celebrates and recommends a certain degree of physical fasting during the Lenten season; yet in the final stanza Herbert seems to undercut this practice by stressing the primary importance of internal "fasting" from sin, externally demonstrated by literally feasting the poor who come to one's door. "To all Angels and Saints" (W, 77) apparently begins by invoking the angels, saints, and the Blessed Virgin, but it ends by rejecting such an invocation in a determination to do only what God clearly commands. "The Priesthood" (W, 160) makes ordination to a sacerdotal office its initial topic, but at the poem's end replaces the external forms of ordination, and the human bishop, with a prayer for personal, direct calling from God. In addition to these poems, "Whitsunday" (W, 59) observes the canonical holy day of Pentecost, but it does so by criticizing the present spiritual state of the British church, calling on God to restore truly Pentecostal fire and inner joy to its preachers, including the speaker himself.[33] Similarly, "Antiphon" (I) (W, 53) could conceivably be set to music and sung as an actual antiphon, but its final lines emphasize inner singing, for "above all, the heart / Must bear the longest part" (ll. 11–12).

In contrast to Herbert's "Protestantizing" devotional strategies, the *Private Devotions* (1626) of Laudian bishop John Cosin recommend

32. "'Setting Foot into Divinity,'" 222, 237. See especially Bell's discussion of how the initial "Passion cycle" of *The Temple* ultimately rejects any attempt at vivid, present-tense evocation of Christ's sufferings.

33. The implicit personal reference here is strengthened by the fact that Herbert's prebendary at Leighton Bromswold required him to preach a Whitsunday sermon each year. See Charles, *A Life of George Herbert*, 121–22.

an emotional reenactment of the Passion in terms that seem to parallel Loyola's *Spiritual Exercises*. Cosin writes, "[A]bout the Time of *His Passion* we should have a sympathie, a *com-passion* and a fellow-feeling with him, being made conformable unto him herein by the exercises of Repentence, which are *The Passion* of every Christian, whereby he dyeth unto sinne; and that the solemne *Joy* of our *Redemption* should be put off till EASTER DAY, the day of his *Resurrection*."[34] Cosin's belief that Christians should conform their feelings to the seasons of the church, shutting out joy every Lent until Easter, differs profoundly from Herbert's already-noted affirmation in "Easter" that resurrection joy should fill every day of the calendar. The gap between "Arminianism" and Herbert's "Old Conformity" is wide, not only in a doctrinal sense, but also in devotional sensibility.

"Sion" (*W,* 106) is the most representative of Herbert's "redefining" or "Protestantizing" group because it is his most global statement preferring inwardness to externality; thus it is his greatest departure not only from Rome and from Laud, but also from Hooker. The first stanza begins its apparent celebration of Solomon's glorious temple and what Hooker would have called its "naturall conveniencie" to the grandeur of God: "Lord, with what glorie wast thou served of old, / When Solomons temple stood and flourished!" (ll. 1–2). He praises the "things . . . of purest gold," and the wood "embellished / With flowers and carvings, mysticall and rare" (ll. 3–5)—mystical carvings, Herbert surely believed, that foreshadowed Christ's coming glory. However, the last line of this stanza introduces a worrisome note. If all of this visible grandeur "show'd the *builders,* crav'd the *seeers* [*sic*] care" (l. 6), then God himself may be overlooked in the exchange. The mystical carvings might even *hide* Christ now, in this age of full revelation.

Calvin and his Puritan disciples protested against such a danger. In their view, as Father McDonnell explains, such grandeur made it "difficult for a man to meet his God and speak with him apart from . . . the sanctuary externality of the official church. The . . . splendor to which the layman contributed only the obedient passivity of awe . . .

---

34. *A Collection of Private Devotions,* 199.

had rendered the believer's contact with God too churchy."[35] In short, the externals could crowd out the living God. Herbert expresses similar feelings in the next three stanzas when he insists that God's "aim" was, and is, not "all this glorie, all this pomp and state" (l. 7) of "Architecture," but the spiritual "frame and fabrick . . . within" the individual believer (ll. 11–12). It is here that the sinful constructions of the heart are pulled down, and here that God lays up his greatest treasure —"one good grone" of real repentance (l. 18). It is precisely Herbert's quest for spiritual "wings" that leads him to devalue the "brasse and stones" of grand sacred architecture. In his own shockingly strong terms, these "heavie things" are "[t]ombes for the dead" (ll. 19–20). Instead of being spiritually "convenient," they are grossly, perhaps fatally cumbersome, like biblical millstones around the neck. In the age of grace, God's favored building site is the heart.

The last and most radical of these "redefining" or "Protestantizing" lyrics are those with a deliberately misleading "vanishing motif." Richard Strier has shown how Herbert displays this "sleight-of-hand" in "The Church-floore" and "Aaron" (*W*, 66–67, 174), in which literal structures or objects—a church's paving-stones, a priest's robes —seem present to the speaker at first, but in retrospect turn out to have been metaphorical all along.[36] "A true Hymne" (*W*, 168) presents itself as formally fit for a musical setting, yet its lyrical content makes it virtually impossible as an actual congregational hymn. The poem begins with an exuberantly hymnic exclamation—"My joy, my life, my crown!"—but immediately takes a perplexing turn as the "hymnist" asserts that this one line may be a true hymn by itself, and that lyric "art" may be unnecessary for real devotion:

> My joy, my life, my crown!
> My heart was meaning all the day,
>   Somewhat it fain would say:
> And still it runneth mutt'ring up and down
> With onely this, My joy, my life, my crown.

35. *John Calvin*, 112.
36. *Love Known*, 127–34, 149–50.

> Yet slight not these few words:
> If truly said, they may take the part
> Among the best in art.
> The finenesse which a hymne or psalme affords
> Is, when the soul unto the lines accords.
>
> (ll. 1–10)

Such a self-reflexive lyric, with its deliberately unmusical lines ("And still it runneth mutt'ring up and down") is designed not to be sung but to be stumbled upon, considered and reconsidered. It works to prevent the antiphonal repetition of which the Puritans often complained, and to illustrate Herbert's stated point: that the true "art" or "finenesse" of a hymn is produced only in the heart of a devoted worshiper, whose "soul unto the lines accords," whose heart "rymes" with the words.[37] "[I]f th'heart be moved," then even if the verse, like Herbert's here, is "somewhat scant, / God doth supplie the want" (ll. 16–18). A "true hymn" need be no formal hymn at all.

The Temple As Vanishing Edifice

This replacement of outer objects with inner experience is not confined to individual lyrics. Indeed, the entire *Temple,* and "The Church-porch" and "The Church" contained within it, can perform this "vanishing act" on the reader who comes to the text expecting to find a collection of analogical meditations on a visibly numinous edifice. When we have come through "The Church-porch" to the "Superliminare," and we read there the invitation to enter and "taste / The churches mysticall repast" (*W,* 25, ll. 3–4), we could easily assume that the Mass is meant. Indeed, the sight of "The Altar" and "The Sacrifice" beyond the "door" seems to confirm such expectations of a reenacted sin offering. However, as we have noted, a close and responsive reading of these two poems and the "Passion cycle" that they begin should overthrow our first impressions.

Still, the materiality of "The Church"'s edifice seems to reassert itself in the liturgical and architectural titles grouped between "Mattens"

---

37. For the Puritans' complaint regarding antiphonal repetition, see Collinson, *Elizabethan Puritan Movement,* 359.

and "The Windows," in the "calendar poems" interspersed through-
out, and in the penultimate eucharistic poems that lead up to the final
communion of "Love" (III) (*W,* 188–89).[38] However, even if we have
carried our misconception of Herbert's intent so far, the final line of
this last lyric should demonstrate to us that he has been speaking all
along of "the temple" within the believer. The communion of "Love"
(III), like the entire "mysticall repast" of "The Church," cannot refer
to the literal sacrament ordered by the Prayer Book, for if it did Her-
bert would never "*sit* and eat" (l. 18, emphasis mine).[39] In *The Coun-
trey Parson,* he rejects such a eucharistic posture, writing that at the
sacrament "hee that kneels, confesseth himself an unworthy [guest],"
while "hee that sits, or lies, puts up to an Apostle" (*W,* 259). Iron-
ically, it is because of Herbert's known loyalty to the Church of En-
gland's external forms that "Love" (III), like the whole of *The Temple,*
must refer to the Christian's internal, eternal fellowship with the risen
Christ.[40]

"Trim Invention" and "Plain Intention"

If, for Herbert, externality and inwardness are so ironically yet pro-
foundly related, can they be reconciled? Reconciliation might at first
seem difficult, given the apparently stark contrast that we have observed
between his appreciation and devaluation of outward forms. Herbert
deals with this problem of ornament obscuring rather than display-
ing truth in "Jordan" (II) (*W,* 102–3), where he retrospectively chides
himself for having fallen prey to the temptation of overembellishing
his expressions of devotion. His was a pious mistake, Herbert says;
he was so taken with the "lustre" (l. 2) of his first spiritual experiences
that he sought to "deck" (l. 6) them in the richness appropriate to
their glory.

38. The architectural titles (*W,* 62–68) include "Mattens," "Even-song," "Church-
monuments," "Church-musick," "Church-lock and key," "The Church-floore," and "The
Windows."
    39. See the discussion of this point in Strier, *Love Known,* 78 n. 41.
    40. The blank-page break in the Bodleian manuscript between "The Church" and
"The Church Militant," along with Herbert's inscription of "Finis" at the end of "Love"
(III), suggests that he considered "The Church Militant" a work separate from *The Temple.*

There is an ironic similarity between Herbert's efforts to "clothe the sun" (l. 11) and Hooker's account of the church's growth in visible glory. As we have noted, Hooker concedes that in the days of primitive Christianity the church's poor surroundings were "suteable unto the nakednes of Jesus Christ and the simplicitie of his Gospell." However, he continues, "[t]ouchinge God him selfe, hath he anie where revealed that it is his delight to dwell beggarlie? and that he taketh no pleasure to be worshipped savinge onelie in poore cotages? Even then was the Lord as acceptiblie honored of his people as ever, when the stateliest places and thinges in the world were sought out to adorne his temple. This most suteable decent and fit for the greatnes of Jesus Christ, for the sublimitie of his Gospell" (*LEP* 5.15.2–3). According to Hooker, "all this glorie, all this pompe and state" was indeed God's aim. The Lord will tolerate "beggarlie" accommodations "when the state of the Church is poore," but he expects fitting outward splendor when he "hath inritched it with plentie." To everything there is a season, says Hooker, and under godly monarchs the season is one of visible glory for the church. For a nation to do less for God when it has the means argues serious irreverence, even blasphemy. Nothing should seem too rich to clothe the sublimity of Christ's gospel.

That Hooker speaks in terms almost identical to those of Herbert's pious error in "Jordan" (II) reveals their profound difference in sensibility, and perhaps in actual principle, over the place of ornament in worship. Like Herbert's earlier self, Hooker proposes to measure devotion by the amount and degree of "trim invention" (l. 3) decking the outward expressions of devotion. For Hooker, the present glorious ascendancy of Christian rulers defines "fitness" as "fineness," even grandeur. However, for Herbert the church's "fit aray" is, as we have seen, that which does not distract from the "fine aspect" of the church's truth, and which does not "show the builders, crave the seeers care" at the expense of the spiritual "frame and fabrick . . . within."

In Herbert's view, Hooker's pious externalism might lead to the consuming "bustle" that conscientiously—and confusingly—embellishes the "plain intention" of reformed worship. Like the blunt "friend" of "Jordan" (II), God would have his worshipers "copie out only that" which clearly expresses the personal, inner "sweetnesse" of Christ's love (ll. 13–18). All other embellishment—the "quaint" traditions and

ceremonial "invention" not grounded in this personal love—is distrac-
tingly "long pretence," which makes the message unintelligible. Mar-
ginal illumination must truly illuminate, not overgrow, the text. Those
baptized in the spiritual "Jordan" ought not to repeat such a mistake.

It is no mere coincidence that Herbert's cautions concerning poetic
and ecclesiastical ornamentation should dovetail so neatly. In both
cases it is the legibility of the plain and powerful gospel message that
concerns him. While God is the ultimate "reader" both of his lyrics
and of the church's "notable and special significations," both "texts"
are meant immediately for finite and fallible human readers. Such
readers need a plain and comprehensible transmission of the truth if
they are to be edified.

Given this principle of legibility, it seems not only possible but also
surprisingly uncomplicated to harmonize "The British Church" with
"Sion," and with the internalizing impetus of the entire *Temple*. Whether
any particular poem praises or denigrates externals depends on the
speaker's rhetorical stance in response to a perceived threat. In the
celebratory "British Church," Herbert answers not only Romanist but
also Puritan complaints by arguing that English moderation in exter-
nals fitly displays her essential saving message by preventing the dis-
tractions of either excess. However, when the externals of worship
are treated as anything more than a decent garment, or an edifying
text—when, in other words, they are emphasized at the expense of
the inner life that they signify, or, worse yet, are equated with it—then
Herbert puts them in perspective. He waves away the brass and stone,
the robes, rites, seasons, days, collects, hymns, even (perhaps espe-
cially) his own poems as the mere figures and shadows that he has
always believed them to be.

For Herbert, the fault or virtue lies not in the externals themselves,
but in the ignorance or understanding that people bring to them. It is
only after the worshiper has followed Herbert in dismissing the church's
outward shadows that he can use them in devotion with a clear con-
science and with joy. Thus Herbert shared the "Old Conformist" *idea*
of a reformed British church: to purify the church's forms meant to
clarify them. Herbert's inclusiveness distinguished him from the Pu-
ritans, with whom he otherwise shared so much. The fact that *The
Temple* is so devoted to "clarifying" these forms by making them dis-

appear suggests that Herbert saw a greater spiritual danger in Laud's reviving devotion to "brasse and stones." For Herbert, the "transparency" of the visible church is not so much that of plain glass—which, after all, might merely show "watrish, bleak, and thin"—but of a plain text or a clear sermon, translucent to the mind, and powerfully moving the heart.

8

"Betwixt This World and That of Grace"

Herbert and the Church in Society

> A church . . . is a Society; that is, a number of men belonging unto some Christian fellowship, the place and limits of which are certain, . . . as the Church of Rome, Corinth, Ephesus, England . . .
>
> —Richard Hooker, *LEP* (3.1.14)

> [The Parson's] children he first makes Christians, and then Common-wealths-men; the one he owes to his heavenly Countrey, the other to his earthly, having no title to either, except he do good to both.
>
> —*The Countrey Parson* (*W*, 239)

Much as Herbert's early biographers idealized him as a devoted celebrant of Britain's national church, so they portrayed him, at least in his last years, as correspondingly estranged from "the world." Walton describes how Herbert's embrace of the one required his reluctant but final rejection of the other:

> [Then died] *Lodowick* Duke of *Richmond, and James* Marquess of *Hamilton* and not long after him, King *James* died also, and with them, all Mr. Herbert's Court-hopes: So that he presently betook himself to a Retreat from *London,* to a Friend in *Kent,* where he lived very privately. . . . In this time of Retirement, he had many Conflicts with himself, Whether he should return to the painted pleasures of a Court-life, or betake himself to a study of Divinity, and

enter into Sacred Orders? (to which his dear Mother had often persuaded him.) . . . [For] ambitious Desires, and the outward Glory of this World, are not easily laid aside; but, at last, God inclin'd him to put on a resolution to serve at his Altar.[1]

Walton's Herbert moves from one pole of conventional hagiography to the other: from "this world," the societal world of power, money, and pleasure, to a haven of spiritual security, a sanctuary for the heavenly "world of grace" on earth. Much as a medieval "religious" would enter a monastery, Herbert the Anglican saint enters the cloister of the British church, represented, significantly, by the solitary eminence of the "Altar."

Admittedly, the spiritual poles that define Walton's Herbert are not the dramatic extremes of the classic "saint's life"—the young rake transformed suddenly into a ragged mystic. However, the dualistic pattern of the traditional saint's life still gives Walton's narrative its structure and provides his explanation for Herbert's inner conflicts and outward actions. In Walton's unambiguous terms, Herbert enters the church because he knows that he will be closer to God as a priest than as a privy counselor. That God personally frustrates Herbert's "court-hopes" in order to ensure Herbert's holiness only emphasizes this dualism between heavenly and earthly employment and reconfirms the British church's uniqueness as an inviolably sacred and sanctifying space, distinct from society and unstained by "the world."

Nevertheless, two overruling facts ultimately make it impossible to view Herbert's entry into the priesthood as a retreat, either in a positive or in a pejorative sense. First, Herbert did not enter the rural ministry to find contemplative peace, since he knew that its exertions offered little of that. Nor did he flee to the church for safety from a disintegrating social order, for in fact the church shared intimately in that larger order and in its decay, which Herbert acknowledged and mourned. Instead, Herbert chose the Bemerton ministry over possibly more lucrative or directly influential places in the church in order to revive publicly the fading Tudor social vision that seems to have helped to revive him personally: the godly calling in the godly com-

1. *Lives*, 276–77.

monwealth. Despite his moderate asceticism and his antimillenialist pessimism about the permanence of human efforts, Herbert felt called by God to do his part in building and rebuilding Christian England according to the Tudor humanist ideal.[2] This ideal, explicit in *The Countrey Parson* and implicit in the didactic strategy of *The Temple,* made the church the chief agent of social cohesion and reconstruction.

Thus the priesthood provided Herbert with the significant "employment" and the "place" in the social and metaphysical order that he had so long sought, but which he could not embrace until he had abandoned his hopes for courtly fame and power. His newfound mission sent him into an institution that he saw as both the chief hope and the potential ruin of the nation. There he sought to exemplify the ideal servant of God and king, and then, in *The Countrey Parson,* to prescribe this model of service for all the pastors in the kingdom. Herbert saw this clerical "brotherhood" as laboring for salvation not only of souls, but also of families, farms, industries, laws, government, and the church itself—in short, of the entire social order. "Edification" was both the pastor's Christian and his patriotic duty.

Even a superficial reading of *The Countrey Parson* reveals a vision of the pastoral calling that is both rigorous and public. Herbert's parson is not only the busiest man in the parish, but also the one involved with the most people, and in profoundly personal ways. Whether preaching to the congregation, counseling a conscience-stricken parishioner, mediating a dispute, or exhorting idle yeomen and gentry to find and practice a calling, the rural minister weaves his presence and his person into the fabric of village life.[3] To follow this ideal himself, Herbert did indeed forsake the bustling courtly world, "the way that takes the town" ("Affliction" [I], *W,* 47, l. 38), but only to immerse himself in a village world of equally intense social activity and, for him, far greater responsibility.

Furthermore, strong evidence in Herbert's poetry suggests that he

2. For a fuller discussion of Herbert's asceticism, see Richard Strier, "George Herbert and the World."

3. For examples of this extensive activity, see Herbert's description of pastoral duties throughout *The Countrey Parson,* especially in chapters 7 (preaching); 5, 15, 24, and 34 (comforting); 8 (mediating); and 32 (exhorting to a calling). See also my discussion of Herbert's pastoral vision in my chapter 5, above.

felt deep ambivalence about the established church of his day as a secure bastion of godliness. His poetic treatments of the church's current condition seem at times to contradict each other, and they in fact lean toward the negative. On the one hand, as we have already seen, "The British Church" (*W,* 109) serenely praises the establishment as uniquely preserved in its ecclesiastical purity. Yet we have noted its opposite number in the Blakean anguish of "Church-rents and schisms" (*W,* 140) at the diseased state of Christendom:

> Brave rose (alas!) where art thou? in the chair
> Where thou didst lately so triumph and shine
> A worm doth sit, whose many feet and hair
> Are the more foul, the more thou wert divine.
> ·
>   Only shreds of thee
> And those all bitten, in thy chair I see.
> ·
>   O Mother deare and kinde,
> Where shall I get me eyes enough to weep,
> As many eyes as starres?
>   (ll. 1–4, 9–10, 24–26)

Here are loss, infection, disgust, near-hysteria. "Debates and fretting jealousies" (l. 16) have done their work; "Your health and beautie both began to break" (l. 20). The "deare Mother" may be dying.

Indeed, "The British Church" is notably outnumbered by poems that lament the decline not only of Christendom in general but also of the British church in particular, even to the point of dreading its impending demise. Along with "Church-rents and schisms," "Decay" and "Whitsunday" (*W,* 99, 59) seem to include England when mourning the present ravages of institutional and spiritual decline in "Asia," Europe, and "Africk." Moreover "The World" (*W,* 84) predicts that inevitably "Sinne and Death" will destroy the church's entire frame before Christ's return and the Last Judgment.

The poem most specifically—and urgently—pessimistic about the ravages of "Sinne and Death" in England is "The Church Militant" (*W,* 190–98). This long didactic prophecy, written before Herbert took deacon's orders in 1624 (*W,* 543), asserts that the "late reformation" (l. 226) in Europe and England is fading rapidly, so that now

Religion stands on tip-toe in our land,
Readie to passe to the *American* strand.
When height of malice, and prodigious lusts,
Impudent sinning, witchcrafts, and distrusts
(The marks of future bane) shall fill our cup
Unto the brimme, and make our measure up;
When *Sein* shall swallow *Tiber,* and the *Thames*
By letting in them both, pollutes her streams:
When *Italie* of us shall have her will,
And all her calendar of sinnes fulfill;

. . . .

Then shall Religion to *America* flee
                    (ll. 235–44, 247)

Herbert's national church, no longer a "double-moated" sanctuary, instead seems doomed to be overwhelmed by papal corruption, and it is already backsliding from the reformed faith toward Rome. In such grim circumstances, the godly poise themselves to flee for the new world.

The question of whether Herbert sympathized with "the Great Migration" led by John Winthrop to Massachusetts Bay in 1630 is a fascinating one. "The Church Militant" itself cannot refer directly to the migration, since Herbert wrote it as early as 1619 and no later than 1624. However, Herbert completed *The Temple* in 1633, and by then he probably knew of the Puritan expedition. Thus his decision to leave "The Church Militant" intact, with its notorious mention of "the *American* strand," might suggest some sympathy with the "errand into the wilderness," insofar as it seemed to confirm his theory of religion's westward flight from corrupt England. Doubtless the New England colonists saw Herbert as a kindred spirit. They frequently quoted "The Church Militant" as a prophecy—though they usually ignored the lines predicting that the Americans "have their period also and their times / Both for their vertuous actions and their crimes" (ll. 261–62).[4] More certainly, as we have noted, the Laudian regime seems to have suspected Herbert's sympathy with New England; as we have noted, in 1633, the vice-chancellor of Cambridge, which was by then under

4. See Sacvan Bercovitch, *The Puritan Origins of the American Self,* 104–5.

Laud's control, nearly refused to license *The Temple* because "The Church Militant" contained those suggestive lines (*W*, 546–47).

In any case, if Herbert held these pessimistic views at the time of taking orders, it is highly unlikely that he embraced the clerical life as a permanent withdrawal into an otherworldly haven of rest and order. In fact, the pessimism of "The Church Militant" raises quite a different question about his motives: why would he so nearly consign his church to destruction, and then enter its service? Fifteen years before John Lilburne called God's elect to "come out" of the irredeemably corrupt "English Babylon" (and four years *after* a shipload of separatists actually did so on the "American strand" at Plymouth Plantation), Herbert took deacon's orders, apparently disturbed by some of the very trends that enflamed the Puritans. If Amy Charles is correct that Herbert composed "The Church Militant" before 1619, then he held these pessimistic ecclesiastical views nearly all his adult life, even while defending episcopacy against the Puritans, serving faithfully as a parson, and writing the most quoted of poems praising his church's *via media*.[5]

However, this seeming contradiction between optimistic nationalism and apocalyptic pessimism becomes far less stark when we look more precisely to the sources of these attitudes. For even at his most adulatory, Herbert never claims that the Church of England is the best of all churches in actual practice, but rather that it is in theory the best of all ecclesiastical ideals. Indeed, his pessimism can be explained in large part as his disappointment in the present-day church for not fulfilling its Elizabethan promise. As much as Herbert decries the imminent triumph of sin and the Roman "Antichrist" (l. 206) in "The Church Militant," he does not blame the coming national apostasy on the British church's distinctive principles of royal supremacy, episcopal government, and church-state union. Indeed, he praises England for at least "[g]iving the Church a crown to keep her state" (l. 90), which, as Malcolm Mackenzie Ross and Richard Strier both note, is "good

5. For the "English Babylon," see John Lilburne, *Come out of her my people*, title page. For the dating of "The Church Militant," see *W*, 543, and Charles, *A Life of George Herbert*, 82. Since "The British Church" appears only in the Bodleian manuscript and in those after it, Herbert probably wrote it after he wrote "The Church Militant." See *W*, 109, textual note.

Hooker."[6] Instead, Herbert sees this church structure—*if* guarded by a godly monarch and Parliament, overseen by godly bishops, and meticulously maintained and expanded by a brotherhood of godly parsons—as the plan most likely to advance the Reformation and save the commonwealth. He can mourn its departing (or departed) glory only because he retains a vision of that glory in his mind's eye. And the ecclesiastical and social order that he mourns he can also hope to restore.

Herbert and the Tudor Godly Commonwealth

Herbert's model for such social edification and reconstruction is essentially that of the Tudor commonwealth. This model, though established and promulgated through *The Book of Homilies* under Edward VI and Elizabeth, was first articulated in England by two increasingly Protestant humanists of the Henrician Reformation, Thomas Starkey and Thomas Cranmer. Starkey's *A Dialogue Between Reginald Pole and Thomas Lupset,* which was not published until modern times, enjoyed major influence in manuscript form on later Henrician social theory, and most significantly on Cranmer, who under Edward VI sought to put Starkey's program into action. In Starkey's *Dialogue,* Lupset defines the guiding principle of the well-ordered Christian nation, where "all labours, business and travail, of wise men handled, in matters of the common weal, are referred to this end and purpose: that the whole body of the commonality may live in quietness and tranquility, every part doing his office and duty, and so (as much as the nature of men will suffer) all to attain to their natural perfection."[7] The anonymous author of *The Homily of Obedience* explains that the order of this perfect social body is innately hierarchical, since "every degree of people in their vocation, calling and office, hath appointed unto them their duty: . . . some are in high degree, some in low, some Kings and Princes, some inferiours and subiects, Priests, and lay men, masters and servants, fathers and children, husbands

---

6. See Ross, *Poetry and Dogma: The Transformation of Eucharistic Symbols in Seventeenth-Century English Literature,* 146; and Strier, "George Herbert and the World," 233.
7. *Dialogue,* 24–25.

and wives, rich and poor, and *every one haue need of other*" (*BH* 1:69, emphasis mine).

Like Hooker after them, these writers appropriate the New Testament ecclesiastical metaphor of the church as "the body" and apply it to the nation as a whole, making the well-ordered church identical with the well-ordered state. Hooker's claim that "the church . . . is a Society" means more precisely that the church is the only society, or rather that political society at large constitutes the church.[8] We see this fusion clearly in *The Countrey Parson* itself, where Herbert states in the passage quoted above that the Christian has "no title" to either his heavenly or his earthly country "except he do good to both" (*W*, 239). Ecclesiastical membership becomes a condition of citizenship, and vice versa, while Christian charity is expressed, at least ideally, by the quiet and faithful discharge of one's calling within the earthly commonwealth.

Thus, as John N. Wall, Jr., writes, Protestant humanist social theory both departs from and preserves the medieval synthesis: "This [humanist] vision . . . of an ordered, hierarchical society, in imitation of God's self-revelation in the order of nature . . . was radical, in that it substituted worldly activity aimed at changing society for the passive devotion typical of medieval images of the Christian life. At the same time, it was conservative, in that it sought no major change in the structure of society, only the perfection of a structure implicit in the existing state of affairs."[9] If we grasp this earthly orientation of the Tudor church, we understand to a great degree how Herbert's ecclesiastical ideals differ from those of the Laudian party with whom Walton aligns him. For while Walton richly details "the excellencies of the active part" of Herbert's life, this activity consists almost entirely of Herbert's observing the many feasts, rites, and outward ceremonies of the church and explaining them to his congregation.[10] In other words, Walton's *Life* nearly equates holy activity with liturgical activity. In contrast, Herbert's pastoral manual, while clearly advocating litur-

8. See George H. Sabine, *A History of Political Theory*, 441.

9. Wall, "Godly and Fruitfull Lessons," in John E. Booty, ed., *The Godly Kingdom of Tudor England*, 67.

10. *Lives*, 307. See 295–307 for Walton's description of Herbert's liturgical diligence.

gical worship, mainly stresses the parson's involvement in the mundane affairs of his people's existence. Like the Tudor humanists, Herbert wishes to transform his parish, and indeed all of England, by permeating and perfecting established social structures with reformed faith and practice. Walton's Herbert sanctifies the community mainly by bringing them within the physical and liturgical structures of the church; Herbert's parson edifies the community at least as much outside these structures as within them.

Herbert's most detailed statement of this Protestant humanist social vision appears in chapter 32 of *The Countrey Parson,* "The Parson's Surveys" (*W,* 274–78). We have discussed this passage as it reveals Herbert's extensive plans for building up the church; from our present perspective, we see that these plans are just as much intended to build up the commonwealth, since the best interests of church and state are, for Herbert, identical. The parson ensures that everyone in his cure, whether yeoman, gentleman, or nobleman, finds "ingenuous and fit employment" that benefits first family, then neighbors, then "Village or Parish" (note the practical identity between secular and sacred jurisdictions), and ultimately the nation at large.

Herbert is particularly concerned that gentlemen and heirs of great houses fulfill their God-given role of conscientious, benevolent leadership both locally and nationally. His parson exhorts these men to serve not only as justices of the peace—"no Common-wealth . . . hath a braver Institution," he writes—but also as members of Parliament. "There is no School to a Parliament," he exclaims, and in his enthusiasm he prescribes behavior far beyond the power of any country parson to supervise: the rural M.P. "must not only be a morning man, but at committees also; for there the particulars are exactly discussed, which are brought from thence to the House but in generall." Regarding the court Herbert is not so enthusiastic; his country gentleman may go "sometimes," but soberly, as to "the eminent place both of good and ill." These words do not seem those of an ascetic hostile to earthly activity. Neither, politically, do they seem those of a Caroline absolutist exasperated with Parliament.

Clearly, the parson still accepts the social hierarchy and the stratification of "callings" that it implies. However, he abides no slackers in the great social chain, reserving his sternest exhortations for the idle "gallants" and "younger Brothers" of the upper classes. To these dangerously "loose" members of the body politic, who "unlawfully" spend their days "dressing, Complementing, visiting, and sporting," the parson commends instead the study of civil law, mathematics ("the only wonder-working knowledge"), fortification, and navigation, all of which benefit the nation. The more adventurous, he says, should channel their energies into the "noble" and "religious imployment" of colonization across the seas, or of traveling "into *Germany,* and *France,* and observing the Artifices, and Manufactures there" in order to "transplant them hither . . . to our Countrey's advantage."

To find such a specific social blueprint in a pastoral manual is surprising only if we had assumed that a parson's calling precludes concern for government, industry, class relations, and national security. But to Herbert's parson, such exhortations to public utility and mutual responsibility are required by his prophetic role. He is "a lover of and exciter to justice in all things, even as *John the Baptist* squared out to every one . . . what to do. . . . [A]s the Husbandman labours for [the gentleman], so must [the gentleman] fight for, and defend [the husbandman], when occasion calls. This is the duty of each to other, which they ought to fulfill." "Each to other," the watchwords of the Tudor commonwealth, bind the unequal classes with equally strong bonds of obligation. The parson, as God's "Vicegerent" (*W,* 225), works to keep "the whole body" in proper health, each member productive in his place.

However, as important as this divinely ordained social cohesion is to Herbert, it serves the yet greater end of advancing the church. True to his Elizabethan roots, Herbert believes that the progress of the Protestant faith is bound up with England's national destiny. In "The Church Militant," Herbert explains more specifically how the "new Plantations" can be considered a "religious imployment." Their colonization, and the resulting technical advancement of the colonized peoples, will pave the way west for the gospel. He writes that throughout church history, imperial

> Prowesse and Arts did tame
> And tune mens hearts against the Gospel came:
> Which using, and not fearing skill in th'one,

> Or strength in th'other, did erect her throne.
>
> ·
>
> Strength levels grounds, Art makes a garden there;
> Then showres Religion, and makes all to bear.
>
> (ll. 75–79, 87–88)

Although, as we will see, "The Church Militant" speaks sharply against imperialist greed, Herbert does not hesitate to claim that in God's providence even the colonists' evil motives and actions create inroads for God's kingdom. He even credits the conquering forces of Spain with leveling such a path in South America (l. 265).

This close linkage between colonial and spiritual purposes can be found expressed more positively by John Donne in his 1622 sermon to the Virginia Company. Preaching on Acts 1:8, he casts London as a new Jerusalem, from which the Protestant colonists go out as ambassadors of King James and apostles of King Jesus to the peoples in the "uttermost part of the earth." "Preach to them Doctrinally," he exhorts, "preach to them Practically; Enamore them with your *Iustice,* and, (as farre as may consist with your security) your *Civilitie* but inflame them with your *Religion.* Bring them to *love* and *Reverence* the name of that King, that sends you to teach them the wayes of *Civilitie* in this world, but to *feare* and adore the Name of that *King of Kings,* that sends men to teach them the waies of Religion, for the next world."[11] Donne acknowledges no possible conflict of interest between earthly and heavenly orders.

Yet he probably crossed King James's will in delivering this sermon. By November 1622, Donne must have known that the Virginia Company was under heavy attack from the King's Council and the king himself. Indeed, a year and a half later, James effectively dissolved the company by royal prerogative, forbidding the Parliament even to consider the matter. One member of that Parliament of 1624 was George Herbert himself, and two of the men most seriously damaged financially and personally by the company's dissolution were Herbert's stepfather, Sir John Danvers, and Herbert's famous kindred spirit, Nicholas Ferrar.[12] Since it is highly unlikely that a cathedral dean like Donne

---

11. *Sermons* 4:280.
12. Charles, *A Life of George Herbert,* 108–10.

held a financial interest in Virginia, his sermon's possibly controversial timing emphasizes his strong belief in transplanting to America English "Civilitie" and "Religion"—the social order and the faith that upheld it.

Herbert's Antielitism

The affair of the Virginia Company also helps to explain why Herbert's explicit pastoral interest in the health of the body politic is accompanied by an unremitting hostility to the aristocratic and mercantile values of the court and the exchange. This hostility had appeared already in "The Church Militant," where he denounced imperialist colonial profiteering as both greedy and ironically futile:

> For gold and grace did never yet agree:
> Religion alwaies sides with povertie.
> We think we rob them, but we think amisse:
> We are more poore, and they more rich by this.
> (ll. 251–54)

It is likely that the Virginia Company's dissolution revolted Herbert even more, since, from his perspective, by royal fiat the colony had been wrested from the oversight of religious and public-minded men and reduced to a mere mercantile adventure.

This, at least, was the view held by Ferrar, Danvers, and Arthur Woodnoth, who blamed the dissolution on the Crown and the "Spanish interest" at court.[13] Ironically, Herbert seems to have been badly mistaken about the colony's affairs. There is strong evidence that despite their good intentions, Ferrar, Danvers, and their partners seriously mismanaged the settling and provisioning of Jamestown, thus indirectly causing hundreds of deaths and giving the king and council good cause to act.[14] However, it is Herbert's probable beliefs about the enterprise, not its actual history, that concern us here. Indeed,

13. Ibid., 109.
14. See Wesley Frank Craven, *Dissolution of the Virginia Company: The Failure of a Colonial Experiment*, 302–3.

Herbert's pro-Parliamentary and anticourt feelings, or at least his close connections to those who held them, probably did as much to end his hopes for secular advancement as did the deaths of his benefactors. The social vision enunciated in *The Countrey Parson,* while monarchist and hierarchical in a limited, Elizabethan sense, is not absolutist, indeed is antiabsolutist, and hence a distinct liability for any would-be Stuart courtier.

This antielitism, which we find in *The Countrey Parson*'s stress on the equality of all before God's laws, is expressed more radically in the lyrics of "The Church," where Herbert identifies himself repeatedly with the simple, poor, and rude. In "Redemption" (*W,* 40), the speaker recounts how he mistakenly adopted elitist expectations about the "rich Lord" to whom he is a "tenant." Quite naturally he sought the lord first at "his manour" in heaven, where he was told that the lord had gone "to take possession" of "some land, which he had dearly bought / Long since on earth" (ll. 1–8). Since the suitor knew the lord's "great birth," he returned immediately and sought him in correspondingly "great resorts"—"cities, theatres, gardens, parks, and courts." The search was long and fruitless until by chance he "heard a ragged noise and mirth / Of theeves and murderers. There," to the speaker's astonishment, "I him espied, / Who straight, Your suit is granted, said, & died" (ll. 9–14). As Richard Strier points out, the narrator is stunned because "he finds his lord in neither a place nor a condition suitable to his lord's 'great birth.' He finds him in totally unlikely and unsuitable company performing a totally unlikely and unsuitable action—dying. . . . The conception of the most glorious and powerful Being in the universe, the King of Kings, dying a humiliating death among 'theeves and murderers' violates decorum in a fundamental way."[15] Like the Magi who go first to Herod's court to find the newborn King of the Jews, the narrator of "Redemption" nearly misses the revelation of God's saving grace because he is bound to earthly notions of hierarchy.

We find similar violations of decorum scattered throughout other lyrics. In "The Storm" and "Gratefulnesse," Herbert casts himself as

15. *Love Known,* 57.

an unmannered beggar thrusting his needs brazenly on his great Lord. "The Storm" (*W,* 132) affirms that

> A throbbing conscience spurred by remorse
>   Hath a strange force:
> It quits the earth, and mounting more and more,
> Dares to assault thee, and beseige thy doore.
>
> There it stands knocking, to thy musick's wrong,
>   And drowns the song.
> Glorie and honour are set by, till it
>   An answer get.
>   (ll. 9–16)

In both the worldly and the spiritual senses, a man under conviction of sin "has no pride." His overwhelming sense of shame causes him shamelessly to force himself on even the person highest above him in rank.

"Gratefulnesse" (*W,* 124), though earlier in "The Church," carries this scene even further. Once God has answered these "[p]erpetual knockings at [his] doore" and admitted the penitent, He must endure his blubbering—"[t]ears sullying thy transparent rooms"—and provide "gift upon gift," for "much would have more, / And comes" (ll. 13–16). This shameless beggar will keep asking as long as he keeps getting. Amazingly, God reacts to this crude opportunist with fond delight. Although the beggar, now identified as "us," has drowned out God's heavenly music,

> This notwithstanding, thou wentst on,
> And didst allow us all our noise:
> Nay, thou hast made a sigh and grone
>   Thy joyes.
>   (ll. 17–20)

No doubt God has

>   still above
> Much better tunes, then grones can make;
> But that these countrey-aires thy love
>   Did take.
>   (ll. 21–24)

This Lord, like a loving father, cherishes the slightest show of repentance or progress in his people. Though he easily could choose to hear better music than coarse "countrey-aires," these groans "take his love" because they come from the heart.

Ironically, for all his trouble God gets more trouble—or so it seems. The beggar is sure of the Lord's indulgence,

> Wherefore I crie, and crie again;
> And in no quiet canst thou be,
> Till I a thankfull heart obtain
>   Of thee . . .
>   (ll. 25-28)

Although expressed as rude bawling, the beggar's demands are music to God's ears because he asks for that which God most wants to give him—"a thankfull heart." As in "Prayer" (II), God is of "an easie quick accesse" for the broken and contrite who long to please him more than themselves. So we can link "The Storm" and "Gratefulnesse" to Herbert's statement in *The Countrey Parson* that "evident miseries have a naturall priviledge, and exemption from all law" (*W,* 245)— or, as I termed it earlier, "the divine right of human need." By identifying himself so strongly with the poor and needy as a spiritual metaphor, Herbert puts himself on a level with the most wretched of his parish on the issues that matter most to a country parson—repentance, faith, and practice.

Furthermore, even when Herbert seems most hostile to the thick-headed foolishness of the country folk, he is working a rhetorical turn. "Miserie" (*W,* 100–102), easily one of Herbert's most pessimistic poems, reads like the long and bitter complaint of a rejected curate. The first stanza sarcastically introduces "Man" as an idiot chanting his drunken "countrey-aire":

> His house still burns, and yet he still doth sing,
> *Man is but grasse,*
> *He knows it, fill the glasse.*
>   (ll. 4–6)

The speaker's complaint grows more vitriolic with each stanza, giving fuller and fuller vent to his disgust:

> Man cannot serve thee; let him go,
> And serve the swine: there, there is his delight:
> He doth not like this vertue, no;
> Give him his dirt to wallow in all night:
> These Preachers make
> His head to shoot and ake.
>   (ll. 43–48)

Sounding every bit like a fastidious parson whose sermons are mocked and whose sensibilities are assaulted by filthy parishioners, the speaker concludes that man, once a "treasure" before sin, is now

> A lump of flesh, without a foot or wing
> To raise him to a glimpse of blisse:
> A sick toss'd vessel, dashing on each thing;
> Nay, his own shelf:
>   (ll. 73–77)

These images of deformity, nausea, and destruction pile one upon another and drive the reader to the striking reversal of the last line: "My God, I mean myself" (l. 78). Except in two lines (34 and 39) buried in the center of the poem, the speaker has stood above the wicked throughout the poem, pointing accusingly at miserable man as "he" and "they." Here, in his final word, the indignant "Preacher" turns the full force of his contempt on himself. Like Paul or Bunyan, he is "the chief of sinners." He has nothing on the bumpkins.

Turning to "Jordan" (I) (*W*, 56–57), we are back to Herbert's typically positive identification of himself with humble country people, and in this case, with their "countrey-aires." Eager to disentangle the pastoral from the "false hair," "enchanted groves," "course-spunne lines," and "vails" of allegory, he claims dryly that "Shepherds are honest people; let them sing" (l. 11). The courtly fictions of poets, says Herbert, put words and songs in shepherds' mouths that shepherds would never actually use. They, like true pastors (and with Herbert the association is unavoidable) are straightforward men who speak their hearts and minds. They show not art, but their meaning. Thus they represent the plain style of Herbert's own "pastoral" poetry—written by a pastor to lead a flock to salvation—which plainly says, "My God, My King" (l. 15).

We may at this point usefully compare Herbert's egalitarian likening of himself to shepherds with Andrewes's treatment of shepherds in his Fourteenth Nativity Sermon, preached before King James. Contrasting the angels' appearance to the shepherds with the star's appearance to the wise men, Andrewes says that the sign of the star is by far the greater:

> The other [sign] (of the Shepheards) was a poore one: poore and meane. This (of the Wise men) a Signe of some State: high and heavenly. . . . [U]pon this [sign] came there to Hierusalem (not a rout of Shepheards, but) a troope of Great Persons. This [sign of the star] is for all. But there is yet more grace offered to some in particular. The Shepheards were a sort of poore simple men altogether unlearned; But, heer come a troope of men of great Place, . . . great Learned men. This (lo) falls somewhat to the Place and Presence, that will be glad to heare it . . . ; that wealth, worth, or wisedome have their parts in Christs birth. It is not only *Stella Gentium* [star of the peoples], but *Stella Magorum,* the Great Mens, the Wise Mens Starr, this.[16]

This indeed is preaching to one's audience. Andrewes displays a special willingness to carry the privileges of "wealth, worth, and wisedome" over into the spiritual realm. The God who sends *Stella Magorum* offers special grace to great men, ordering the cosmos according to the affairs of kings and scholars. He hardly seems the kind of God who would ignore all the heavenly music to hear a beggar groan.

Yet, just as Herbert would perpetuate the church hierarchy that he criticizes, he also considers a divinely ordained class structure to be the only reasonable pattern for society. "All equal are *within* the churches gate," he warns the lordly in "The Church-porch" (*W,* 22, l. 408, emphasis mine); but outside the gate, social hierarchy still obtains.[17] Still, at least by the mid-1620s, Herbert had become revolted by the indolence and vain display of the gentry, nobility, and court, behavior sanctioned and even necessitated by the increasingly corrupt patronage system.[18] Herbert knew that one who hopes to win favor

16. *XCVI Sermons,* 130.
17. See Strier, "George Herbert and the World," 230.
18. Cristina Malcolmson discusses Herbert's adversarial relationship to this system of patronage in "Society and Self-Definition," 156–57. As to dating the poems of "The Church," this enterprise is of course largely speculative, but Amy Charles seems correct in concluding that the lyrics that lament Herbert's lack of employment were written

and fortune by wit, fine dress, or flattery—as he himself had tried to do in his Cambridge days—had to neglect the mundane details of socially edifying employment, whether as Lord Chancellor, member of Parliament, estate manager, village justice—or even as a clergyman. As we saw in chapter 5, Herbert reserves some of his most scathing language for chaplains who flatter their noble patrons and thus neglect their prophetic role, comparing them to Judas (*W,* 226). While Herbert does not utterly reject patronage, he criticizes its grave and growing abuses, which weaken or destroy the mutual bonds of respect and responsibility that knit together the social hierarchy.

Herbert's critique of patronage is remarkable for two reasons. First, these views distance him yet further from the Caroline court and the party of Laud, who personally owed much of his advancement in the church to the favor of that most notorious Stuart patron, the Duke of Buckingham.[19] Second, Herbert's views are remarkable because, while conservative in their call for a return to the founding "middle way" of Elizabethan England, they sound potentially revolutionary in their immediate context: such a return would overthrow Stuart absolutist theory and practice.

Herbert's Individualism and the Lyric Genre

Despite the decidedly political edge of such statements, few of Herbert's readers have found a social vision expressed in the main body of his poetry, "The Church." Indeed, until recently the opinion of Herbert's turn-of-the-century editor, George Herbert Palmer, has prevailed:

> In religion Herbert, with most of the devout men of his time . . . is . . . an individualist. The relations between God and his soul are what interest him. . . . Any notion of dedicating himself to [others'] welfare is foreign to him. Perhaps his poem THE WINDOWS comes nearest to expressing something like human responsibility. But such moods are rare. Usually his responsibility

---

before he took deacon's orders in 1624. See Charles, *A Life of George Herbert,* 81–82, 112–13. It is not unlikely that he was developing contempt for courtly values even before his final loss of "court-hopes"; yet after making the final break by taking deacon's and priest's orders, his contempt for and rejection of those values probably grew to find their fullest expression in the later poems and *The Countrey Parson.*

19. Trevor-Roper, *Laud,* 52, 60–61.

is to God alone; and this, passionately uttered in AARON and THE PRIEST-
HOOD, is the farthest point to which his self-centered piety carried his verse.
The mystic forgets himself in the thought of God; the philanthropist, in the
thought of human needs. To Herbert—at least to the poet Herbert—the per-
sonal relationship of the soul to God is the one matter of consequence.[20]

As one-sided as such a conclusion may seem in the light of *The Coun-
trey Parson,* we should not dismiss it lightly, for some more careful
readers of Herbert's work have shared it—and with some cause.[21]
Few of the poems in "The Church" deal with church or society as a
body of people. Instead, nearly all portray the individual, as Palmer
says, in personal conversation with God.

Yet integration of "The Church"'s lyrics into the social vision of
The Countrey Parson, while not initially easy, is indeed possible if we
bear in mind the generic differences of the two works. The pastoral
manual is straightforward didactic prose, and it therefore teaches by
explicit precept how the pastor should edify church and society. On
the other hand, the poems in "The Church" belong to the genre of
personal devotional lyric, which Earl Miner calls a "private mode"
virtually defined as individual, intimate expression to God. However,
it is a mistake to hear the individual voice of the lyric speaker as ex-
cluding other voices. Indeed, as Barbara Kiefer Lewalski has written,
this voice is probably inclusive. She argues that "the great biblical
model" for the religious lyric is the psalmist, whose voice frequently
includes all the grieving or rejoicing voices of God's people.[22]

Chana Bloch has demonstrated that throughout "The Church" Her-
bert depends heavily on scripture, and especially on the Psalms, for a
language that "prevails against the pretensions of human speech."
Even more importantly, Herbert also turns to the Bible for specific
strategems and scenarios that interpret his experience. For example,
Bloch writes:

> The speaker of "The Quip" [*W,* 110–11] makes no attempt to match the
> scoffers' repartee with the "quick returns of courtesie and wit" ["The Pearl.

20. Palmer, ed., *The Life and Works of George Herbert* 2:111.
21. Including Malcolm Mackenzie Ross. See Ross, *Poetry and Dogma,* 147–48.
22. For the "private mode," see Miner, *The Metaphysical Mode from Donne to Cowley,*
3–47. For the Psalmist as model, see Lewalski, *Protestant Poetics,* 4.

Matth. xiii.45," W, 88–89, l. 12], as we might expect him to do. He declines to speak in his own defense, and even in declining he does not choose his own words. His "quip," repeated four times over—"But thou shalt answer, Lord, for me"—is a quotation from one of the penitential psalms: "For in thee, O Lord, have I put my trust: thou shalt answer for me, O Lord my God" (Ps. 38:15). . . . [T]he psalm verse . . . stands emphatically apart from the taunting voices of the world, refusing to engage them on their own terms but appealing instead to a different order of reality.

Bloch notes that other poems besides "The Quip" depend on the Psalms in similar ways: "Jordan" (I) ("My God, My King"), "The Posie" ("Lesse then the least / Of all Gods mercies"), and "The Forerunners" ("Thou art still my God").[23]

Even though many of the lyrics do not include such explicit psalmic references as refrains, the great emotional range of "The Church" enables the reader to treat the lyrics much as Calvin does the Psalms—as "An Anatomy of all the Parts of the Soul: for there is not an emotion of which anyone can be conscious that is not represented here as in a mirror."[24] While Herbert's poems, like the Psalms, are often marked by the author's particular circumstances, they nevertheless invite us to read ourselves into the text.

"The Church," Places, and Power

From this generic perspective we can better understand the public purpose of "The Church." In chapter 5 we noted, with Camille Slights, that these lyrics are unified by a didactic strategy—one that generally works, not by stating explicit precepts, but by dramatizing crucial scenes along the Protestant spiritual pilgrimage, scenes in which the reader can find his experience mirrored and thereby gain comfort or learn vicarious lessons.[25] The individual speaker of the poems, while not the Protestant Everyman, nevertheless is typical of the "church" as a whole—that is, the invisible church, the entire body of the elect struggling to trust God in the face of a hostile world. Furthermore, these lyrics often portray virtues and vices that contribute, respec-

23. "Spelling the Word: Herbert's Reading of the Bible," 17–18.
24. John Calvin, *Commentary on the Book of Psalms*, xxxvi–xxxvii.
25. *Casuistical Tradition*, 3, 186, 194–95.

tively, to societal edification or disintegration. So it is important that Herbert's social consciousness appears most prominently throughout "The Church" in the poems dealing with his best-known "affliction": his sense of exclusion from a meaningful "place" in the body politic.

Herbert's ideally virtuous "common-wealths-man" is personified in "Constancie" (*W,* 72–73). This exemplar is praised above all because he knows his position in the social order and unflinchingly fulfills the duties incumbent on that position: he is "To God, his neighbor, and himself most true"; "neither force nor fawning can / Unpinne, or wrench [him] from giving all their due"; and "What place or person calls for, he doth pay" (ll. 3–5, 15). This character sketch recognizes certain divinely ordained inequalities in the commonwealth, but it assumes an equality of obligation up and down that scale—the "each to other" of Starkey's *Dialogue* and of *The Countrey Parson* itself. This universal "Mark-man" could be a yeoman bound to show deference to his local lord or a King's Justice obligated to uphold a poor man's right against the encroachment of the mighty. The poem also hints at the constant possibility of social collapse, so imminent in "The Church Militant": this man of duty and place knows how apt the "wide world" is to "runne bias from his will," but "though men fail him, yet his part doth play" (ll. 32, 30).

In contrast, we find "Constancie's" relation of self to society ironically reversed in "Employment" (II) and "Affliction" (I) (*W,* 78–79, 46–48). Here it is the "wide world" that officiously works at its business, while the speaker feels the pain of his uselessness and exclusion. The "Mark-man's" calm and confident sense of "place" is nowhere to be found. Indeed, these lyrics lament this exclusion in similar terms:

> Oh that I were an Orenge-tree
> > That busie plant!
> Then should I ever laden be,
> > And never want
> Some fruit for him that dressed me . . .
> > ("Employment" [II], ll. 21–25)

> Now I am here, what thou [God] wilt do with me
> > None of my books will show:
> I reade, and sigh, and wish I were a tree;

>   For sure then I should grow
>   To fruit or shade: at least some bird would trust
>   Her houshold to me, and I should be just.
>   ("Affliction" [I], ll. 55–60)

In Herbert's poignantly repeated wish we see his imagined relief from the psychic pain of his idleness. Trees, with their natural place in the order of things, produce their useful commodities without the agonized self-consciousness of human toil, especially the toil of the academic over his "lingring book" (l. 39).

Furthermore, the context of these lines reveals Herbert in the process of rejecting the courtly values that he had followed to this failure. These "court-hopes," though disappointed, still smoulder in his fiercely competitive, commercial language. "Employment" (II) claims cynically that

>   Life is a businesse, not good cheer;
>   Ever in warres.
>   The sunne still shineth there or here,
>   Whereas the starres
>   Watch an advantage to appeare.
>   (ll. 16–20)

Herbert likens the heavens to the Jacobean court, where his own "quick soul" had long watched for "an advantage to appeare" and had sought to "trade in courtesies and wit" (ll. 3–5). But to the budding courtier's dismay, "The Man is gone, / Before we do our wares unfold" (ll. 27– 28). Unawares, the vigilant courtly pitchman loses his goods —his full, mature potency—and must leave the corridors of power, his strategems thwarted. Herbert here expresses a despair made almost complete by the lines that follow: "So we freeze on, / Untill the grave increase our cold" (ll. 29–30). Because he does not cry out to God at the poem's end—an uncharacteristic and therefore striking departure for him—"Employment" (II) expresses without relief the desolation brought by pursuing a courtly place through competition and self-display.

"Affliction" (I), while expressing the same frustrated desire for courtly glory and using the same language of ambitious striving for a "place," pulls back from the final despair of "Employment" (II) by addressing its complaint to God. Throughout the lyric, Herbert half-confronts and half-avoids his past misreadings of God's character.[26] He acknowledges that in his youth he was foolish to think of the Lord as a mere "King of pleasures" presiding over a courtly "world of mirth" (ll. 13, 12). However, until the final lines he speaks not as a penitent, but as a well-meaning dupe, and to God as his seducer. From this temporarily warped perspective he sees all of God's gifts—the early joys, the "Academick praise" (l. 45)—as baits to false optimism. God has "enticed" (l. 1) Herbert's heart, raising his expectations of smooth spiritual and political advancement, so that "argu'd into hopes, my thoughts reserved / No place for grief or fear" (ll. 15–16). Then God cruelly "didst betray" (l. 39) him to disease and banishment in academe. The passionate, heartbroken reversal of the concluding couplet breaks this spell of bitterness while heightening the pathos of exclusion: "Ah my deare God! though I am clean forgot, / Let me not love thee, if I love thee not" (ll. 65–66).

This paradoxical ending fuses the language of unrequited love with that of disappointed courtiership. Yet it transcends both of these vocabularies by acknowledging how thoroughly inadequate, even dangerous, his analogies have been. Throughout the poem he has struggled to understand the nature of his early "love" for God, but he has found that this love was shot through with the "fiercenesse" of self-interest. He concludes by pleading that God would enable him to "love" Him in a manner worthy of the name—with a love that depends not on uncertain hopes and human circumstances, but on the sure ground of God's re-creative, sovereign grace. The fact that this plea is in the negative—that Herbert is willing to be excluded utterly from human and divine benefits rather than be a hypocrite—underlines his longing for a pure and simple love, free from mercenary motives.[27]

26. Helen Vendler has noted instructively that "Affliction" (I) "depends on a series of inconsistent metaphors for a single phenomenon, God's treatment of his creature." In the poem, Herbert portrays God variously as a seducer, a sovereign, an enchanter, a wage-paying master; then as a sender of sickness and famine, a cruel physician, and even a murderer. See Vendler, *The Poetry of George Herbert,* 42.

27. My view parallels that of Barbara Leah Harman, who writes that the speaker of "Affliction" (I) "would rather be forgotten than be false" with God. See Harman, "George Herbert's 'Affliction' (I): The Limits of Representation," 267–85, especially 279.

The fear of being "clean forgot" appears also in "Employment" (I) (*W*, 57). This fear is in one sense even more pathetic here than in "Employment" (II) and "Affliction" (I) because Herbert feels excluded not only from the court but also from the whole created order:

> All things are busie; onely I
> Neither bring hony with the bees,
> Nor flowres to make that, nor the husbandrie
> To water these.
>
> I am no link of thy great chain,
> But all my companie is a weed.
>
> (ll. 17–22)

Yet this lament takes Herbert one step further in his redemptive rejection of "court-hopes." He is pleading no longer for secular glory as evidence of God's blessing, but for nothing more (or less) than lowly preferment in the kingdom of heaven:

> Lord place me in thy consort; give one strain
> To my poore reed.
>
> (ll. 23–24)

The conception of "place" expressed here differs fundamentally from that in the poems discussed above. Those value "place" on a scale of rank and power, the highest and strongest being best. Conversely, "Employment" (I) values "place" as mere inclusion in an overall harmony. The only joy sought is that which comes from playing one's part—any part—in an order that praises and pleases God. Unlike the pleasure of courtly superiority and conquest, this joy can be shared with fellow subjects, and with the divine Sovereign himself. Indeed it must be shared; for by implication the "one strain" of praise will please the heavenly King—and the true worshiper—only if it blends submissively with the rest of the heavenly "consort." To seek to raise one's strain above the others would be to spoil the harmony and therefore the unique joy of inclusion.

Herbert expresses this hard-earned and easily forgotten wisdom in "Submission" (*W*, 95):[28]

---

28. "The Church" deliberately portrays the Christian's relapses into worldly ambi-

How know I, if thou [God] shouldst me raise,
   That I should then raise thee?
Perhaps great places and thy praise
   Do not so well agree.

(ll. 13–16)

We have noted that in 1619 Herbert wrote in a flush of pride to his stepfather Danvers that the "dignity" of the Cambridge Orator's place —"the finest in the University"—had "no such earthiness in it, but it may well be joined with Heaven" (*W*, 369–70). In "Submission," he has come to abandon his hopes for the even finer place at court to which he thought the oratorship would lead. He has also come to admit that such a place might not have "joined" him with heaven, but rather cut him off from it.

However, "Submission" does not categorically deny the compatibility of "great place" and heavenly virtue. The court is, after all, "the eminent place *both* of good and ill" (*W*, 277, emphasis mine). However difficult it is to imagine a Stuart official obtaining a high position without practicing the flattering, deceitful "courtship" that Herbert found so spiritually deadly, Herbert seems to have believed it possible for rarely virtuous "Mark-men" to do so. They must be constant against the "force" and "fawning" of court life, its "ruffling windes," "glittering looks," "close tentations," and ever-changing fashions ("Constancie," *W*, 72, ll. 4, 7–8, 22). The tentative "perhaps" in line 15 of "Submission" suggests that "places" are not corrupt as such, but that men seek and use them corruptly. Herbert knows his particular weakness for the "close tentations" offered by power, and he has come to see his own exclusion from the royal graces as a deliverance from evil.

---

tion and ingratitude. The humble "Employment" (I) is soon followed by the bleak and bitter "Employment" (II), then eventually by the repentant "Submission," which in turn gives way to a number of angry complaints, most notably "The Collar" (*W*, 153–54). "The Flower" (*W*, 165–67) offers a maturer, more resolved understanding of the soul's mutability and utter dependence on God's grace—"We say amiss, / This or that is: / Thy word is all, if we could spell" (ll. 19–21)—yet even this celebration of God's love ends with an admonition to vigilance against "self-raising": "Who would be more, / Swelling through store, / Forfeit their Paradise by their pride" (ll. 47–49).

Herbert's Private and Public Vision

These poems of "place" and "employment" all teach, whether by positive or negative example, that a humble sense of office and duty in a larger social and metaphysical order is essential for individual happiness. The qualities of constancy, diligence, submission, and harmonious participation celebrated by these and many of Herbert's other lyrics are fundamentally social virtues, applying between persons. Throughout "The Church," the person with whom Herbert "has society" is primarily God himself; however, the inwardness of the lyrics need not and should not be read as indifference to human society. Rather, this stress on the individual's encounter with God can be consistent with the Protestant humanist program: personal conversion and private devotion are not only ends in themselves, but also prepare the Christian for service and make possible the combination of individuals into a commonwealth.

As Cranmer writes in his homily of "true, liuely, and Christian Faith," "true faith cannot be kept secret, but when occasion is offered, it will breake out, and shew itself by good workes. [It] cannot long bee idle: For as it is written, The iust man doeth liue by his faith. Hee neuer sleepeth nor is idle, when hee would wake, and be occupied" (*BH* 1:22–23). A later homilist, like Herbert himself in *The Countrey Parson,* attacks upper-class idleness in particular, and specifies how true inward devotion will "breake out" to affect the commonwealth as a whole:

> [E]uery one . . . ought . . . in some kind of labour to exercise himselfe . . . whether it be by gouerning the common weale publikely, or by bearing publike office or ministry, or by doing any common necessary affaires of his countrey, or by giving counsell, or by teaching and instructing others, or by what other meanes soeuer hee bee occupied, so that a profit and benefit redound thereof unto others, the same person is not to be accounted idle. (*BH* 2:250)

In chapter 3 we saw that Herbert's inward devotion in "Lent" finally produces his call, at the end of the poem, literally to feast the hungry poor at one's door. While such moments of explicit social awareness are rare in "The Church," nevertheless what is true locally of "Lent" may well be true of "The Church" as a unified whole. The same Tudor humanist notion—that a transformed spiritual and intellectual life will overflow naturally in good works of "profit and benefit unto others" —may provide the key to reconciling the private utterances of "The Church" with the public vision of *The Countrey Parson.*

However, while Herbert repeats and further articulates the Elizabethan mandate to build the godly commonwealth, we have already noted that he did not share the millenialist optimism of many sixteenth- and early seventeenth-century English Protestants, who generally believed in the inevitable, progressive triumph and permanence of their efforts.[29] William Lamont has demonstrated how John Foxe's enormously influential *Acts and Monuments* conditioned generations of Englishmen—not only separatist Puritans but also the cultural mainstream, including bishops, nobility, and monarchs themselves— to believe their nation destined to crush the Roman "Antichrist" and bring in the reign of Jesus Christ.[30] Conversely, Herbert predicts that Rome will prevail and force the flight of true religion to America.

A juxtaposition of Herbert's sturdy, if not quite full-blooded, humanism with his historical pessimism reveals the complexity of his mature attitude toward life in this world.[31] He was at once joyful and stoic; immersed in the private griefs and trials of a whole parish, yet intimate with no one but, perhaps, his wife and Ferrar; convinced of imminent collapse, but committed to enormous constructive effort; full of foreboding, and of hope. Few contemporaries of Herbert described this complex mentality as well as did New England's John Cotton: "There is another combination of virtues strangely mixed in every lively, holy Christian: and that is, diligence in worldly businesses, and yet deadness to the world. Such a mystery as none can read but they that know it."[32] While Cotton did not share Herbert's institutional pessimism, they did share this seasoned indifference to the earthly outcome of their labors. Herbert had loved the world and its

29. See Ernest Tuveson, *Millenium and Utopia: A Study in the Background of the Idea of Progress,* 75–85.

30. *Godly Rule,* 13–27; see especially 23–24.

31. See Ross, *Poetry and Dogma,* 135–57.

32. Cotton, as quoted in Perry Miller, ed., *The American Puritans: Their Prose and Poetry,* 171.

glories with fierce ambition, and, having had his advances rejected, he fell at times to loathing both the world and himself. However, in his brief maturity he seems to have learned to love both self and the world again, though differently, with "weaned affections"—to use another New England phrase—no longer for their own sakes, but for the sake of their Creator.[33]

Herbert would not set his heart on the institutional church that he loved, any more than he would on any other earthly institution or thing. He believed that in a world bound to decay no success is lasting, even the success of those who had settled and established the ecclesiastical order under Elizabeth. Reward and full success, he believed, will be realized only in heaven, where the diligent Christian's seemingly futile labors will be remembered by God and transformed into permanent, glorious gain. Beyond the confusion and collapse of the present and the disasters of the future lies complete divine restoration on "the last and lov'd, though dreadfull day" ("Home," *W*, 108, l. 58).

Yet in his own time, where most of Herbert's spiritual and social concern centered, his renewed sense of a calling to rebuild the church provided positive relief from the worst of his torments, as described in "Affliction" (IV) (*W*, 89–90):

> Broken in pieces all asunder,
> Lord, hunt me not,
> A thing forgot,
> Once a poore creature, now a wonder,
> A wonder tortur'd in the space
> Betwixt this world and that of grace.
> (ll. 1–6)

Herbert's ecclesiastical ideal gave him meaningful "employment" in which he would no longer be "forgot"; it also gave him a model for reintegrating his own fragmented inner "body politic," which seems to have mirrored disintegrating English society itself.[34] Because the brokenness of the old social order had so imprinted itself on him,

---

33. On "weaned affections" see Miller, *American Puritans,* 172.
34. See Ross, *Poetry and Dogma,* 137, 141.

Herbert could not seek personal restoration without seeking to restore that public order as well. He did not expect any human constructions or reconstructions to last forever. He only desired a space to comfort and encourage those who, like him, were diligent in this world for the sake of another.

Epilogue

Moderation . . . is not an halting betwixt two opinions, when the through-believing of one of them is necessary to salvation. . . . Nor is it lukewarmnesse in those things wherein Gods glory is concernd. . . . But it is a mixture of discretion and charity in ones judgement. . . . The lukewarm man eyes onely his own ends, and particular profit; the moderate man aims at the good of others, and unity of the Church. *Yet such moderate men are commonly crush'd betwixt the extreme parties on both sides.*
—Thomas Fuller, *The Holy State,* "Of Moderation."[1]

Answered questions may satisfy, but it is the unanswered and, most of all, the unanswerable, that fascinate. Some poets have died fascinatingly young—Sidney, Keats, and Shelley come to mind—and they seem the greater for having done so. Their precocious masterworks rise toward death like clifftops toward the sea; the eye may register the sudden fall, but the imagination traces the ascending ridge further up into mountains of thin air.

For Herbert, dying in 1633 at a youngish forty, the question is not only one of lost artistic potential—though it is that, too—but even more of his relation to the national upheaval that followed. Can we imagine him at forty-one, ordered by Canterbury to enforce Laud's neomedieval reforms and preach up the king's divine right? Yet can we imagine him at fifty-two, commanded by Parliament to abandon the Prayer Book or lose his church? Above all, can we imagine him at fifty-six, reacting to the king's death warrant, signed by Sir John Dan-

---

1. *The Holy State and the Profane State* 1:205–6.

vers, his sometime stepfather? No doubt the bad season would have made the poet sad, but would he, could he, have chosen sides?

There are to these questions the shadows of an answer—though not an answer itself—because history has provided a kind of understudy for George Herbert: Thomas Fuller, a younger contemporary (1608–1661) whose early theological and political trajectory closely paralleled Herbert's, but did not end abruptly in 1633. Instead, through the crisis years and into the Restoration, Fuller kept to the old Elizabethan middle way (or what was left of it), and he was repeatedly embraced and rejected by both sides in the conflict. His likeness to Herbert seems to have grown out of some uncannily similar associations and experiences. Like Herbert, Fuller seems best described as an "Old Conformist" churchman; he remained tenaciously loyal to episcopacy and the Prayer Book, but in points of doctrine he tended toward moderate Puritanism. Indeed, his best-known work, *The Holy State and the Profane State* (1642), names Elizabethan Calvinists William Whitaker and William Perkins as the exemplary divine and the ideal preacher, respectively.[2] Like Herbert, Fuller was a Cambridge man, and he benefited from the attentions of John Davenant, Herbert's ordaining bishop at Salisbury and Fuller's uncle; the Calvinist Davenant oversaw his nephew's schooling and early career, appointing him a prebendary in Salisbury during Herbert's few years at nearby Bemerton, when the two may have met.[3] Also like Herbert, Fuller was on warm terms with Nicholas Ferrar and the Little Gidding community, who transcribed his *Holy State* before publication.[4] Furthermore, Ferrar seems to have shared with Fuller the as-yet-unpublished manuscript of *The Countrey Parson:* Fuller's profile in *The Holy State* of the "faithfull Minister" clearly echoes Herbert's pastoral manual. In fact this profile ends by quoting—imperfectly, as if from personal memory—Herbert's then-unpublished verses "To my Successor," which are still to be seen carved over the street entrance to the old Bemerton rectory.

I do not mean to claim that there existed between the two men a

2. Ibid., 65, 88, 80, 87.
3. William Addison, *Worthy Dr. Fuller,* 34, 8–9, 64.
4. *DNB,* "Fuller," 756a.

substantial personal relationship, or even any strong personal resemblance. Herbert—meticulous in appearance, spare of flesh, by some accounts choleric in temper, by all accounts unsparing in literary craft —could never have been taken in the street or the study for the slovenly, bulky, affable, and absent-minded Fuller. As writers, they do share a gift for the pithy aphorism, but overall the one excels at the burnished, tightly wound lyric poem, while the other is best known as Coleridge's "dear old" antiquary, weaving loose prose backdrops for his earthy anecdotes.[5] Their great resemblance lies in shared ecclesiastical and political principles.

And indeed, after 1633 Fuller and all the parsons in England had their principles sifted and ground between the upper and lower millstones of Laudian and Puritan policy. Fuller, while not exactly crushed between these extremes, was badly pinched. On the one hand, in the spring of 1640, he subscribed out of episcopal principle to Laud's new canons, while objecting strongly to the severity of the "Canon for the restraint of sectaries"—thus incurring suspicions of holding pro-Puritan sympathies.[6] On the other hand, in the spring of 1643, he swore an oath of loyalty to Parliament, but because of his continued loyalty to the king's person, he came under Puritan suspicion and felt obliged to withdraw from London to the king.[7]

Yet once at Oxford, Fuller quickly fell into disfavor with ardent absolute monarchists, and for good reason; in *The Holy State* he had cautioned against "unbounded power" in kings, stating, "God alone makes things lawfull by willing them, whilest the most calmest Princes have sometimes gusts of Passion, which meeting with an unlimited Authority in them may prove dangerous."[8] So, under a cloud, Fuller eked out a living as chaplain to Sir Ralph Hopton, the most moderate Royalist general, until 1644, when King Charles, out of personal fondness, made Fuller chaplain at Exeter to the newborn Princess Henrietta.[9] With Exeter's surrender to Fairfax in April 1646, and the effective collapse of the king's forces, Fuller cobbled together a series of

5. Addison, *Worthy Dr. Fuller,* 201.
6. *DNB,* "Fuller," 756a.
7. Addison, *Worthy Dr. Fuller,* 108–10.
8. Fuller, *Holy State,* 353.
9. Addison, *Worthy Dr. Fuller,* 128.

London church lectureships, under intermittent Puritan scrutiny, while producing a string of highly successful devotional and historical works, including *A Pisgah-Sight of Palestine* and *The Worthies of England.*[10] These books made him, like Herbert, one of the best-selling authors of the century, admired on all sides of the conflict.

But the defining moment of the civil war, especially for a limited monarchist like Fuller, came in January of 1649, when his monarch met with the most absolute of limits; for Charles's death meant not only the decapitation of the king, but of kingship itself. Fuller, as both a loyal subject and friend of Charles, grieved deeply after the execution, putting his work aside and preaching a eulogistic sermon at Waltham Abbey on "The Just Man's Funeral."[11] Yet remarkably, in the depths of his grief, he did not break off his long-standing friendship with a man in the first rank of those who tried Charles and signed him over to death—Sir John Danvers.

It is here, at Fuller's strangest intersection with Herbert's world, that he would seem to part company most sharply with Herbert himself; for it seems virtually unimaginable that Herbert could have played the role of intimate to a regicide. Nevertheless, this regicide had been his mother's husband and his friend; and amid the upheavals of the Interregnum, the unimaginable happened to many people more than once. Civil wars are of course proverbial for dividing houses and friends, and Herbert might conceivably have broken with Danvers. However, even more alarming than a divided family or friendship is a divided mind, which must break with itself. Herbert's mind encompassed loyalty to a king who, constitutionally speaking, was soon to violate the bounds of his power; as well as loyalty to a Parliament that, constitutionally speaking, would then cut off its own head. Such a mind sets out armed to engage the approaching enemy, only to meet itself coming the other way. In 1649 Fuller, with his inner loyalties massing for battle, called an inglorious but lasting inner truce: as the *via media* vanished, he found a modus vivendi. Whether discretion or charity had determined Fuller's decision, we do not know. We do know that in 1633 Herbert, his tuberculosis prevailing in the dank air of

10. *DNB*, "Fuller," 757–58.
11. Ibid., 757a.

Bemerton, was spared these most crushing confrontations, both without and within.

I have claimed that Herbert, in writing *The Temple* and *The Countrey Parson,* was involved in regenerative nostalgia, attempting to refound the faltering Elizabethan church in the small spaces of the heart and of the rural congregation. By comparison, Fuller's *Holy State* and *Worthies of England* display such nostalgia at work on a significantly larger scale. Writing during and after the old regime's final collapse, Fuller paces out dimensions not just for a parsonage or a parish, but for every room, office, and institution in the commonwealth, and he then provides portraits of the men and women who have best filled them. Herbert hopes that his mustard seeds will grow and that, parish by parish, the kingdom will revive. Fuller, working in more desperate times, puts gradualism aside, and calls out to the entire disintegrating kingdom at once. There is, of course, more careful craftsmanship in a single poem by Herbert than there is in pages and pages of Fuller. Yet both were animated by the same Tudor humanist social vision: that in the increasingly chaotic present one must look to the best of the past in order to build the future.

Any institutional remains of the past Elizabethan ideal by which Herbert lived were buried with Charles I. Stuart absolutism had done as much as anything to kill the old regime, yet at the king's death the broken body of that regime lost its last human face. Ironically, the future did not actually belong, as it seemed at the time, to Cromwell and the Puritans; but neither would those scattered dry bones of Tudor church and state rise again. The old order had not been wise enough to resolve its contradictions or to prevent its own suicide; but, as we have already noted, Herbert did not expect any human constructions or reconstructions to last forever. And on this last point, at least, the old middle way had been wise enough: like one of Herbert's self-aware lyrics, it acknowledged its own temporality, its own limits, pointing beyond itself, indeed beyond this most changeable world.

Bibliography

Addison, William. *Worthy Dr. Fuller.* London: J. M. Dent, 1951.

Andrewes, Lancelot. *A Learned Discourse of Ceremonies Retained and used in Christian Churches.* London: Charles Adams, 1653.

————. *XCVI Sermons.* London: 1629.

Bainton, Roland H. *Here I Stand: A Life of Martin Luther.* New York: Abingdon Press, 1950.

Barish, Jonas. *The Anti-Theatrical Prejudice.* Berkeley: University of California Press, 1981.

Baxter, Richard. *The Reformed Pastor.* Edited by J. I. Packer. London: Puritan Paperbacks, 1973.

Becon, Thomas. *The Early Works of Thomas Becon.* Edited by John Ayre. Cambridge, Mass.: The Parker Society, 1843.

Bell, Ilona. "'Setting Foot into Divinity': George Herbert and the English Reformation." *Modern Language Quarterly* 38 (1977): 219–41.

Benet, Diana. *Secretary of Praise: The Poetic Vocation of George Herbert.* Columbia: University of Missouri Press, 1984.

Bercovitch, Sacvan. *The Puritan Origins of the American Self.* New Haven: Yale University Press, 1975.

Bernard, Richard. *The Faithfull Shepheard.* London: 1607.

Blackstone, B. *The Ferrar Papers.* Cambridge: Cambridge University Press, 1938.

Bloch, Chana. "Spelling the Word: Herbert's Reading of the Bible." In *"Too Rich to Clothe the Sunne": Essays on George Herbert,* edited by Claude J. Summers and Ted-Larry Pebworth, 15–21. Pittsburgh: University of Pittsburgh Press, 1980.

Booty, John E., ed. *The Godly Kingdom of Tudor England.* Wilton, Conn.: Morehouse-Barlow, 1981.

Bourne, E. C. E. *The Anglicanism of William Laud.* London: S. P. C. K., 1947.

Bouwsma, William J. *John Calvin: A Sixteenth-Century Portrait.* New York: Oxford University Press, 1988.

Bradshaw, Paul F. *The Anglican Ordinal.* London: S. P. C. K., 1971.

Bridges, John. *A Defence of the government established in the Church of England for ecclesiastical matters.* London: 1587.

Brook, V. J. K. *A Life of Archbishop Parker.* Oxford: The Clarendon Press, 1962.

Calvin, John. *Commentary on the Book of Psalms.* Translated by James Anderson. Edinburgh: Calvin Translation Society, 1845.

————. *Institutes of the Christian Religion.* 2 vols. Translated by Ford Lewis Battles. Edited by John T. McNeill. Philadelphia: Westminster Press, 1960.

Carlton, Charles. *Archbishop William Laud.* London and New York: Routledge and Kegan Paul, 1987.

Cartwright, Thomas. *The Second Replie of Thomas Cartwright: Agaynst Maister Doctor Whitgiftes Second Answer, Touching the Church Discipline.* London: 1575.

Chambers, R. W. *Thomas More.* New York: Harcourt-Brace and Co., 1935.

Charles, Amy M. *A Life of George Herbert.* Ithaca, N.Y.: Cornell University Press, 1977.

Church of England. *Articles of Religion.* London, 1571.

————. *The Book of Common Prayer, 1559: The Elizabethan Prayer Book.* Edited by John E. Booty. Charlottesville: University Press of Virginia, Folger Shakespeare Library, 1976.

————. *Certaine Sermons or Homilies Appointed to be Read in Churches in the Time of Elizabeth I (1547–1571). A Facsimile Reproduction of the Edition of 1623.* 2 vols. in 1. Gainesville, Fla.: Scholars' Facsimiles and Reprints, 1968.

————. *Constitutions and Canons Ecclesiastical, 1604.* Edited by H. A. Wilson. Oxford: The Clarendon Press, 1923.

————. *Synodalia. A collection of articles of religion, canons and proceedings of convocations in the province of Canterbury . . . 1547–1717.* 2 vols. Edited by Edward Cardwell. Oxford: Oxford University Press, 1842.

Church of Scotland. *The First and Second Booke of Discipline.* Edinburgh: 1560. Reprint. London: 1641.

Cobbett, William, ed. *The Parliamentary History of England.* 36 vols. London: 1806–1820.

Collinson, Patrick. *The Elizabethan Puritan Movement.* Berkeley: University of California Press, 1967.

————. *The Religion of Protestants: The Church in English Society, 1559–1625.* Oxford: The Clarendon Press, 1982.

Coolidge, John S. *The Pauline Renaissance in England: Puritanism and the Bible*. Oxford: The Clarendon Press, 1970.

Cosin, John. *A Collection of Private Devotions*. Edited by P. B. Stanwood. Oxford: The Clarendon Press, 1967.

Coverdale, Miles, ed. *Letters of the Martyrs*. London: 1564.

Craven, Wesley Frank. *Dissolution of the Virginia Company: The Failure of a Colonial Experiment*. Gloucester, Mass.: Peter Smith, 1964. Reprint of 1932 edition.

Dalton, Michael. *The Countrey Ivstice, Containing the practice of the Ivstices of the Peace out of their Sessions*. 2d ed. London: 1622. Reprint. New York: Arno Press, 1972.

Davies, Horton. *Worship and Theology in England*. 4 vols. Princeton: Princeton University Press, 1970–1961.

DiCesare, Mario and Rigo Mignani. *A Concordance to the Complete Writings of George Herbert*. Ithaca: Cornell University Press, 1977.

Dickens, A. G. *The English Reformation*. New York: Schocken Books, 1964.

Doerksen, Daniel. "Recharting the *Via Media* of Spenser and Herbert." *Renaissance and Reformation* 8 (1984): 215–25.

Donne, John. *The Complete English Poems*. Edited by A. J. Smith. Harmondsworth: Penguin, 1971.

———. *Devotions upon Emergent Occasions*. Ann Arbor: University of Michigan Press, 1959.

———. *Devotions upon Emergent Occasions*. Edited by Anthony Raspa. Montreal: McGill-Queens University Press, 1975.

———. *The Satires, Epigrams, and Verse Letters*. Edited by Wesley Milgate. Oxford: The Clarendon Press, 1967.

———. *The Sermons of John Donne*. 10 vols. Edited by George R. Potter and Evelyn Simpson. Berkeley: University of California Press, 1953–1962.

Edwards, Philip et al., eds. *The Revels History of Drama in English*. Vol. 4, *1613–1660*. London: Methuen, 1981.

Eliot, T. S. *Complete Poems and Plays, 1909–1950*. New York: Harcourt, Brace, and World, 1952.

Ellrodt, Robert. *L'Inspiration personelle et L'Esprit du temps chez les poetes metaphysiques anglais*. Paris: n.p., 1973.

Elton, G. R., ed. *The Tudor Constitution: Documents and Commentary*. Cambridge: Cambridge University Press, 1962.

Elyot, Sir Thomas. *The Book Named the Governor*. Edited by S. E. Lehmberg. London: Dent and Dutton, 1962.

Fish, Stanley E. "Herbert's Hypocrisy." Unpublished paper delivered at Newberry Library, Chicago, 1989.

―――. *The Living Temple: George Herbert and Catechizing.* Berkeley: University of California Press, 1978.

―――. *Self-Consuming Artifacts: The Experience of Seventeenth-Century Literature.* Berkeley: University of California Press, 1972.

[Fulke, William.] *A Brief and plaine declaration, concerning the desires of all those faithfull Ministers, that have and do seeke for the Discipline and reformation of the church of Englande. Which may serve for a just Apologie, against false accusations and slaunders of the adversaries.* London: n.p., 1584. Often called by its subtitle, *A Learned Discourse.*

Fuller, Thomas. *The History of the Worthies of England.* London, 1662.

―――. *The Holy State and the Profane State.* 2 vols. Cambridge, 1642.

―――. *A Pisgah-Sight of Palestine.* London, 1650.

Gardner, W. H. *Gerard Manley Hopkins, 1844–1889.* 2 vols. London: Secker and Warburg, 1949. Reprint. London: Oxford University Press, 1961.

Garraty, John A. and Peter Gay, eds. *Columbia History of the World.* New York: Harper and Row, 1972.

George, Charles H. and Katherine George. *The Protestant Mind of the English Reformation, 1570–1640.* Princeton: Princeton University Press, 1961.

Gerrish, Brian. "John Calvin on Luther." In *Interpreters of Luther: Essays in Honor of William Pauch,* edited by Jaroslav Pelikan, 67–96. Philadelphia: Fortress Press, 1968.

[Gilby, Anthony.] *A Pleasaunt Dialogue, Between a Souldior of Barwicke, and an English Chaplaine.* . . . N.p., 1581.

Grant, Patrick. *The Transformation of Sin.* Amherst: University of Massachusetts Press, 1974.

Greenwood, John. *The Writings of John Greenwood, 1587–1590.* Edited by Leland H. Carlson. London: Published for the Sir Halley Stuart Trust by G. Allen and Unwin, 1962.

Halewood, William H. *The Poetry of Grace: Reformation Themes and Structures in English Seventeenth-Century Poetry.* New Haven: Yale University Press, 1970.

Hall, Joseph. *Works.* 12 vols. Oxford: D. A. Talboys, 1837.

Haller, William. *The Rise of Puritanism.* New York: Harper and Row, 1957.

Hardwick, Charles. *A History of the Articles of Religion*. London: George Bell and Sons, 1888.

Harman, Barbara Leah. "George Herbert's 'Affliction' (I): The Limits of Representation." *ELH* 44 (Summer 1977): 267–85.

Hart, A. Tindal. *The Country Clergy, 1558–1660*. London: Phoenix House, 1958.

Herbert, George. *The Complete Works in Verse and Prose*. 3 vols. Edited by Alexander B. Grosart. London: Robson and Sons, 1874.

———. *The Latin Poetry of George Herbert: A Bilingual Edition*. Translated by Mark McCloskey and Paul R. Murphy. Athens: Ohio University Press, 1965.

———. *The Williams Manuscript of George Herbert's Poems*. Edited by Amy M. Charles. Delmar, N.Y.: Scholars' Facsimiles and Reprints, 1977.

———. *The Works of George Herbert*. 2d ed. Edited by F. E. Hutchinson. Oxford: The Clarendon Press, 1964.

Hill, Christopher. *The Century of Revolution, 1603–1714*. Edinburgh: Thomas Nelson and Sons, 1961.

———. *Society and Puritanism in Pre-Revolutionary England*. London: Secker and Warburg, 1964.

Hooker, Richard. *Of the Laws of Ecclesiastical Polity*. 4 vols. Edited by W. Speed Hill. Cambridge: Harvard University Press, 1977.

Hudson, Winthrop S. *John Ponet (1516?–1556): Advocate of Limited Monarchy*. Chicago: University of Chicago Press, 1942.

Hunter, Jeanne Clayton. "Herbert's 'The Water-Course': Notorious and Neglected." *Notes and Queries* 34 (1987): 310–12.

———. "'With Wings of Faith': Herbert's Communion Poems." *Journal of Religion* 62 (January 1982): 57–71.

James I, King. *Works*. London: R. Barber and I. Bill, 1616.

Journals of the House of Commons. London: 1547–.

Kendall, R. T. "The Puritan Modification of Calvin's Theology." In *John Calvin: His Influence in the Western World*, edited by W. Stanford Reid, 199–214. Grand Rapids, Mich.: Zondervan, 1982.

Kenyon, J. P., ed. *The Stuart Constitution, 1603–1688: Documents and Commentary*. Cambridge: Cambridge University Press, 1966.

Kip, William Ingraham. *The History, Object, and Proper Observance of the Holy Season of Lent*. 2d ed. Albany, N.Y.: Erastus Pease, 1844.

Knappen, M. M. *Tudor Puritanism*. Chicago: University of Chicago Press, 1939.

Knox, John. *Works*. 6 vols. Edited by David Laing. Edinburgh: Wodrow Society, 1846–1895.

Lake, Peter. *Moderate Puritans in the Elizabethan Church*. Cambridge: Cambridge University Press, 1982.

Lamont, William. *Godly Rule*. London: Macmillan, 1969.

Laud, William. *The Works of the Most Reverend Father in God, William Laud*. 7 vols. Edited by W. Scott and J. Bliss. Oxford: Library of Anglo-Catholic Theology, 1848–1860.

Legg, J. W. *English Orders for Consecrating Churches in the Seventeenth Century*. London: Henry Bradshaw Society, 1911.

Lein, Clayton D. "Art and Structure in Walton's *Life of Mr. George Herbert*," *University of Toronto Quarterly* 46 (Winter 1976–1977): 162–76.

Lewalski, Barbara Kiefer. *Protestant Poetics and the Seventeenth-Century Religious Lyric*. Princeton: Princeton University Press, 1979.

Lilburne, John. *Come out of her my people*. London: 1639.

Little, David. *Religion, Order, and Law: A Study in Pre-Revolutionary England*. New York: Harper Torchbooks, 1969.

Luther, Martin. *The Bondage of the Will*. Translated by J. I. Packer and O. R. Johnston. London: James Clarke and Co., 1957.

McDonnell, Kilian, O.S.B. *John Calvin, the Church, and the Eucharist*. Princeton: Princeton University Press, 1967.

McNeill, John. *A History of the Cure of Souls*. New York: Harper and Brothers, 1951.

Malcolmson, Cristina. "George Herbert's *Country Parson* and the Character of Social Identity." *Studies in Philology* 85 (1988): 245–66.

———. "Society and Self-Definition in the Works of George Herbert." Ph.D. diss., University of California at Berkeley, 1983.

Marcus, Leah Sinanoglou. *Childhood and Cultural Despair: A Theme and Variations in Seventeenth-Century Literature*. Pittsburgh: University of Pittsburgh Press, 1978.

Martin, Brian W. *John Keble: Priest, Professor, and Poet*. London: Croom Helm, 1976.

Martz, Louis L. "The Generous Ambiguity of George Herbert's *Temple*." In *A Fine Tuning: Studies of the Religious Poetry of Herbert and Milton*, edited by Mary A. Maleski, 31–56. Binghamton, N.Y.: Medieval and Renaissance Texts and Studies, 1989.

———. *The Poetry of Meditation*. New Haven: Yale University Press, 1954.

Mather, Cotton. *Magnalia Christi Americana*. Edited by Kenneth B. Murdoch. Cambridge: Harvard University Press, 1977.

Maycock, A. L. *Nicholas Ferrar of Little Gidding*. London: S. P. C. K., 1938.

Mayer, John. *The English Catechism Explained*. 5th ed. London: 1635.

Miller, Perry. *Errand into the Wilderness*. Reprint. New York: Harper and Row, 1964.

————. *The New England Mind: The Seventeenth Century*. New York: Macmillan, 1939.

————, ed. *The American Puritans: Their Prose and Poetry*. New York: Anchor Books, 1956.

Miner, Earl. *The Metaphysical Mode from Donne to Cowley*. Princeton: Princeton University Press, 1969.

Mitchell, W. Fraser. *English Pulpit Oratory from Andrewes to Tillotson*. New York: Russell and Russell, 1962.

Murray, James A. H., ed. *The Oxford English Dictionary*. 10 vols. New York: 1888.

Nardo, Anna K. *The Ludic Self in Seventeenth-Century English Literature*. Albany: State University of New York Press, 1991.

Nevinson, Charles, ed. *The Later Writings of Bishop Hooper*. Parker Society Series, no. 21. Cambridge, Mass.: The Parker Society, 1852.

Newman, John Henry. *Tracts for the Times, Remarks on Certain Passages in the Thirty-Nine Articles*. No. 90. 4th ed., rev. London: Rivington, 1842.

Newman, John Henry, Cardinal. *Apologia Pro Vita Sua, Being a History of His Religious Opinions*. New York: Longmans, Green and Co., 1947.

Palmer, George Herbert, ed. *The Life and Works of George Herbert*. 3 vols. Boston: Houghton Mifflin and Co., 1907.

Parker, Matthew. *A brief examination for the tyme, of a certain declaration, lately put in print in the name and defence of certaine Ministers in London, refusyng to weare the apparell prescribed by the lawes and orders of the Realm . . .* n.d.

Patrides, C. A., ed. *The English Poems of George Herbert*. Totowa, N.J.: Rowman and Littlefield, 1975.

————, ed. *George Herbert: The Critical Heritage*. London and New York: Routledge and Kegan Paul, 1983.

Perkins, William. *The Workes of . . . William Perkins*. 3 vols. Cambridge: I. Legett, 1612–1613.

———. *The Workes of . . . William Perkins.* 3 vols. Reprint. Cambridge: I. Legett, 1626–1631.

Reeves, Troy D., ed. *Index to the Sermons of John Donne.* 3 vols. Salzburg: Institut fur Anglistik und Amerikanistik, Universitaet Salzburg, 1979–1981.

Robinson, Hastings, ed. *The Zurich Letters.* Cambridge, Mass.: The Parker Society, 1842.

Ross, Malcolm Mackenzie. *Poetry and Dogma: The Transformation of Eucharistic Symbols in Seventeenth-Century English Literature.* New Brunswick, N.J.: Rutgers University Press, 1954.

Rushworth, J., ed. *Historical Collections of Private Passages of State.* 8 vols. London: 1659–1701.

Rymer, T. and R. Sanderson, eds. *Foedera, conventiones, literae et cuiuscunque generis acta publica.* 3 vols. London: 1704–1732.

Sabine, George H. *A History of Political Theory.* New York: Holt and Co., 1937.

Schoenfeldt, Michael C. *Prayer and Power: George Herbert and Renaissance Courtship.* Chicago: University of Chicago Press, 1991.

———. "Standing on Ceremony: The Comedy of Manners in Herbert's 'Love (III).'" In Claude J. Summers and Ted-Larry Pebworth, eds., *"Bright Shootes of Everlastingnesse": The Seventeenth-Century Religious Lyric,* 116–33. Columbia: University of Missouri Press, 1987.

———. "'Subject to Ev'ry Mounters Bended Knee': Herbert and Authority." In *The Historical Renaissance: New Essays on Tudor and Stuart Literature and Culture,* edited by Heather Dubrow and Richard Strier. Chicago: University of Chicago Press, 1988.

Shakespeare, William. *The Complete Works of Shakespeare.* 4th ed. Edited by David Bevington. New York: Harper Collins, 1992.

Sherwood, Terry G. *Herbert's Prayerful Art.* Toronto: University of Toronto Press, 1989.

Sibthorpe, Robert. *Of Apostolique Obedience.* London: 1627.

Skinner, Quentin. *The Foundations of Modern Political Thought.* Vol. 2, *The Reformation.* Cambridge: Cambridge University Press, 1978.

Slights, Camille Wells. *The Casuistical Tradition in Shakespeare, Donne, Herbert, and Milton.* Princeton: Princeton University Press, 1981.

Stanford, William. *An Exposition of the King's Prerogative.* London: 1567.

Starkey, Thomas. *A Dialogue Between Reginald Pole and Thomas Lupset*. Edited by Kathleen M. Burton. London: Chatto and Windus, 1948.

Stephen, Sir Leslie and Sir Sidney Lee. *The Dictionary of National Biography*. 22 vols. Oxford: Oxford University Press, 1917.

Stewart, Stanley. *George Herbert*. Boston: Twayne Publishers, 1986.

Strier, Richard. "George Herbert and the World." *Journal of Medieval and Renaissance Studies* 11 (Fall 1981): 211–21.

———. "History, Criticism, and Herbert: A Polemical Note." *Papers on Language and Literature* 17 (1981): 347–52.

———. "'Humanizing' Herbert." *Modern Philology* 74 (1976): 78–88.

———. *Love Known: Theology and Experience in George Herbert's Poetry*. Chicago: University of Chicago Press, 1983.

———. "'To All Angels and Saints': Herbert's Puritan Poem." *Modern Philology* 77 (November 1979): 132–45.

Summers, Joseph. *George Herbert: His Religion and Art*. Cambridge: Harvard University Press, 1954.

Taylor, Thomas. *Works*. London: J. Bartlet, 1653.

Thompson, Elbert N. S. "*The Temple* and *The Christian Year*." *PMLA* 54 (1939): 1018–25.

Trevor-Roper, H. R. *Archbishop Laud, 1573–1645*. 2d ed. London: Macmillan, 1963.

Turner, H. E. W., ed. *The Articles of the Church of England*. London: A. R. Mowbray, 1964.

Tuve, Rosemond. *A Reading of George Herbert*. Chicago: University of Chicago Press, 1952.

Tuveson, Ernest. *Millenium and Utopia: A Study in the Background of the Idea of Progress*. Berkeley: University of California Press, 1949.

Tyacke, Nicholas. "Puritanism, Arminianism, and Counter-Revolution." In *The Origins of the English Civil War*, edited by Conrad Russell, 119–43. London: Macmillan, 1973.

Tyndale, William. *The Obedience of a Christen Man*. Antwerp: 1528. Facsimile reprint edition. Amsterdam and Norwood, N.J.: Walter S. Johnson, 1977.

Veith, Gene Edward, Jr. *Reformation Spirituality: The Religion of George Herbert*. Lewisburg, Pa.: Bucknell University Press, 1985.

———. "The Religious Wars in George Herbert Criticism: Reinterpreting Seventeenth-Century Anglicanism." *George Herbert Journal* 11 (1988), 19–35.

Vendler, Helen. *The Poetry of George Herbert*. Cambridge: Harvard University Press, 1975.

Wall, John N. *Transformations of the Word: Spenser, Herbert, Vaughan*. Athens: University of Georgia Press, 1988.

Walton, Izaak. *The Lives of John Donne, Sir Henry Wotton, Richard Hooker, George Herbert, and Robert Sanderson*. Edited by George Saintsbury. London: The World's Classics, Oxford University Press, 1962.

Welsby, Paul A. *Lancelot Andrewes, 1555–1626*. London: S. P. C. K., 1958.

Wesel-Roth, Ruth. *Thomas Erastus*. Lahr/Baden, Switzerland: M. Schauenburg, 1954.

Whitgift, John. *The Works of John Whitgift*. 3 vols. Edited by John Ayre. Cambridge, Mass.: The Parker Society, 1851.

Wood, Thomas. *Five Pastorals*. London: S. P. C. K., 1961.

Woodhouse, A. S. P. *Puritanism and Liberty*. 2d ed. Chicago: University of Chicago Press, 1974.

Index of Herbert Poems

"Aaron," 141–44, 147, 175, 199
"Affliction" (I), 131, 170, 183, 201–3, 204
"Affliction" (IV), 208
"The Agonie," 28n34, 151n3
"The Altar," 4, 151n3, 172, 176
"The Answer," 92
"Antiphon" (I), 173

"The Banquet," 28n34, 29, 30, 151n3,
   168
"The British Church," 1, 70, 149–50,
   165–67, 179, 184

"Christmas," 151n3, 168
"The Church": didactic strategy of, 122,
   200; Williams and Bodleian MSS of,
   171; antielitism in, 193; dating of poems
   in, 197n18; and individualism, 199–
   200; and spiritual relapses, 204n28;
   mentioned, passim
"The Church-floore," 175, 177n38
"Church-lock and key," 172, 177n38
"The Church Militant": separate from
   The Temple, 177n40; and Herbert's
   pessimism, 184–87; dating of, 186n5;
   mentioned, 28n34, 148, 190–91, 192,
   201
"Church-monuments," 167–68, 177n38
"Church-musick," 168, 177n38
"The Church-porch. Perirrhanterium,"
   91, 122, 151n3, 176, 197
"Church-rents and schismes," 1, 70, 73,
   184
"The Collar," 122, 169, 204n28
"Confession," 170–71
"Conscience," 170
"Constancie," 201, 205
"The Crosse," 170

"Death," 151n3
"Decay," 184
"Deniall," 93
"Divinitie," 28
"Dooms-day," 151n3

"Easter," 92, 151n3, 168, 170, 174
"Easter-wings," 169, 170
"Employment" (I), 123, 204
"Employment" (II), 123, 201, 202, 203,
   204
"Euen-song" (Williams MS), 171
"Even-song," 171, 177n38

"The Flower," 129, 204n28
"The Forerunners," 200

"The Glance," 101
"Good Friday," 151n3
"Gratefulnesse," 193, 194–95
"Grief," 93

"Heaven," 151n3
"The Holdfast," 6, 21, 94, 95, 136, 169
"H. Baptisme" (I), 168
"H. Baptisme" (II), 168
"The H. Communion," 28n34, 29n37,
   30, 134, 168
"The H. Communion" (Williams MS),
   28n34
"Home," 208

"The Invitation," 28, 29n37, 151n3

"Jordan" (I), 93, 196–97, 200
"Jordan" (II), 93, 94, 177–79
"Judgement," 151n5
"Justice" (II), 130n3

"The Knell" (Williams MS), 168

"Lent," 4, 5, 28n34, 44, 64–86, 121, 127,
   151n3, 173, 206
"Love" (II), 131
"Love" (III), 21, 28n34, 94, 95, 100,
   151n3, 177
"Love unknown," 28n34

"Mattens," 171, 176, 177n38
"Miserie," 195–96

Musae Responsoriae, 20, 24, 44, 45, 72, 78, 151, 154

"The Pearl. Matt. xiii. 45," 91, 199–200
"Perseverance" (Williams MS), 22–24
"The Posie," 91, 200
"Prayer" (I), 92
"Prayer" (II), 195
"The Priesthood," 30, 126, 127–41, 142, 143, 147, 173, 199
"The Pulley," 169

"The Quidditie," 91
"The Quip," 91, 92, 199

"Redemption," 151n3, 193
"The Reprisall," 21, 94, 151n3

"The Sacrifice," 151n3, 176
"Sepulchre," 151n3
"The Sinner," 151n3
"Sion," 4, 150, 174–75, 179
"The Storm," 193–94, 195

"Submission," 204–5
"Sunday," 151n3, 168
"Superliminare," 151n3, 176

The Temple: and courtly strategies, 6, 91, 140; licensing of, 21, 24, 186; humiliation of eloquence in, 90–95; catechistical strategy of, 118, 183; praised by Baxter, 152; and externals of worship, 164–77; and "Anglican" meditation, 167–68; as "vanishing edifice," 176–77; mentioned, *passim*
"The Thanksgiving," 94, 136, 151n3
"To all Angels and Saints," 121–22, 151n3, 173
"Trinitie Sunday," 151n3, 169
"A true Hymne," 175–76

"The Water-course," 16–17, 21, 24, 28n34
"Whitsunday," 151n3, 173, 184
"The Windows," 99, 132, 172, 177, 198
"The World," 184

General Index

Abbot, George, Archbishop, 75, 103
Alphonsus of Aragon, King, 161
Ames, William, 106n5, 120n34
Anabaptism, 32, 145
Andrewes, Lancelot, Bishop, 11, 15, 106, 110, 112–14, 150n1, 151, 159–61, 162–63, 197
Anglicanism, 10, 17, 18, 25, 26, 31, 120n34, 150, 152, 182. *See also* Anglo-Catholicism
Anglo-Catholicism, 10, 110, 150, 151n3. *See also* Anglicanism; Oxford Movement
Anti-Calvinism. *See* Arminianism; Laudianism
Anticlericalism, 145
Antinomianism, 145n16
Archytas, 42
Arminianism: and Laudianism, 15–16; origins of, 15–16; at Cambridge, 21; and Herbert, 21, 23, 24, 69, 85; and divine-right monarchy, 34, 35, 147; and divine-right episcopacy, 48, 107, 147; and enforcement, 59, 125; and sacerdotalism, 62; and social class, 62; and preaching, 62–63, 110, 113n22; at Oxford, 75; and pastoral theory, 106; as "new" doctrine, 136; and externals of worship, 159, 162, 163; mentioned, 5, 11, 110n12, 121, 139, 157. *See also* Conformity, New; Episcopalianism; Laud, William, Archbishop; Laudianism; Monarchy
Arminius, Jacob, 15, 23. *See also* Arminianism
Arnobius, 159
Articles of Religion, 9–33 *passim*, 54, 105–6, 109, 127, 134, 135, 153
Augustine of Canterbury, Saint, 160
Augustine of Hippo, Saint, 4, 14, 83

Bainton, Roland H., 25n27
Bancroft, Richard, Archbishop, 106
Basil the Great, 76

Bastwick, John, 49
Baxter, Richard, 107, 113n22, 116, 117, 119, 120n34, 125–26, 144–45, 147–48, 152
Becon, Thomas, 39–40, 68–69, 76–77, 82, 83
Bell, Ilona, 10, 152, 173
Bellarmine, Robert, Cardinal, 160
Benet, Diana, 10
Bernard, Richard, 106, 110n11, 133
Beza, Theodore, 12, 14, 20, 22
Bloch, Chana, 199–200
Book of Common Prayer, The, 54, 66–67, 78, 149, 150, 151, 153, 159, 164, 171, 177, 210, 211
Book of Homilies, The, 49–51, 60–66 *passim,* 74, 115, 155, 162, 187–88, 206
Bourne, E. C. E., 150n1
Bouwsma, William J., 32
Bradford, John, 105n4
Brent, Sir Nathaniel, 59
Briefe Notes on Valdesso's Considerations. See Herbert, George: Prose
Brownists, 55. *See also* Non-Conformity; Puritanism
Bucer, Martin, 10, 17, 20
Buckingham, George Villiers, first Duke of, 34, 198
Bullinger, Heinrich, 10, 17
Bunyan, John, 4, 79–80, 143, 196
Burton, Henry, 49

Calvin, John, 5, 9–33 *passim,* 41n18, 49, 62, 103, 108, 109, 119, 134, 145, 153, 154, 163, 174, 200. *See also* Calvinism
Calvinism: hyper-Calvinism, 5; and theological speculation, 12–16; English episcopal, 34, 35–36, 62, 63, 75, 103, 114n23, 153, 211; and resistance theory, 41n18; mentioned, 9–33 *passim,* 48, 96n6, 106, 108, 110nn11,12, 113, 114, 120, 139, 147, 150n1, 151, 163. *See also* Calvin, John; Conformity, Old; Episcopalianism; Monarchy

Canons of 1604, 54–55, 57, 58, 119, 122–23
Canons of 1640, 58, 212
Cartwright, Thomas, 45–46, 55, 106, 161
Charles, Amy M., 128, 173*n33,* 186, 197*n18*
Charles I, King, 16, 34, 35, 42, 48, 58, 63, 75, 85, 103*n1,* 123*n39,* 124, 138–39, 147, 156, 157, 212, 213, 214
Charles II, King, 104
Chrysostom, John, Saint, 83
Coleridge, Samuel Taylor, 212
Collinson, Patrick, 34*n2,* 36, 163–64
Conformity, New, 11, 48–50, 65–66, 107. *See also* Arminianism; Laud, William, Archbishop; Laudianism
Conformity, Old: and Herbert, 37–47 *passim;* origins of, 37–43, 50–54; and Puritanism, 45–47, 162, 163, 164; and enforcement, 47–50; and scripturalism, 50–53; and lay authority, 53–59 *passim;* failure of, 86; and externals of worship, 161–64 *passim;* mentioned, 3, 11, 48, 104, 140, 152–53, 172, 179, 211–14. *See also* Calvinism: English episcopal
Constantine, Emperor, 160
Coolidge, John S., 45, 46
Cornaro, Luigi, 68
Cosin, John, Bishop, 59, 167, 173–74
Cotton, John, 207
Counter-Reformation, 5. *See also* Roman Catholicism
Countrey Parson, The. See Herbert, George: Prose
Cranmer, Thomas, Archbishop, 5, 10, 17, 19, 50–52, 53, 54, 60, 62, 74, 149, 152–62 *passim,* 187, 206, 214

Dalton, Michael, 56*n43*
Danvers, Sir John, 90, 191, 192, 205, 210–11, 213
Davenant, John, Bishop, 21, 63, 75, 139, 143, 211
Davies, Horton, 162–63
Dickens, A. G., 37, 38, 52, 53
Doerksen, Daniel, 10
Donne, John, 34, 36, 42, 105*n4,* 110–12, 125, 131, 156, 165–66, 168, 173, 191–92

Edward VI, King, 27, 39, 40, 43, 187
Eliot, T. S., 113, 156
Elizabeth I, Queen, 40–41, 43, 48, 55, 69, 72, 106, 124, 187, 208
Ellrodt, Robert, 12*n5*
Elton, G. R., 40, 41
Elyot, Sir Thomas, 38
Episcopalianism, 32. *See also* Arminianism; Calvinism: English episcopal; Laudianism; Oxford Movement
Erasmus, 23, 38
Erastianism, 37, 38*n9,* 49, 52
Erastus, Thomas, 38*n9*
Eucharist, 10, 12*n5,* 24–32 *passim,* 58–59, 109–10, 133–35

Fairfax, Baron Thomas, of Cameron, 212
Ferrar, Nicholas, 122, 156–58, 166, 191, 192, 207, 211
Fish, Stanley E., 5, 89*n3,* 117, 118–19, 122
Foxe, John, 207
Fuller, Thomas, 210, 211–14

Gardner, W. H., 2*n3*
George, Charles H., 110*n12*
George, Katherine, 110*n12*
Gerrish, Brian, 12
Gifford, George, 163–64
Gilby, Anthony, 66
Gilpin, Bernard, 106
Grant, Patrick, 151
Greenwood, John, 164
Gregory the Great, Pope, 160
Grindal, Edmund, Archbishop, 48, 124

Halewood, William H., 10
Hall, Joseph, Bishop, 106, 114*n23,* 124
Hamilton, James, Marquess of, 181
Harman, Barbara Leah, 203*n26*
Henrietta, Princess, daughter of Charles I, 212
Henry VIII, King, 37–41 *passim,* 43, 50, 52, 54, 62
Herbert, George: his "regenerative nostalgia," 1, 2, 33, 214; appeal across denominations, 2, 152; and Puritanism, 2–3, 20, 45, 46, 52, 55, 65–71 *passim,* 85–86, 90, 96–97, 104, 107, 109, 110, 115, 116, 117, 128–29, 144, 151, 152, 172–73, 175, 179, 185–86, 207–8; as Reformation poet, 8; and

Calvinism, 9–33 *passim*, 136, 151, 166; and eucharist, 10, 12*n5*, 27–32, 58–59, 109–10, 133–35; and predestination, 20–24; and Massachusetts Bay colony, 21*n22*, 185–86; and church-state relations, 36–37, 43–45, 46, 52–60 *passim*, 64–86 *passim*; and Old Conformity, 37–63 *passim*, 172–73, 174, 179; as defender of established church, 45, 49; and Laudianism, 47, 55–59, 65–66, 69, 85–86, 104, 107, 108, 112, 113*n22*, 115, 128, 147, 152, 166, 172–73, 174, 180, 185–86, 188–89; and hagiography, 47, 138–39, 156, 181–82, 188–89; and scripturalism, 52–53; and private conscience, 60–63; and fasting, 64–86 *passim*; "Anglican" readings of, 65, 127, 138–39, 149–51, 152, 181–82, 188–89; and customs, 72, 154–55; and "divine right of human need," 82–85; and postures in worship, 87–88, 138*n4*, 177; and preaching, 87–90, 95–102, 110–15 *passim*, 129–33; and surveillance, 95–101 *passim*; and catechizing, 115–20 *passim*; and casuistry, 120–22; and visitation, pastoral, 122–23; and church discipline, 124–25; and calling to priesthood, 135–41; and architecture of churches, 138*n7*, 155–56, 157–58, 162, 167–68, 172–77 *passim*; and courtly ambition, 140, 200–205; and lay priesthood, 141–46; and Roman Catholicism, 166, 173, 174, 179, 186, 207; and Tudor "godly commonwealth," 187–92; and Virginia Company, 191–93; and anti-elitism, 192–98; and patronage, 197–98; and individualism, 198–200; and lyric genre, 198–200; and Psalms, 199–200; private and public vision, 206–9
—Poetry. *See* Index of Herbert Poems
—Prose: *The Countrey Parson*, original title, 1*n1*; purpose of, 44, 88, 104–6, 183; origins of, 104–6; pastoral theory of, 104–26 *passim*, 183*n3*; models for, 105*n3*; quoted and mentioned, *passim*; *Briefe Notes on Valdesso's Considerations*, 53, 157
—Translation: *A Treatise of Temperance and Sobrietie*, 68
Herbert, Magdelene, 182

Herbert, Philip, fourth Earl of Pembroke, 75, 138–39
Herbert, William, third Earl of Pembroke, 75
Herod the Great, King, 161, 193
Heylin, Peter, Bishop, 59
Hill, Christopher, 70, 71, 120, 124
Honorius, Emperor, 161
Hooker, Richard, 1, 41–42, 43, 45, 46, 49, 52, 66, 75, 85, 108, 153, 159, 161–62, 163, 166, 172, 174, 178, 181, 187, 188
Hooper, John, Bishop, 105*n4*
Hopkins, Gerard Manley, 2
Hopton, Sir Ralph, 212
Huguenots, 41*n18*. *See also* Monarchy
Hunter, Jeanne Clayton, 3, 10, 21, 25–30 *passim*
Hutchinson, F. E., 90, 150, 154*n8*

Instructions of 1633, 63
Isaiah, prophet, 83–84, 85

James, Saint, 132
James I, King, 6, 11, 15, 34, 41, 42, 48, 49, 52, 55, 56*n43*, 61, 75, 85, 106, 108, 110*n12*, 113, 124, 140, 147, 181, 191, 197
Jerome, Saint, 114
Jewel, John, Bishop, 10
Jonson, Ben, 146
Joyce, James, 3

Katherine of Aragon, Queen, 37
Keats, John, 210
Keble, John, 151*n3*, 167
Kempis, Thomas à, 31
Kendall, R. T., 14*n7*, 15*n8*, 17*n12*
Kenyon, J. P., 48
Knox, John, 163

Lamont, William, 103*n1*, 207
Laud, William, Archbishop, 2, 11, 15, 21, 34, 35, 47–49, 56–59 *passim*, 61–63, 65, 69, 75, 85, 103–4, 106–7, 114, 123*n39*, 124, 136, 138–39, 147, 150*n1*, 151, 157, 158–59, 162, 163, 164, 167, 168, 172, 180, 186, 198, 210. *See also* Arminianism; Conformity, New; Laudianism
Laudianism, 3, 16, 48–50, 55, 57–58, 61–63, 78, 103–4, 106–8, 110, 112–15,

125, 138, 147, 148, 156, 158–61, 166, 168, 173, 185–86, 188–89, 212. *See also* Arminianism; Conformity, New; Episcopalianism; Laud, William, Archbishop
Lessius, Leonard, S.J., 68
Lewalski, Barbara Kiefer, 10, 111, 199
Lilburne, John, 186
Lindsell, Augustine, Bishop, 106
Little, David, *52n34*
Lupset, Thomas, 187
Luther, Martin, 9, 12, 13, 25, 26, 27, 38–39, 124, 157. *See also* Lutheranism
Lutheranism, 5, 25, 27, 68, 109, 120n33. *See also* Luther, Martin

McCloskey, Mark, 1n1
McDonnell, Kilian, O.S.B., 32n41, 163, 174
McNeill, John T., 41n18
Malcolmson, Cristina, 6, 88, 105n3, 146, 168n25, 197n18
Marcus, Leah Sinanoglou, 1n2
Martyr, Peter, 9, 17, 20
Martz, Louis L., 5, 9, 10, 12, 16–18, 19, 21, 22, 24–30 *passim,* 151
Mary I, Queen, 40, 43
Mather, Cotton, 2n3
Melanchthon, Philip, 12
Melville, Andrew, 20, 151, 154, 161
Miller, Perry, 208n33
Milton, John, 11
Miner, Earl, 199
Mitchell, W. Fraser, 110n12, 113n22
Molière, 88
Monarchy: absolute vs. limited, 34–63 *passim. See also* Arminianism: and divine-right monarchy; Calvinism: and resistance theory; Huguenots
Montague, Richard, Bishop, 59, 106
More, Thomas, Saint, 38
Murphy, Paul R., 1n1
Myrc, John, 105n3

Nardo, Anna K., 1n2
Newman, John Henry, Cardinal, 4, 17–18, 27
Non-Conformity, 52, 55, 107. *See also* Puritanism

Oley, Barnabas, 1n1, 156, 157, 158

Oxford Movement, 2, 127. *See also* Anglo-Catholicism; Episcopalianism

Packer, J. I., 144
Palmer, George Herbert, 198–99
Parker, Matthew, Archbishop, 19, 72
Patrides, C. A., 10, 31
Paul, Saint, 13, 107, 145, 168, 196
Pelagianism, 15. *See also* Pelagius
Pelagius, 23. *See also* Pelagianism
Perkins, William, 14, 22, 88n1, 90, 96–97, 102, 106, 110, 115n25, 119, 120n34, 133, 150n1, 211
Petrarchanism, 173
Pierce, William, Bishop, 106
Plato, 118
Pole, Reginald, Cardinal, 187
Ponet, John, 41n18
Predestination, 16–24, 63, 75, 103
Presbyterianism, 11, 34, 55, 104, 107, 144, 161, 163. *See also* Non-Conformity; Puritanism
Preston, John, 21
Protestantism, Continental, 4, 5, 9, 10, 17, 20
Prynne, William, 49
Puritanism: moderate, 11, 211; crypto, 48; separatist, 55, 59, 136; and "lecturers," 57; and Laudianism, 59, 148, 212; and Old Conformity, 63; and Lent, 66–86 *passim,* 121; and preaching, 96n6, 110, 115; and catechizing, 119, 123; and casuistry, 120n34; and church discipline, 124, 125; and Commonwealth Parliament, 125; and anti-clericalism, 145; and Civil War, 147; and ceremonies, 151, 153, 160; as fanatical, 156; and externals of worship, 161–64 *passim;* and liturgy, 163–64, 176; and Sunday "sports," 168n27; and architecture of churches, 174–75; mentioned, 3, 10, 172, 179, 214. *See also* Herbert, George: and Puritanism; Non-Conformity; Presbyterianism

Quakerism, 145

Reeves, Troy D., 105n4
Restoration, 71, 104, 156, 211
Richmond, Lodowick, Duke of, 181
Ridley, Nicholas, Bishop, 10
Roman Catholicism, 3, 4, 5, 9–33 *pas-*

sim, 31, 97, 109, 110, 121, 150, 157, 160, 166, 173, 186, 207
Ross, Malcolm Mackenzie, 186, 208*n34*
Rutherford, Samuel, 41*n18*

Sanderson, Robert, 106*n5,* 120*n34*
Schismatics. *See* Non-Conformity
Schoenfeldt, Michael C., 6, 89, 91, 140
Separatism, 55, 59, 136, 145*n16,* 164, 207. *See also* Non-Conformity
Servetus, Michael, 32
Shakespeare, William, 88
Sheldon, Gilbert, Archbishop, 71
Shelley, P. B., 210
Sherwood, Terry G., 10*n2*
Sibbes, Richard, 21
Sibthorpe, Robert, 61
Sidney, Sir Philip, 93, 173, 210
Six Articles, Henrician, 39–40
Skinner, Robert, Bishop, 106
Slights, Camille Wells, 120, 122, 200
Socrates, 117, 119
Somerset, Edward Seymour, Duke of, Protector, 54
Spenser, Edmund, 94
Stanford, William, 41
Starkey, Thomas, 187, 201
Stewart, Stanley, 5, 10, 25–29 *passim,* 151
Strier, Richard, 4, 10, 94, 121, 141–42, 143, 166*n24,* 170*n29,* 175, 177*n39,* 183*n2,* 186, 193
Summers, Joseph H., 1, 170*n28*

Taylor, Edward, 152
Taylor, Jeremy, 106*n5,* 120*n34*
Taylor, Thomas, 123
Trevor-Roper, H. R., 57, 59

Tuke, Thomas, 96*n6*
Tuve, Rosemond, 5, 10, 151
Tuveson, Ernest, 207*n29*
Tyacke, Nicholas, 34*n2,* 36, 62
Tyndale, William, 39

Ussher, James, Archbishop, 48
Uzzah, Old Testament priest, 135–36, 141

Valdes, Juan de (Valdesso), 20, 157
Vaughan, Henry, 152
Veith, Gene Edward, Jr., 5*n7,* 10, 11, 32*n42*
Vendler, Helen, 4, 65, 80, 203*n26*

Wall, John N., 4, 9*n1,* 10*n2,* 188
Walton, Izaak, 47, 68, 112, 122, 127–28, 137–39, 149, 151, 152, 156, 157, 158, 181–82, 188–89
Welsby, Paul A., 106*n6*
Whitaker, William, 14, 15, 20, 211
Whitefield, George, 144
Whitgift, John, Archbishop, 15, 45, 48, 52
Williams, John, Bishop, 75, 157
Winthrop, John, 185
Wolsey, Thomas, Cardinal, 38*n10,* 62
Wood, Thomas, 150*n1*
Woodnoth, Arthur, 138, 192
Wren, Matthew, Bishop, 59
Wycliffe, John, 124

Yeats, William Butler, 4

Zwingli, Ulrich, 25, 26, 27. *See also* Zwinglians
Zwinglians, 38*n9. See also* Zwingli, Ulrich